Love's Journey

ALSO BY MICHAEL GURIAN

Emptying (*poetry*)

Mothers, Sons, and Lovers: How a Man's Relationship with His Mother Affects the Rest of His Life

The Prince and the King: Healing the Father-Son Wound

Love's Journey

The Seasons and
Stages of Relationship

Michael Gurian

SHAMBHALA
Boston & London
1995

Shambhala Publications, Inc.
Horticultural Hall
300 Massachusetts Avenue
Boston, Massachusetts 02115

9 8 7 6 5 4 3 2 1

First Edition

Printed in the United States of America on acid-free paper
Distributed in the United States by Random House, Inc.,
and in Canada by Random House of Canada Ltd

Library of Congress Cataloging-in-Publication Data

Gurian, Michael.
    Love's Journey: the seasons and stages of relationship/Michael Gurian.—1st ed.
    p.   cm.
    Includes bibliographical references.
    ISBN 1-57062-105-5 (acid-free paper)
    1. Love.   2. Interpersonal relations.   3. Man-woman relationships.
I. Title.
BF575.L8G87   1995   95-3899
152.4'1—dc20   CIP

To Gail, who has inspired so many love stories

CONTENTS

Acknowledgments   ix

Introduction   1

PART ONE: THE SEASON OF ENCHANTMENT

Story: The Enchanted Ring   23

Stage 1. Romance   29
Stage 2. The Fall into Disillusionment   55
Stage 3. Power Struggle   67

PART TWO: THE SEASON OF AWAKENING

Story: The Big People at the Bottom of the World   91

Stage 4. Awakening   101
Stage 5. The First Conscious Descent   125
Stage 6. Refined Intimacy   149

PART THREE: THE SEASON OF INTERDEPENDENT
                    PARTNERSHIP

Story: Isis and Osiris   171

Stage 7. Creative Partnership   178
Stage 8. The Second Conscious Descent   203
Stage 9. Radiant Love   225

Contents

PART FOUR: THE SEASON OF NONATTACHMENT

Story: The Living and the Dead 243

Stage 10. The Elder's Solitude 248

Stage 11. The Third Conscious Descent 261

Stage 12. Initiation into Cosmic Consciousness 274

Epilogue *283*

Selected Readings *285*

ACKNOWLEDGMENTS

Those who know me know that for me, community holds the key to lasting wisdom. This book grows from community, standing on the shoulders of those many who made it possible. In this small space I give special thanks to the mentors and personal teachers from whom I've gained vision fundamental to this book. Some of them wish to be named, some not. Some of them remain in my memory as aspects of the place they inhabited.

Many lessons about the quest for joy have remained with me from the people of India, whom I knew during my boyhood years there, the women carrying bundles on their heads on rural roads, Brahmans wandering in white with begging bowls and staff in Madras, men herding sheep in Bombay, children smiling for cameras in New Delhi, professors speaking fluently their view of life at conferences where my father taught at the University of Hyderabad—from these people in India I gained my first sense that there are seasons and stages of life and love, that there is a structure in the human journey that provides it with much-needed spiritual discipline. I offer them my profound gratitude, giving special thanks to Aiya, Balwant, and Mahmoud.

My thanks are due also the people of the Southern Ute reservation, where I spent part of my early adolescence. An ancient people, no matter how long oppressed, carries in its body the spiritual discipline it needs to survive. From the lives of some of them I gained a felt sense of the seasons and stages of a hard-lived life. My special thanks to my shamanic teacher, Jim McNeill, and my Cheyenne teacher, Clayton Small.

Ahmet Uysal, Necla Aytur, Yusuf Eradam, Aykut Misirligil, and many others in Turkey helped me integrate a joyful vision of the world that is so completely Turkish—one that stands, like that country, half in contemporary Europe, half in medieval Asia.

Thanks are also due Shmuel ben-Dor, who has long been a family friend, and Gabi Ben-Ezer, who gave me a place to begin my explorations into this subject in Israel. My gratitude also to the people of Kibbutz Dorot who showed me a way of life that can bring great joy.

I give special thanks to my parents, Jay and Julia Gurian, whose personal work spawned me and whose professional work spawned sociological and anthropological data important in the field of family relationships. Many thanks to Michael Herzog, whose mentoring helped shape my future and who allowed me to join an extended family system on which I would later model some of my thinking. Profound thanks also to Rod Stackelberg, who paved the way for my time in Berlin to be life-changing.

The assistance of certain hands-on professionals made this book possible. Jeff Hedge, D.O., gave me important scientific documentation and advice. Richard Dalke's technological help was invaluable. Al Turtle and Kari Wagler inspired very helpful pieces of my thinking. Dave O'Neal, my editor, remains, as always, my friend and ally.

My profound thanks to Gail, my wife and companion, and our daughters, Gabrielle and Davita. Nurturing them is often reason enough for me to search for spiritual truth.

Finally, I thank the many clients; the seminar, workshop, and retreat participants; and the church members, agency staff, businesspeople, and prison populations who have invited me to help with their spiritual growth, intimacy training, and community process. They have let me serve them, and, in letting me do so, they have blessed and renewed my work.

Love's Journey

INTRODUCTION

*Our creative struggle, our search for wisdom and truth,
is a love story.*
—Iris Murdoch

When I was a young teenager, living in Colorado, I knew an
elderly couple, the Harrisons. Mrs. Harrison was a retired
nurse who wore aprons and knee-high nylons and thick-
soled white shoes. Mr. Harrison, a neighborhood poet and
former English teacher, wore overalls and thick glasses and
could play chess for hours. The Harrisons lived a few doors
down from us, and after school I often preferred playing
chess with Mr. Harrison and eating Mrs. Harrison's cookies
to wrestling with friends my age. The Harrisons missed their
children and childrens' families who lived far away. They had
a lot to give and wanted to give it. They chose me somehow
among all the neighborhood kids to be "auntie" and "uncle"
to. They became my mentors.

I remember one life-changing conversation with them
that took place on a Saturday afternoon, over the chessboard.
Mr. Harrison asked me, "Why are you alive, Michael? Do
you know?" Since he was always asking me questions like
that, it wasn't surprising. I answered, "To be a good person,
I guess. To do good."

He frowned. "Okay, but why do you think *you're* here?
You, Michael Gurian?"

1

"To help people, I guess. I want to teach when I grow up."

Still he wasn't satisfied. He painted a picture for me. "Suppose you're looking into a dark forest. There's only one thing you can take out of that forest. You're gonna have to go in there and maybe risk getting killed, so the thing you take out better be the most important thing in the world to you. What would it be?"

I tried to see the picture, the forest. I saw myself walking in it. I saw a castle and I saw a maiden. I had my answer. Love, it had to be love, right? "Someone to be in love with the rest of my life," I said to him. "I'll go in there and find my Mrs. Harrison." In the context of my own parents' troubled marriage and my limited experience with girls, the Harrisons represented to me the essence of real love.

Mrs. Harrison smiled her pleasure, but her husband was still not satisfied. "Tell me this, Michael." He took off his glasses. "My eyes look different when the glasses aren't magnifying them, right?"

I nodded. His glasses were so thick that when he had them on, his eyes looked like balls.

"So that's what I want you to do with 'being a good person,' and 'helping other people,' and 'being in love.' What's behind all those ways of loving people? What's the eye that's trying to see out of all of those?"

I had no idea what he meant and told him so.

"Joy!" he cried. "The search for joy! Everyone misses that. Everyone thinks 'love' and 'goodness' are the keys. They're the door. Joy is the key that opens the door. If you don't love with joy in your heart, your love is false. It's that simple. If you're smart, Michael, what you'll want out of your life is joy. Do you know what joy is?"

I shrugged like kids do. Joy wasn't something I thought about much. When I did, I assumed it was something adults had, or older people, or maybe only prophets and wise people had it. They sang about joy in church.

I said honestly, "I don't know."

"You're too young to know now anyway. Don't worry about it. But just remember what I'm saying, because one day you'll wake up to it. Just remember that an old man told you to find joy in your life. Will you do that?"

I promised I would.

"All right, then," he nodded, "now let's play chess."

I did not realize it then, but Mr. Harrison, at that moment, with words whose passion I remember quite clearly to this day, existed in my childhood as a kind of sacred force. The Harrisons hoped I would become a person of vision, an adult they could be proud of. "Joy" was that "vision," that original eye behind the glasses. A year later we moved away from that neighborhood, and I never saw them again. For many years, I simply forgot them.

Then, a few years ago, I had a dream. The Harrisons were in their living room by the chessboard. It was as if they were stuck in that house, frozen in time, long after they should have been dead. They were like ghosts, waiting to be released. Who was supposed to release them? Well, since I had dreamed them, I must be their captor. Why, I wondered, had they come to me? What did it mean?

Upon awakening from the dream, I found myself floating through memories of the Harrisons, the old neighborhood. I pondered what I had done with my life since being with the Harrisons. I remembered the philosophical conversations. I sat with my journal and wrote down dialogue we had had, as if I were writing my own memoirs. I remembered and wrote down the conversation about joy.

Rereading it there in bed, in the quiet blue of the early morning, I had an awakening. I realized I knew very little about joy. I had been given a mission by the Harrisons but hadn't really fulfilled it. If I were honest, I would have to say I had grown into an adult who believed it was impossible to find joy, that I did not deserve it, that no one but a saint could ever really achieve it.

This realization brought me to free-write in my journal whatever came to me.

"You live in a culture that's terrified of experiencing true joy," I wrote. "There are things about love you won't experience until you give yourself to the quest for joy. . . . Mr. and Mrs. Harrison have come back in the dream to show you that you're frozen, stuck. It's time to move!"

As my morning of spiritual work continued, I came to these realizations:

As a child of my generation, a child of a dysfunctional family and a culture in chaos, I was initiated into my youth and my manhood through the spiritual work of *woundedness*. "Being a man" meant, for me, being in constant naked touch with my wounds and working to heal them. My own particular story of woundedness included these elements: I had been sexually abused as a ten-year-old. I had been a hyperkinetic child, on and off medication. My mother—a woman of great love—was also a violent authoritarian; my father—a man of great compassion—nonetheless did not protect me. Beaten, abused, betrayed, I was a physically and psychologically damaged child. Spiritually sensitive, I entered many spiritual paths over two decades ago. I grew, I found healing. I became a writer, teacher, and therapist; all blended my healing with my ability to help others. I married and had children. I had become a good man, a helper, and a husband, all of the things I told Mr. Harrison I should become.

Still, I viewed the world as a place based in woundedness. I viewed the world as a place based in sin. I viewed the world as a place based in the negative, *via negativa*. I had not yet understood that my love of others, my goodness, my hard work were based primarily in my woundedness, thus they were all done to cure my own pain.

This insight stunned me. It filled me with the kind of soulful shame that brings new life. I sat back and remembered Mr. Harrison's words: "Find joy." I repeated them to myself almost as if they were doing the talking. "How?" I asked. I did not know yet, but I knew it was time to initiate myself into the next phase of my life through something more than woundedness—something called joy.

Exhausted, I lay back, looked out the window at the sky, and felt tears in my eyes.

That was three years ago. From that, and the spiritual work that insight has taken me through, I have learned much about how afraid I can be of joy. Doesn't that sound crazy? Why should I be *afraid* of joy? Yet I have found that most people are often afraid to experience the joy of belonging, of being who they are, of really living. Over the last few years I have noticed that, in the same way woundedness is a lifelong journey, I still have much more to learn about joy than can be learned in one lifetime. But I have also come to notice that much of my professional and personal life has been a quest for joy, even long before I had the consciousness to recognize it. This is true for many people. We are on the quest for joy whether we know it or not, but if we are not conscious of the quest, we can go years, even decades, without fully *experiencing* joy.

During my own personal work of releasing the Harrisons to their joyful destination, I was aware of a professional yearning to meet cartographers of the quest for joy. As I re-thought my whole life and noticed all the moments of joy I had, moments too often ignored, I felt certain that had I had a map of joy's way early on in life, I would have been able to live more consciously, more joyfully. The book you are reading is about the lifelong quest for joy. It is a kind of map.

As I've seen clients and lectured and led workshops around North America over the last few years, I've had the privilege of helping thousands of people explore their own quests for joy. Some of their lives appear in these pages. These people found the material very helpful and pressed me to put it in book form. Here is that book. In the workshops I ask participants to listen to voices within them and around them that say, "You were put on this earth to be joyful!" That single statement, fully lived, has been most powerful for many participants. It is also a grounding statement for this book.

Having lived for many years in other cultures, and being a professional and personal researcher into tribal ways, I have gravitated toward searching for tribal attitudes and maps about joy. Much of what I found is in this book: myths, stories, legends.

With the help of many sources and feeling grateful to them, I have "created," or "discovered," or "visioned" a map of the journey human beings seek to make when they love in joy and through love seek joy. That map is the core of this book. I offer it not as a final statement, but as a compass. Your own way of living and loving is your map. Use this compass, and your love will be enriched. That is its promise.

THE LONG QUEST FOR JOYFUL LOVE

"If you don't love with joy in your heart," Mr. Harrison told me, "your love is false." That statement haunts me still. The model, stages, and stories presented in this book focus on the joy we can discover through the seasons and stages of loving. The model guides individuals and couples toward what the book calls "joyful love." When we speak of loving, we will speak of the whole spectrum of loving—loving ourselves, others, mates, children, community, the earth. But wherever they wander in their story about the quest for joy, the chapters always wander back to how we are practicing that quest for joy in our love relationships, our marriages, our families—how we are creating joyful love *with* intimates. In my own search for cartography about the quest for joy, I found myself flowing with the energies of the fairy tales—"And they lived happily ever after."

I came to understand that the fairy-tale ending—"They lived happily ever after"—is not just saying, "They got married." It is about much more than teaching us that we, like the fairy-tale couples, should learn to be good, helpful people, and marry; it is the spiritual statement, "If you go through what these characters went through, you will find joy." The stories teach what the Harrisons tried to teach: joy is the great quest. It can be our daily quest.

This daily quest has always been hard, in any culture. Yet in some ways it's harder today than it has ever been. We live, as we end this millennium, for the first time in 7 millon years of prehuman and human history, in a society whose most biologically essential alliance—the male/female alliance—the one on which the future of the race, through the birth and care of its children, depends—exists without a clear design or story. We don't have any clear plan for family, coupling, even child raising. Quite simply, we occupy a society in which thousands of years of human effort to create tribes and set family structures and strict gender roles have given way to a chaos that was inevitable, a chaos that comes to a culture that decides to seek joyful, intimate love rather than arranged marriage and strict gender roles.

But we haven't gotten to the "joyful love" part yet. One out of two marriages ends in divorce. Our culture is in a gender war that destroys relationships. Male chauvinism is alive and well, while many women have discovered a new female chauvinism. Stereotypes rule dialogue. Working through the chaos of our age, we search for joyful love in a time of spiritual revolution. We turn to the Judeo-Christian past as well as to Eastern traditions. Through therapy, new age practices, the rebirth of tribal rituals, the women's movement, the men's movement, gestalt, psychic readings, couples workshops, mythopoetic consciousness, individual life journeys, vision quests, Total Quality Management training, changing workplaces, self-help books, we've been trying to integrate all the different currents of wisdom flowing in the age of information.

Through this vast multitude of modern forms of spiritual education, what we are seeking is joyful love, whether we've defined it as such or not. Standing in both the best of the ancient and religious past and the most sacred work of the recent past, we are developing a new kind of love story—though we haven't organized it too well yet—a love story that makes sense to us as late twentieth-century lovers who, for the first time in human history, have the economic freedom to find the joyful love promised long ago by such books as the Bible. We are wrestling with our responsibilities once we find this promised love. We are seeking maps for it that meet the needs of our time. We have come to that place in human social development when, filled with courage, we seek deep within ourselves that essential center of our beings that is capable of joyful love, like a fountain that keeps replenishing itself. In Jungian psychology and in mythology that "center," that "fountain" is called the Lover archetype.

THE LOVER ARCHETYPE

The Lover archetype is that part of our psychospiritual configuration that represents unconditional love, delight, and joy. It's the Lover in you that enjoys a sunset, or basks in the glow after sex, or looks into your child's eyes and weeps for joy.

The Lover, like the archetypal symbols of Warrior, Goddess, King, Magician, Crone, Wild Woman, Wild Man, Explorer, and many others, is a metaphor for one of those mysterious aspects of yourself you really can't define except by "making up" a story and character for it. The Lover in you and its story about the way you love, the way you experience being loved, the way you feel delight and express joy, inform the activities of every other "part" of you.

Every culture, whether it speaks overtly of a Lover archetype or not, is well aware of the Lover, for the symbol pops up in every culture's stories. Most cultures spend more time telling stories about the way its people love than any other subject! Our culture is no exception. From novels to MTV, from e-mail to Hallmark cards, we are accessing and activating the Lover archetype at a frenzied pace.

Unfortunately, in our culture much of our frenzy to access the Lover is a cover-up. We are concealing how little we know about the Lover. We make the Lover a superficial character, then we get angry at it and at the process of loving when we don't find, in love relationships, the joy we want and need.

The Lover seeks joy but usually hides when faced with a frenzy or hysteria of activity. The Lover in us is tender, vulnerable, and in need of much careful, sensitive nurturing. The frenzy of superficial romance and the hysteria of hopelessness that often rule our present-day relationships with mates, and thus our relationship with the Lover in us, send the Lover underground, back into the forest, where it awaits our return to sanity. The Lover wants more connection from us. The quest for joy is a doorway into that deeper connection.

As we develop the Lover more consciously in ourselves, we find ourselves able to take more personal responsibility for our lives and actions. For joy comes from personal empowerment rather than from being a victim and waiting for others to save us. The more spiritually disciplined our love lives become, the more strength we have to notice a cessation of blaming and an increase of joy.

For the Lover to develop in us, the Lover needs a love story to live in. Otherwise—as the Lover does so often in our culture, which has a million love vignettes about romance and disillusionment but few long quests for joy—the Lover lives in chaos. The Lover's Journey, which follows, is a love story about the long quest the Lover archetype makes during a human lifetime.

THE LOVER'S JOURNEY

The Lover's Journey takes place over four seasons in the lifetime of an individual and of a relationship. Although my model is a new way of organizing this journey for our culture, I have found it and echoes of it in our own ancestral past and throughout the world. The Lover's Journey has truly been in progress for millennia, developing through everything from the Bible to rap music.

In my effort in this book to capture the Lover's Journey in a single model in written form, I am especially grateful to Joseph Campbell's *Hero with a Thousand Faces*. In it Campbell saw millennia of development of a "Hero's Journey," from various sources, East and West, and risked putting that Hero's Journey structure into the written cycle of language. The Lover's Journey, like the Hero's Journey—and overlapping with it, as becomes clear in this book—is an unfolding of a large portion of the Great Life Story that began countless thousands of years ago with the first syllable uttered in search of story about life's spiritual design. The Hero's Journey is the evolutionary step that embraces many of the activities that culminate in the civilization-building of the last few centuries. I hope the Lover's Journey now acts to return hidden spirit and joy to what the Hero has built.

THE SEASONS AND STAGES OF LOVING

The structure in this book is a new paradigm built on messages from the past, confirmed by new information on the science of human loving, observed by me in tribal cultures still extant and cultures around the world (specifically Central European, Middle Eastern, East Indian, and Native American, with which I have personal experience) and integrated by a hopeful, searching mind. I am the author of this vision, this paradigm, this book, so I take ownership of organizing the human journey toward joyful love into the structure of this book. I do not pretend, however, to have plumbed the actual depth and breadth of a spiritual structure that has been millions of years in the making. I shall speak as if I know, but the ultimate test will be in the actual application of these seasons and stages to your own life.

Even when you are not conscious of it, you are on a Lover's Journey. Even when you are in a divorce, facing your partner's death, suing someone for sexual harassment, living in widowhood, you are on the journey. Even when you are single, you are on it. Some lovers are better uncles and aunts than they would be parents. Some are better at loving many than loving a few. Some never find the human mate they desire but kiss the earth in a thousand ways. They are all on the Lover's Journey.

The seasons and stages of the Lover's Journey are not rigid constructs. We move in and around them in various ways and sometimes find ourselves experiencing several at once. Yet if you study your own life closely through the lens of the Lover's Journey, you will notice how particular periods of your life are definitely dominated by specific stages of growth.

In tribal cultures, like the Shavante of Brazil, the Lover's Journey is lived in what are called *age sets*. Often these age sets are about five years in length. Thus, the twelve stages of the Lover's Journey might take up a person's lifetime: sixty years.

In much of India, a life span is spiritually divided into four periods, ending in sannyass, a time when the elder sets off alone to discover what mystical nonattachment truly is. By this model, we might say the four seasons of the Lover's Journey take up fifteen to twenty years each, spanning a sixty- to eighty-year life.

No one model works for everyone. Some of us spend an inordinate amount of time in one season—for example, the season of dependency. Many of us never discover the season of interdependence. Many of us stay in power-struggle relationship all our lives. In our culture, we often don't mature to psychological adulthood until well into our midlife. In tribal cultures, the first two seasons of life, in which young people are led to mature into full adulthood, tend to happen in the first two decades of life.

In the Lover's Journey, we can move beyond one season, but then, because of crisis, return to it. For example, we can mature beyond dependence on our partner and even beyond the power-struggle cycle, but when our partner has a one-night stand, we return to power struggle. In a case like this, our consciousness of the Lover's Journey makes it possible for us to make each crisis a *descent* into new truth, not merely a regressive return to an earlier pattern.

Clients and workshop participants often tell me that what they find most puzzling about their journey is this: what do we do if we find ourselves in one stage and our partner in another? We will explore this difficulty as we make the journey together. Resolving it is one of life's greatest challenges. Many of us have some knowledge of the early stages of loving. If you find that the first two chapters seem to present familiar material, push on.

As we make the journey, you'll notice that each stage comes with a lesson of trust, a focus for an individual's and a couple's spiritual discipline, and suggestions for integrating the stage into your life. Hopefully, each piece of spiritual discipline you practice as you make your own journey will lead you to a sense of yourself as ever more joyful.

Each of the four seasons of the Lover's Journey is grounded in principles of development psychology. The Lover evolves from dependency (childhood) to independence (young adulthood), independence to interdependence (adulthood), interdependence to nondependence (elder years). This does not mean we're stuck to this formula. Many of us experiment with nondependence, or nonattachment, in our youthful spiritual searches or in middle-age years spent in monkishness. Many of us confuse dependency with interdependence, thinking we are sharing power when in fact we are taking power, sometimes taking it by pretending we are victims or that we have surrendered to another. Many of us seek independence as a primary goal throughout our lives, then wake up feeling lost and isolated just before we die. Most of us do not get beyond the tug-of-war between dependency and independence. But we can learn from the Lover's Journey that there is much more to life, waiting just around the corner.

STORIES OF THE LOVER'S JOURNEY

Throughout my life, like all of you, I've listened to love stories. Grandparents tell these stories from their lives, from their sacred books, from folklore; aunties tell them, uncles tell them, parents tell them, neighbors tell them, other kids tell them, the radio tells them, the television tells them, books tell them, poems tell them, nursery rhymes tell them.

The seasons and stages of the Lover's Journey often reach into our souls with the most clarity when we hear them in myths, stories, and fairy tales. In *Women Who Run with the Wolves,* Clarissa Pinkola Estés, the Jungian analyst, writes: "Stories do not require that we do, be, act anything—we need only listen. The remedies for repair or reclamation of any lost psychic drive are contained in stories. . . . Stories are embedded with instructions which guide us through the complexities of life."

The earliest story I can remember involved two kids, Jack and Jill, who went up a hill to fetch a pail of water. Jack fell down and broke his crown, and Jill came tumbling after. If ever there was a story of awkward love, that one was it, but I didn't know that as a four-year-old. Sometime in my late teens, when I awakened to the power of stories, I thought back to that nursery rhyme. With a lot of sexual interpretation—love meant sex to me in that hormonally resplendent stage of my life—I wrote this in a high school paper: "Jack and Jill went up the hill to get it on. The water symbolizes their primal love. But Jack tries to contain it in a pail. But he doesn't get it—love can't be contained! He stumbles, his love stumbles. Jill, maybe to be polite so Jack doesn't feel lonely in his stupidity, tumbles down with him."

As far as I know, that was the first time I tried to apply what I call "the storyteller's psychology" to a love story. I listened to a story and tried to understand what its drama meant to me, to my community and world, without stealing the story's energy and integrity. When I went to college and graduate school, where I studied philosophy, literature, mythology, and psychology, I developed the idea that every story has *one* interpretation, and an *objective* one at that—that if you get smart enough, you'll understand the one meaning of the tale. Fortunately, I had a lot of wise teachers who helped me gain mythologist's tools by which to develop the gifts of that early innocence we all have toward stories, that innocence which does not want to steal the story's energy but rather to bring the story's energy to our own lives.

I've selected the stories in this book for their depth of soul, their richness of revelation about how identities mature, how love embraces life energy, how communities become wise, and how the cycle of life moves round and round. They are stories that reveal secrets of loving too long submerged in our culture—secrets we have betrayed as we have grown upward but not inward.

These stories speak the language of allegory, metaphor, and archetype. Their metaphors reveal mysteries about ourselves we have not fully understood; their allegories reveal journeys we have been making and striving to make; their archetypes reveal energies within ourselves we have not yet contained or fully enjoyed. Ordinary objects of everyday life become magnificent, dark, animated, wise. Sand and water, fish, people's eyes, souls, bodies, hands, underground places, mountaintops—all of them take on special significance, all become teachers. They can do this because in the world of these stories, we and every *thing* around us are sacred, interconnected, in an interdependent web. Everything teaches us, we teach everything.

Magical characters appear in these stories: giants, dragons, sea-creatures, genies, sorcerers. Places and people from past times and old stories appear—the Goddess Isis, the Knights of the Roundtable, Cinderella, even the Little Mermaid, whose celluloid life is a conglomeration of old characters. Archetypes appear—Lover, Warrior, Goddess. In the storyteller's psychology, there is no "right way" to use archetypes. Archetypes are fluid; they change as you interpret them in flux. Yet each storyteller develops his own family tree for archetypes, his own way of using them, his own felt sense of what each represents in the psyche. Hopefully, his story is grounded in the spiritual life of his times, so the way he finds to interpret archetypes will be confirmed by the inner vibrations of the listeners' minds. The storyteller yearns to tell stories people need to hear.

In a storyteller's psychology, archetypes, seemingly ordinary objects, extraordinary characters, and figures from the past and from folklore come to us as in a dream. In dreams, every character can be viewed as a part of yourself, hidden in your unconscious mind, speaking out its truth to your busy, conscious life.

Sometimes we don't get a needed message about our lives unless, in a story, we hear a rock tell us what to do. Then we sing about the Rock of Ages, and each time we give voice to its spirit, we give voice to our own spiritual safety.

Sometimes we don't know how to assert our needs until we dream about two lions, like the ones in Walt Disney's *Lion King,* fighting each other, and one prevailing, and that one victor carrying in his teeth the elements of our own deep need to feel fully centered in the cycle of life.

Sometimes we don't heal our wounds unless, like a client of mine who was working with a Wise Woman story, we go home that night, meet a wise woman named Grandma who comes to us in a dream when we are very depressed, and gives us permission to forgive ourselves and to be healed.

In archetypal stories, just as in a sacred place or sacred book or wise parent's advice, life glows. Things take on important meaning, people sing songs to you, life is structured and worthwhile, thus you are worthwhile, and everything exists on this earth to help you learn spiritual discipline so that, in the interdependent web of life, your spiritual discipline will guide you to support the growth of everything on this earth.

LOVE AS SPIRITUAL DISCIPLINE

The stories in this book have been brought together with the purpose of providing readers with ways to make love a spiritual journey. There is wisdom in them about how romance works; how to move out of power struggle; how to move through grief in love and experience joy; how to heal wounds you received as children; how to communicate with others and do conflict more effectively; how to honor others without losing yourself; how to raise kids; how to mentor other couples; how to survive deaths of children; how to make solitude a part of your life; how to help a loved one die; how, yourself, to die.

The stories in this book provide form and content by which you can revision the way you love into a spiritual discipline whose focus is joy. In this model called the Lover's Journey, *spiritual discipline* is whatever spiritual practice you establish for yourself to achieve joyful living and joyful love. That practice may be Christian based, Buddhist based, or based in one of the other major world religions. It may be Goddess based, earth based. It may even be agnostic or atheistic.

Joyful living and joyful loving imply that you approach life with enough spiritual *attachment* to your own worth and to the worth of others and the earth that you can gain support for the nurturance of your own identity and sacred self. Joyful life also implies that you give support to others and the earth for the nurturance of theirs. And it implies that you practice enough spiritual *detachment* to hold the boundaries of your established identity and help others and the earth hold the boundaries of theirs. Joyful life and love, then, are about being in tune with but not overwhelmed by what is needed for happiness to flourish in your world.

Whatever form it takes, spiritual discipline requires these four external elements:

1. spiritual guides (in person and in story)
2. sacred place(s)

3. an accepting community

4. daily practice

Many of us go to church several times a week but do not feel attached to the spiritual guides we worship. We appear to practice spiritual discipline but are, in fact, going through the motions. And more and more these days we are meeting people who have become addicted to religion. They do not approach their search for joy as a spiritual discipline but rather as a regressive dependency.

Many others go to church once in a while or pray once in a while but do not have a spiritual discipline—they lack the necessary attachment to and detachment from one or more of the primary elements. Perhaps most of all, we see in the mirror and around us the kind of person Thomas Moore writes about in *Care of the Soul*. Moore writes that because most of us lack depth and sacredness in everyday life, we overemphasize entertainments, emotional isolation, power struggle; we feel lost—akin, really, to no one and nothing; empty of divinity; frightened by our own families; unable to understand ourselves.

In whatever way we do not practice life as a spiritual discipline, we can be equally sure we are not practicing love as a spiritual discipline. And so we often find love elusive, meaningless, disturbing, dark, vicious, impossible, impractical, something that drains our life energy rather than feeding it.

The Lover's Journey offers you a disciplined but flexible way of loving. Power struggle becomes a small part of your spiritual discipline rather than the dominating factor in relationships.

So *Love's Journey* is written in the belief that joyful love is not something waiting for us in the future. It is available now, if we would just make it conscious. It is in and around us everywhere, waiting for us to practice it and, by that practice, change not only ourselves but our world.

There's a story waiting for us. Let's begin it.

Part One

THE SEASON OF ENCHANTMENT

Story: The Enchanted Ring

This story comes from my father's people in Russian Georgia. It is the story of two people who shared a love so great the whole world knew of it. It is also a story of things that lay behind that great love, things the world knew nothing of. What need would there be for stories if we knew everything already? This story molds its enchanted metal with hidden truths.

Once upon a time there lived a princess named Katia who was known far and wide for her beauty. Just as she came of age, her mother died. On her deathbed, her mother called her close and whispered, "Katia, you will marry a man whom you will love and who will love you dearly. I see it. He has great magic. Love him, my child, love with all your heart, give yourself utterly, but find the source of his magic and take it when you can, so that you do not lose your heart in his. It is the only way to be happy. And do not tell your father of this conversation."

Throughout her mother's funeral, her words rang in Katia's ears. She even looked at her father a little differently because of them.

Meanwhile, nearby, there lived a wealthy merchant and his wife. They had a son, Nikolai, who was just coming of age. One day Nikolai returned from a trip to find that his father had died. After he had mourned his father, Nikolai asked his mother for the money his father had left him. With that money he went in search of an old peasant his father had told him about some months before. This peasant, his father had said, would show him the ways of the world. "One day, Nikolai," his father had said, "you will love and be loved by a beautiful woman. But she will try to steal your heart. You must learn the great lesson of love: to seem to give your heart completely, but never give it at all. There is an old man who will help you."

On the edge of the forest, Nikolai found the old man. From him, Nikolai bought a dog and a cat, which he took home to his mother. His mother raised her eyebrows. "Why have you given money for that dog and cat?" she said. "This is foolishness! Your father should not have trusted you with this money!"

Nikolai said, "Don't worry about the money, Mother; somehow it will always come back to us." With that, he took the last chunk of his money and set out on the road. From the old peasant, he had heard of a princess in a faraway land who would soon die in possession of an enchanted ring. "With this ring in his possession," the peasant had said, "a young man can find the everlasting love he seeks and always be safe from love's harms."

Nikolai came to the princess's castle and bribed the guards so he could come near her bier. When he saw her lifeless face, he saw a beauty like he had never known before. Though he knew she could never love him, he fell in love with her. He took the ring off her finger and left the castle, returning home. He had no money, but he had the dog, the cat, and the ring—all the things the old peasant had told him he would need. Unfortunately, the old peasant had told him nothing more, and now, as Nikolai searched for him, he found the old man nowhere.

One day, not too long afterward, while walking in the graveyard where her mother was buried, Katia met Nikolai, who was there paying respects to his father. The young people saw each other and fell into a love so deep it frightened them. Yet they stood together, talked together, and each felt a sense of levitation and joy, as if an eternal hand had finally lifted them to the exalted place reserved only for lovers, the place both had dreamed of.

When Katia got home, she sent servants to discover who this handsome, tender man could be. They had spoken many words of love together but still did not know each other's names. Even as her servants sought Nikolai's identity, Katia thought she must test this young man to discover how close he came to her ideal.

When Nikolai got home, he knew who Katia was. The whole realm knew the king's daughter. He pulled out the ring again, the enchanted ring which, in truth, had done nothing enchanting at all since he had gotten it. But now, as he turned it and turned it on his finger, dwarves and knights appeared to him. "We are at your service," they said. "What do you want?"

"I want you to build my own house into a grand one. Then I want you to find things so precious, even the king and his daughter would know nothing of them." They did these things, and Nikolai's mother, happily surprised, embraced her son with pride. "Mother," he said, "you must help me woo Princess Katia." He did not want to go himself. He was afraid he would, upon seeing her again, not see the princess he had fallen in love with, but see someone less fine, less worthy.

So his mother took the precious jewels to the king and explained Nikolai's wish for an audience to ask for Katia's hand. Katia came out. She had learned that he was not a prince. If he wanted her, she had decided, remembering her mother's words, he would have to do something extraordinary.

Her father said to her, "What shall we ask this young man to give you for your hand?"

Katia said to Nikolai's mother, "Tell him to build in one night in the king's sacred meadow a new palace more splendid than my father's own, and to hang a crystal bridge from one palace to the other, and to cover the crystal bridge with all kinds of embroidered rugs. If he does this I will marry him."

Then her father said, "And if he does not fulfill this task, he shall be put to death. That will teach young men not to waste my time."

Katia's heart stopped for a second. She had not expected this last part! But what could she do?

Nikolai's mother went home in tears, yet he calmed her. "Fear not, Mother, nothing will happen to us, and we shall not be bested." He twirled the enchanted ring and bid his allies to build what the princess had requested. This they did, and the next morning, Katia and her father saw how powerful Nikolai's magic was. The king asked Nikolai to his castle, where the young people were married with great joy.

Things went well at first in the crystal castle, but soon their love began to show strain, like little cracks in the walls. Sometimes Nikolai looked at Katia and recalled the face of the dead princess, his first love, and in this state turned away from Katia, often going on interminable hunting trips. He knew his distance and his absence frightened her, but he did not know what else to do. He did not know that they made her recall her mother's words.

Sometimes, for her part, Katia sat in gloomy silence, trying to understand how Nikolai could have built this place all in one night. She envied his powers, even as she knew her envy and her nagging to know his magic made him recoil from her. Katia's father and Nikolai's mother often saw their children's gloom and tried to help but could not, and then, of course, things would turn back to joy again, and all would be well between the two lovers for a time.

One day, as the glass walls were cracking again, Nikolai prepared for a long hunting trip. Katia begged him to stay, for in the night her mother had come to her in a dream. "Promise him eternal love," her mother had said, "in return for his secret. And be ready to give what you've promised." So Katia said to Nikolai, "Let us start again. We have both had secrets. Let us tell them, and start again." Nikolai wanted to feel the joy of love again too, so he agreed. Katia confessed that she had been a nag over his magic and knew it and apologized. Nikolai confessed that the ring was the source of his magic.

Feeling deep love again, the lovers danced and drank well into the night and then fell asleep. Katia, waking up first, could not resist taking the ring off her husband's finger. She put it on her own and twirled it three times. Fairies and witches appeared to her. They said, "What is your bidding?" Before she could stop herself, Katia said, "Make this castle whole again, fix all its cracks, and take it to some kingdom far away where there is a prince who will love me completely and utterly and never go away from me on trips." Her allies did as she asked.

That morning, when he woke up, Nikolai lay in a stupor in the king's now-empty meadow. Finding his daughter gone, the king arrested his son-in-law, who, in truth, could explain nothing. Nikolai even thought he might be to blame for her disappearance. He mourned her loss. From his dungeon he cried out, "Find the ring, find the ring," but no one knew what he was talking about.

Unbeknownst to him, his dog and cat had witnessed everything that had happened while he was asleep. They had mysterious powers by which they were able to sense where the ring had gone. They followed their sense to the kingdom far away where the princess had gone. They found her there and worked their way into her and her new husband's lives by doing tricks. They were not surprised to see that the princess missed her own world and was not quite happy. Nor were the dog and cat surprised to see that the prince had taken the ring from the princess. At night, he slept with it in his mouth.

One night, bewitching him with tricks, music, and drink, they got the ring from him. They returned to their master's dungeon. There, overjoyed, Nikolai put the ring on his finger and twirled. He bid his allies bring the princess and the castle back, which they did. Katia confessed what she had done, and Nikolai told the dog and cat to take the ring back to the old peasant, wherever he was.

Nikolai and Katia were reunited and for a time lived quite happily together.

STAGE 1

ROMANCE

I feel so beautiful, so free
I need nothing but you
You are everything to me . . .
—SONG HEARD ON A MANHATTAN SUBWAY

When I was a boy, I had my share of puppy loves, but Jocelyn was my first real romance. At seventeen, I wanted to experience "free love." Unfortunately, Jocelyn, a fundamentalist Christian, had other plans. She needed me to take Jesus into my heart before she would kiss me. She already had a romance—with God. I needed her love to show me I was worthy of being alive. Neither of us could really come through for the other, though for months we tried hard to love each other. What, really, did we know about love? Our families hadn't taught us much. We knew what we knew from songs and books and fantasies. We knew romance, kids' style.

One morning, frustrated, I wrote this poem:

THE BEST YEARS

When I was a boy
  they said
  these are the best years of your life.
When I was a youth in love
  they said
  these are the best years of your life.

29

When I was in college, alone
   they said
   these are the best years of your life.
When I got married
   they said
   these are the best years of your life.
When I retired
   they said
   these are the best years of your life.
Now I am old
   and aged
   and can no longer hear them
   these are the best years of my life.

For me, at this stage of my life, there was either the tumult of romance, the attraction of enchantment, the surrender to dependency, the lust of infatuation—or there was aging and silence. There was either true love or cynical defeat.

It would be a long time before I left this first stage of loving. This first stage, romance, in all its ardor and splendor, is psychologically a mask for the way we learned to relate as children—through dependency. I didn't know that. All I knew was that, when I loved Jocelyn, I was in a garden of love, and I didn't want to leave.

THE FIRST GARDEN

There is perhaps no more famous story about stage 1 of the Lover's Journey than the story of Adam and Eve in the Garden of Eden. There they were, two blessed beings who did not have to work at being blessed, who did not have to struggle to communicate with each other. They were in a state of perfect love and harmony. They knew God. In their garden, light was light and dark was dark, and they knew the difference, for there were no gray areas, and they chose the light.

They experienced that beauteous effusion we all experience when we're first in love—new flowers seemed to grow everywhere, for their personal enjoyment. Creatures came out from trees and bushes to bask in the glow of their passion. The sun was not too hot for them nor the moon too lonely.

They had enough to eat and drink, just as we always seem to do when we're romantically entranced, even if we're in financial poverty. The ardor provides our sustenance, doesn't it? Who needs money? How can we not feel this way, for what else as powerfully as romance makes us feel we have actually, no matter how ugly or poor we've felt in the past, been born in divine image?

Adam and Eve had it all, and, like each of us in our first stage of love, they had not eaten from the tree of knowledge yet; they did not know what shadows really lay inside themselves (shame at their nakedness), inside each other (betrayal and blaming), inside even the world of the divine (Satan); and they did not know that their sense of freedom from all worry was based, in fact, in a deep dependency that, soon, would feel like a cage.

DEPENDENCY: THE ROOT OF ROMANCE

Dependency is about needing another's *care* for my own physical survival and/or psychological growth and/or spiritual fulfillment. *Another* here can mean person, group, divine being, or political principle. When "another" makes us feel worthy, we are dependent.

During our childhoods, we need to relate to caregivers through dependency systems. As we grow up, we seek to leave dependency behind. One way we do this is by developing a romance, "falling in love with" another person and, through the other, moving away from previous caregivers.

Yet the romance that begins that process of loving is, like Janus, the character from Greek mythology, a two-faced being. The front face embraces a new lover who will, perhaps, be our doorway into future growth. The second face looks back at childhood ways for information and direction about how to love. Our romances play out patterns of dependency.

In the garden, Adam and Eve were dependent creatures. Everything was given to them and because of that, they could focus purely on loving each other.

Likewise, in childhood dependency and in romance, everything feels given to us. Love takes care of itself. It just is; it not only is, it is awesome in scope. We have no worries, we focus only on each other. We do not realize the subtlety of our dependency on each other yet. Nor do we realize we can take the dependency too far—making our relationship with this other a matter of enmeshment, confusion, and lifelong struggle.

THE ENCHANTED RING: PART ONE

Imagine for a moment that you are Katia. Your mother dies, leaving you with a vision that feels like prophecy. In that vision she sees you in passionate love with another. She implores you to love this other with all your heart, to find the source of his magic, and to make sure you capture it. In capturing it you will keep him close to you, and you will not have to give yourself up to him. This vision and advice your mother gives on her deathbed are so powerful they cannot be spoken to your father, and they make you see your father differently from then on.

In each of us, male or female, there is "romantic history"

and "romantic prophecy." We are Katia. From our caregivers, each of us gained legends, advice, exhortations about how to love. Often, those legends, that advice, those pleas came from our same-sex parent. And they often came from this parent unconsciously. We watched our parents relate and aligned with our same-sex parent as we got older, modeling that parent's Way. We didn't really understand what we were modeling and learning until we came of age. Even then we only thought we understood it—in every move we made to rebel against it—we still had a long way to go.

Katia gains from her mother the deep, archetypal idea that to be happy she must give utterly in love, yet at the same time, she must learn the source of her spouse's power and, at the right moment, capture it. "Power" in her world of love means "magic." Whoever controls the magic, that ability to sway the other, enchant the other, manipulate and control the other, will gain what s/he needs from the relationship.

Katia lived long ago, but certainly she lives in us still.

Nikolai, too, encounters a caregiver's advice about the enchantments of love. In his case, a dying father leaves him the wealth to pursue a lover's course and find the mentor from whom to get advice. Nikolai connects with a trinity of assistants—dog, cat, peasant—and through that association, gains the power over enchantment by which he will master romance. His father has told him to love utterly, but still not give his heart. The peasant directs him to the dead princess who possesses the enchanted ring.

Was it planned that he fall in love with the visage of the princess? Was it planned that he carry that visage of perfection in his mind throughout his romance even with Katia? Who knows what the unconscious plans for us? What we can be sure of is this: Nikolai, like Katia, pursues his family's legend, a romantic legend passed on to him by his same-sex parent.

Isn't each one of us somewhat like Nikolai in our early stages of loving? We have learned to beware of the other as much as adore him, seek the enchanted ring by which to woo her, yet carry within us an image of perfection that she will never be able to satisfy.

As men we tend to associate with Nikolai and as women with Katia. These associations are fruitful. At the same time, Nikolai and Katia are both parts of each of us. A woman can associate with Nikolai and a man with Katia. At their core, the two young people are very similar when it comes to the romantic histories they bring to love—both want the bliss of love, both have learned to be wary of too much dependency on their partner, both know they each have personal powers and magic that will, deep in the unconscious, do battle with their lover's power for sovereignty.

The story continues. Nikolai and Katia meet at their parents' graves—what better way to show how powerfully they love each other? Their infatuation is enormous, the kind that can surpass all griefs, even the deaths of beloved parents. We too have felt the power of this "love at first sight." We've felt that electrical charge of energy transfer that truly makes us feel we have become the most powerful beings on earth.

After the *moment* of infatuation comes the *process* of infatuation—the wooing. Nikolai is nervous and enlists his mother's aid; Katia accepts her father's. These two lovers are still deeply dependent on caregivers to carve for their young hearts a path through the wilderness of love. Mother is pessimistic, Father is authoritarian—both parents in their way are afraid of losing their children. Through the emissary of his mother, Nikolai is offered a test by Katia that does not, for her, carry any lethal penalty. Her father, to protect her, makes sure Nikolai understands the gravity of his wooing.

Now the enchanted ring is put to use. Now the need for enchantment in the romance process becomes clear. In this same way, each of us in our romance accepts challenges, pursues lovers, sets forth challenges, acts coy. We use all tools and allies available to us. We seek to gain the love and trust of the other, often by doing things that, before our romantic attachment, would have seemed impossible. For us in our world, building a crystal palace is comparable to taking a risk we would never take except to prove our love for our new mate. It is about committing ourselves to marriage, giving up our virginity, breaking off from a parent who stands in the way of our romance, building a dream house for our lover, moving to another city and giving up a good job just so we can be with our lover.

The magic of Nikolai's enchanted ring shows itself in the *relationship building* we do. The magic of the challenges Katia sets forth shows itself in the *sacrifices* we expect of our partner. Male or female, we all expect sacrifices of our partner; we all expect to make sacrifices in order for love to grow. We show the extremes of our expectations and our abilities during the romance stage. We build crystal palaces, or at least promise to.

So there's an interpretation of part I of an "enchanting" little tale. Two people with a little bit of baggage fall in love. So what's new?

Let's go even deeper. What is this moment in the graveyard when we know we're in love? What is infatuation made of? What can it teach us about joy?

And even beneath that—what is the moment of infatuation in the graveyard hiding from us? What lies in those graves under the surface of the earth?

INFATUATION: THE LEAP OF FAITH

When Katia and Nikolai fall in love, they make a leap of faith. In our infatuation with another—in the flower-giving, promise-making, song-singing process of the first days, weeks, months of a romance—we reach across a void into the other person's heart. That leap of faith, that falling in love, sexual lust, eyes meeting across a crowded room, is a kind of fear bypass by which we biologically and psychologically get up the guts to circumvent our basic survival fear of meshing our life with another life that can, potentially, destroy us.

This is what both Katia's dying mother and Nikolai's dying father were trying to tell their children. Watch out or you'll lose yourself. Beware, your lover will want to steal your heart from you. Love is dangerous. Kids know it themselves, too—their utter nervousness, awkwardness, fear, is about that sense of danger, the danger of losing oneself in rejection, being consumed, devoured. Without the long moment of infatuation, we wouldn't go beyond the danger.

To be more literal about it, the human brain, evolved over millions of years in an ecosystem as physically and psychologically dangerous as ours, is not an entity that easily trusts others of potentially equal power or seemingly greater power. It needs a fear bypass. It needs a leap of faith. The brain needs it in religion where without a leap, faith isn't possible. And the brain needs it in human love.

The process by which we do this bypass in stage 1 is the process of *illusionment*. My brain (disguised on Hallmark cards as "the human heart") decides to love a mate by molding that mate into an illusion of my own creation. My brain decides I can depend on this someone else because it projects directly onto him or her the illusions it needs for trust between us to build—illusions about who the mate is, based on what I need him/her to be. The more I learn about how my brain projects these illusions, the more I gain from romance, the more I understand my own capacity for magic, and then, the better prepared I get for the full, twelve-stage cycle of love.

THE BIOLOGY OF ROMANCE

As I describe the way we fall in love, I talk about "the brain," rather than "the heart." I'm not trying to steal the magic of romance. When I refer to the brain in this process, I am doing the same sort of thing we've done for centuries with the heart—I'm creating a metaphor. We know too little right now about how the brain works to pretend we can speak of it in pure scientific terms, yet we also know that the heart has little to do with the magic of loving. The brain is in charge.

Here's a very clear, culture-wide example of how the human brain, in the process of romance, has engaged in illusionment—how it creates illusions so it can make the leap of faith into romance. This clear-cut way is seen in basic gender-different approaches to romance. Men and women create, for the most part, different initial illusions by which to make their leaps of faith. In "The Enchanted Ring" we see this pattern of gender difference in illusionment. In fact, it is a pattern so common in fairy tales, we can be pretty sure the same brain that leads us into the illusionment of romance is also the source of the stories about illusionment that can enable us to grow beyond them.

According to psychological studies in clinical literature as well as surveys in popular magazines like *Vogue,* romantic enchantment occurs most frequently in women (about 65 percent of the time) when the man they've fallen in love with is financially and socially successful—has the magic to create the crystal palace; the same occurs most frequently in men (about 70 percent of the time) when the woman they've fallen in love with is young and pretty. As men we tend, initially, to make women into sex objects; as women we tend, initially, to make men into success objects.

Why? It's not all just stereotype. It's rooted in biology, the place where a lot of magic is rooted. For both males and females, the biological imperative of life is procreation. Males tend to find magic in younger, more beautiful women because the bodies of those women indicate fertility. One reason many women have often chosen to live in pursuit of a "beauty myth," as Naomi Wolf has called it, is because they know at a cellular level how males want the magic in the young, beautiful body.

To be attractive to females, males have generally had to live a "performance myth." Attraction to females is based very much on how well a male competes with other males for the female. Females know that a man's fertility is not generally dependent on his physical beauty or youth. Most important to female biology is his physical/mental prowess, and proof of that prowess in his competitive standing in the community. Quite simply, if he's not a success, he's not worth betting her and her children's lives on.

Men didn't make women what they are, nor did women make men what they are. Our culture, in the face of its own biological and sociological trends, has tended to encourage dialogue in which each sex blames the other for its problems.

It would be of infinitely greater benefit for everyone to get to the biological roots of why we make the romantic leap as we do. Until we do this, we are unable to navigate stage 1 romantic attractions with wisdom, and unable to teach young people to do so as well.

When we honestly look at how our own sexual biology works, each of us, male and female, sees a lot of Katia and Nikolai in the mirror.

Women often honestly admit at my workshops how hard it is for them to be romantic with someone who they feel will simply be a drain on them, financially, emotionally, socially. They want someone who is vital, who performs, who masters the situation. "I went too far with my first husband," one woman admitted in a workshop. "I had expectations of him I didn't know I had. I wanted him to prove himself all the time but didn't know I did. No one ever had the good sense to show me some of my actions and reactions came from biology."

Many men have come forward in workshops to admit their attraction to beautiful women. In a recent workshop, one man spoke for a lot of men when he said, "I like women, pure and simple, and I have my own taste in what I like, and yes, I tend to like women who are a little more passive than me and who take care of themselves, and who care about how I see them. I don't use women—I've been married ten years and I'm monogamous—but I married a woman who fit my bill, and I look around a lot at other women. I have a lot of fantasies, it's just who I am. I used to be ashamed of being a man. I'm not anymore. To me, being a man means being myself while I stand by my commitments."

As you can imagine, this statement resulted in a lot of discussion. The man's wife was present and spoke of her resentments, but also of her pride in her husband's loyalty and honesty. We do not live in a perfect world. Because some people want biology to be different than it is, or to go away, doesn't mean it will. When we really explore how we fall in love and why, we encounter shame about our fantasies and tastes. We blame others for theirs. Knowledge about sexual biology helps us let go of the shame, and it makes it easier for all of us, male and female, to spend more energy on standing by commitments and building nurturing community.

Along with basic sexual biology, brain chemistry has more to do with stage 1 romance than we realize. Here's an example. Researchers Michael Liebowitz and Donald Klein at the New York State Psychiatric Institute work with PEA (phenylethylamine), an amphetamine-like chemical in the body that speeds up the flow of information between nerve cells. Researchers like Liebowitz and Klein have discovered that when two people are attracted to each other, PEA is what creates the physical euphoria, the ecstatic "I love you, I adore you, I'll do anything for you!" feeling. Liebowitz and Klein have worked with "PEA junkies," people who seem to need romance all the time in order to get the amphetamine-like reaction and feel excited by life. These people meet, have sex, and move on to the next romance quickly.

In a groundbreaking experiment, Liebowitz and Klein gave antidepressants that help control PEA to a group of "attraction junkies." The result: the "junkies" were no longer junkies. They did not need a mate a month to feel whole. Brain chemistry, these researchers found, has a great deal to do with that magical leap of faith we all make into the cycle of love.

And it just gets more fascinating. Vasopressin and oxytocin are brain chemicals linked to monogamous activity in primates. In a recent issue of *Nature,* Dr. Thomas Insel revealed that in studying these brain chemicals "we have the first evidence of a neurochemical basis for attachment." Studies have mainly been done on rodents, but as Dr. Sue Carter, Insel's colleague, put it, "The possible implications for humans are enticing." Only 3 percent of mammals are monogamous. Is there a neurochemical basis not only for attraction, but even for actual long-term commitments that begin in the enchantment of romance?

Through physiological factors like hormones, brain chemicals, PEA, and biological strategies of sexual commitment, we push out of ourselves toward deep surrender to another. These biological guides move us toward choices that are biologically sound for us, choices that may well be socially and psychologically sound as well.

By incorporating biological information into our spiritual discipline and lifelong quest for joy, we have a chance, especially in stage 1 where biology is so clearly active, to heal a psychic and spiritual wound most of us suffer—a wound that keeps us and our culture from joy. This wound is the soul/body split.

Our cultural heritage has split our basis for personal action into "soul principles" (i.e., moral principles) and "bodily urges" (i.e., physical drives). The split is given its clearest voice in the religions many of us practice. Freud and early psychologists supported the split, perhaps without wanting to. Through the soul/body split, religions and social psychologies could teach us morality, and how to trust a partner. We benefited from the split. We became civilized.

But splitting soul and body is no longer adaptive. We are able now, as we enter the next millennium, to see how the soul/body split has forced us to suppress much of the wisdom of our own bodies, turning us toward abstract principles to guide our magic—"I should only love so-and-so who is pure in such-and-such a way and I should only love him/her in such-and-such a way"—but thereby leading us into centuries of communal shames and damaged self-esteem.

We can also see that, just as often, in reaction to rigid moral principles, or in ignorance of the need for moral guidance, we have gone through times, many of them quite recent, of giving credence to the undisciplined magic of our bodies—"I can love whomever I want whenever I want in whatever way I want and there will be no consequence"—leading to tragic abuse and death.

Over the last few years, our culture is rediscovering the importance of wise integration of the biology of loving. In that rediscovery are many clues for many people about how they love—whether they are biologically suited for monogamy, for instance, or homosexuality, or whether they are prone to attraction addiction. There is new wisdom about how soul and body are utterly united in their quest for joy, their pull toward love, their leap of faith, their romantic enchantments.

THE PSYCHOLOGY OF ROMANCE

The poet and researcher Diane Ackerman has written, "Love develops in the neurons of the brain, and the way it grows depends on how those neurons were trained when we were children. Evolution hands out a blueprint for the building of the house of one's life. But, as with a house, much depends on the skill and experience of the builders; the laws and codes of society; the qualities of materials. . . . How we love is a matter of biology. How we love is a matter of experience."

As Nikolai and Katia experienced that first "falling in love" feeling, their PEA was probably sky high. Nikolai may have desired Katia, initially, because of her physical beauty; or the two lovers may have chosen monogamous marriage in a way guided, not only by societal norms, but also by their vasopressin and oxytocin levels. Nikolai and Katia were biological creatures in stage 1 romance.

That's not the whole story, of course, because it does not take into account their psychological history, a history beautifully symbolized by the graves the two young lovers stood near—their parents' graves.

"It wasn't until a year later," a client of mine told me, "that I realized the woman I wanted to love was not really Sabrina, she was my mother at Sabrina's age."

Said a female client, "When I met Jack, he was everything my father wasn't."

And another: "I had given up on ever finding someone. Finding Eric was like finding myself."

Our biology gives us the tools for the magic of romance; psychology is about how we use those tools. In stage 1, neurochemically catalyzed by biological factors, we psychologically project old images, most often images of primary caregivers, onto lovers. We know no other deep psychological method of doing romance. Mom, Dad, or other caregivers have been our dependency objects. We've learned how to love by being loved by them. In stage 1 it feels utterly right to make our lover into the mother and/or father and/or other primary caregiver who raised us.

No one can avoid this in stage 1. It's just the way romantic psychology works. To what degree does each of us do it? That's for each of us to answer. Becoming conscious of your own particular psychological strategies means gaining an in-depth understanding of how your dependency on early care-givers was managed, and how you want to handle its mani-festations in your romances.

If our dependency on caregivers during our childhood took place in the context of a healthy, well-boundaried, well-nurtured family life, and if we experienced a transition from those healthy dependencies into independence during ado-lescence and young adulthood, we enter stage 1 of an adult relationship with projections, but also with the inherent knowledge that one day the projections will have to dissolve, and on that traumatic day life will not be over.

If dependency on our caregivers was not healthy, not well boundaried, not well nurtured, and/or if we experienced traumatic transitions from those dependencies into indepen-dence, and/or did not really separate from those childhood dependencies—if, in other words, we are like the vast major-ity of people in our culture, people who have significantly unresolved issues with parents—we will enter the depen-dency season and the romance stage of an adult relationship cleaving to projections and weaving an unconscious, com-plex web with them that we become dependent on through-out the life of the relationship. When, two months or two years or twenty years into a relationship, our partner mildly or deeply disappoints us, betrays us, or confuses us, we will probably avoid our terror of that failure by abusing, control-ling, distancing from, or abandoning our partner.

We have to remember that this psychology of dependency and the magic of romance are based in the immature, often damaged psyche's belief that someone else holds the key to our sense of safety and self-worth. Our psyche is saying, "If I can be rescued by him/her I will feel worthy and I will re-ward him/her with emotional safety." And: "If I can rescue him/her I will feel worthy and s/he will reward me with emotional safety." Or a million "ifs" like that.

What this comes down to is that in stage 1, no matter our sex, we are quite literally willing to say, "You are more important to me than myself," because in surrendering to another this way we think s/he can become not only a lover whom we will care for, but also a residual caregiver to whom we can safely attach our developing and wounded selves.

To bring this psychological material to the concrete, see if anything feels familiar in the following list of behaviors that reflect the psychological magic we experience during stage 1.

• Before we even meet our lover, we spend a lot of time visualizing the perfect partner. We do what is made into metaphor by Nikolai's idealization of the princess who holds the ring. Our own visualizing is based in biological, familial, social, and personal standards of beauty, safety, and security developed culturally over millennia and personally throughout our own life history.

• Before we even meet a potential partner, we have already projected onto him/her one or more of our parental figures. We usually set a base for our projection by starting with same-sex parents—projecting Dad onto men and Mom onto women—but this is just a base; it depends on our family histories and generally expands to a point where we are projecting imagery onto lovers that is not limited to the caregiver of their sex.

• The moment in the graveyard occurs. We meet (even if not face to face, i.e., through letters with a pen pal), we "fall in love," we have those first talks, dances, sexual moments that "blow our minds."

• The romance grows until we have a feeling of utter

closeness with the other—"We are one!" We don't realize that this feeling is idealized dependency, laden with baggage from the past that weighs each of us down. We think we're beyond all that; we think this "we are one" feeling is about utter interdependence between two equals.

• We discover the other as our perfect mirror—that is, "You are the one who shows me who I am. Without you I would not have an identity."

• We surrender ourselves to the other through adoration, flattery, gift giving, and personal change, and by saying what the other wants to hear. If we are both "in love" with each other, we are both doing this surrender. We make promises of endless love: "I will love you forever."

• We justify to ourselves and to concerned others in our support systems that our loss of self with this man or woman is just fine. "I know what I'm doing. Get out of my life, you guys, I've found everything I want."

• A first disturbance occurs—a first disillusionment—but we deny it quickly. "We don't have common interests, but who cares? We'll be fine, just fine."

• We inculcate a belief that we and our mate have magically joined in an intimacy system agreed upon between us in preverbal union. This intimacy system is specifically *not* accessible to anyone but us, and is accessible to us without effort: "We have something no one else understands, something beyond words. We just *are*. It feels so easy. I never knew love could be this easy." We are like Nikolai and Katia, who create with their love a crystal palace all their own, a place no one else will live in—at least not in the beginning.

Without the biological and psychological process of enchantment, we wouldn't give up our natural safety boundaries, we wouldn't copulate; there would be no species survival. We need the hormones and brain chemicals to push us; we need the illusions to be projected onto mates; we need to pretend our mates will give us everything our parents gave us, or more. It is how stage 1 romance works. By taking that first, infatuated leap of faith, we begin our quest for joy, our journey through the cycle of mature love.

ROMANTIC LOVE WITHOUT DEEP TRUST

Take a moment to focus on these nine questions.

1. Do you spend a good deal of time fantasizing a "perfect other"? You may do this whether you're married or single.

2. Do you ask your mate(s) to fill in the emotional space left by the departure from your emotional core of the attentions of one or more of your parents?

3. Is the maintenance and growth of your self-esteem dependent on the opinion of one or more of your immediate family members (mate, children, parents) and/or on success in some other primary aspect of your life (e.g., religious practice or work)?

4. Do you believe that to truly be alive you must feel that "I am completely one with" or "I have surrendered to" someone or something else—mate, family member, religion, work, addiction?

5. Do you feel that you lack an internal map for finding wholeness and must wait for the right lover, guru, divine being, object, or practice to show you the way to wholeness?

6. Do you tend to give whatever your parent or mate or

child or religious practice or work asks in order to be loved by him, her, or it?

7. Do you feel primarily responsible for making things work in emotional relationships and primarily at fault when they don't work?

8. When you're alone, do you focus on and brood about your inadequacies?

9. Are others completely or mostly to blame for your problems?

Read the questions as many times as you need to. They're tough questions. Let them settle in you until you're sure of your answers. If you answered any of them with a "Yes," you are like most people you know.

Most of us were brought up in troubled families. These families were usually nuclear families, so they existed— especially where their dark secrets were concerned—in isolation from community support and assistance; thus, we were brought up in troubled families and felt we had nowhere to turn.

When we as children were brought up in families and communities where we could not adequately trust our care- givers—whether because of their addiction, divorce, emo- tional crises, distance, absence, abusiveness, abandonment, inability to bond, emotional or physical incest, or incompe- tence—we can't, without years of profound spiritual work and discipline, trust others and ourselves later in life.

If we can't trust ourselves and others and build interdepen- dent relationships based in that trust, we replay distrusts and dependency patterns, trying to get throughout our later lives the love we didn't get as kids. In replaying those patterns, *we become dependent on "trusted" lovers whom we do not, at our core, actually trust.* As we were as children, we have become adults who want desperately to be loved for "who we are" but can't trust a lover enough to let him/her see who we are. We practice love not as a spiritual discipline but a regressive emotional state. Our family systems did not give us the sense of attachment we needed as kids, so we hang on to those families—through idealizations and through complaints—as if to a cliff. Most therapeutic strategies developed since the institution of the nuclear family have been about helping people resolve issues with families that did not give them the love they needed.

ROMANCE AS A COMMODITY

Unfortunately, we've created a whole culture to make us feel okay about being regressive, okay about not having been taught our value while we were dependent children, and okay about remaining dependent children the rest of our lives.

From films to song lyrics to music videos to e-mail, our popular culture is dominated by the promise of gardens of Eden. All the promised relationships and products help us feel somewhat better about ourselves (usually better about what we often call our *false selves,* for dandruff shampoos and new boats and $2,000 dresses have little to do with anything but the continuation of a false existence). The more we watch and listen, the more we become adults dependent on others and commodities. We have made lovers into our spiritual salvation and material goods into sacred objects. During childhood, our most active teacher, after our parents, is popular culture; during adolescence, our most active teacher, especially through peer group process, is popular culture. Especially during late childhood and throughout adolescence, we have few spiritual mentors with whom we're intimate and through whom we learn, by intimate process, how to find ourselves. Instead, we are taught that adult life in society depends on commodities. Other people swiftly become commodities, as do natural resources. When the enchantment provided by these people, resources, or things wears off, we discard them, seeking new people, resources, and things through whom to get our needs met. Many of us take decades to realize that even many of those needs are needs of a false self. We don't know what our true needs are. The irony of all this is that we are training ourselves through popular culture to remain eternally in the romance of stage 1, but our romance is a romance with what is not really us.

THE FIRST TASK

What you've just read is pretty bad news. It argues that most of us are psychologically damaged human beings; mindful mainly of stories that promise a lie; compelled, for our psychic survival as children and then as adults, to remain in dependency on spouses or lovers for our psychological and spiritual sustenance. It argues that the cult of romance we've created in our culture and the frenzy to be "in love" that we live by in our relational lives are indicators of this crisis of dependency. If, as you move through this book, you discover that you are dependent on primary relationships to a greater or lesser degree the way you were dependent on parents, know that you are not alone.

That camaraderie is, for many people, good news. The more every one of us compares the cult of romance we live in to the spiritual challenges of mature love, and the more we come together as a culture to find ways out of eternally replaying dependencies on others and commodities, the more our whole culture will rise up in unity, toward joy. Finding joy in stage 1, the time of romance, is a sacred task, which we can accomplish with conscious effort, and a leap of faith.

Toward the end of each chapter of this book, beginning with this one, I'll point out the specific spiritual task the Lover is going through during the particular stage of loving. The Lover's spiritual work in each stage is about new *lessons of trust*, and new *foci for personal energy*. With each task accomplished, we mature more and more. Sometimes the lessons of trust and foci for energy will be obvious, sometimes more subtle. In stage 1 they are relatively obvious. In every stage the Sacred Tasks are good news.

Stage 1 of the Lover's spiritual discipline gives us our first lesson in trust: *bonding*.

In much the same way as when I was a child, to trust in love I must be able to depend on another. I must be able to feel safe to mature my being with this other by the other's act of opening himself or herself to me and my accepting that embrace.

Many of us have been so hurt that we can't accomplish this trust, this bonding, even as our hormones and brain chemicals give us attractions to others. Many of us, too, go the opposite route. We don't just bond, we enmesh. We follow our initial and normal projections of parental or past figures onto our lover by inculcating them and never letting them go. We set about depending on the other as if on a parent. We've seen these patterns in this chapter, but, nonetheless, the Lover's task remains; the Lover must bond and explore bonding as stage 1 spiritual discipline.

Stage 1 of the Lover's Journey also provides us with the

first element of focus for the Lover's spiritual discipline: *surrender*. These elements of focus in each stage are ways of focusing our internal energies.

To practice love as a spiritual discipline, I must be able to surrender myself to another, if only momentarily. I must be able to focus my energy toward interpersonal bonding through the act of surrender.

As you recall your time of romance, or pass through it now, or renew it at ritual times every year, or mentor young people in its practice, you bless yourself and the world by being conscious of the grace you feel when you surrender utterly. It is the great risk. It is that first act of initiating joyful connection. It is not meant to last long, but it must occur. We must feel its bio-psychological surge of energy coursing through us, and, with hope, we will experience moments of surrender all through our lives.

How do you practice your surrender? If you are a person who is often lonely, take a moment to discover how you may have been hurt so often you've bypassed romantic surrender as quickly as you can. After only a few days or weeks of romance, do you break things off? Or do you get married too quickly, surrendering too much too soon?

Do you commit yourself to someone, but then rebel against him/her every chance you get—acting out sexually, demeaning your lover in public? If so, you may not actually be surrendering.

If you discover you or your partner have bypassed romance, scared of its magic, your task and your partner's task is to relearn how to be romantic. Many people do this on anniversaries, on vacations, at candlelight dinners, through valentines and other rituals of romance. If you are the kind of person who looks down on these sentimentalities, you have probably been badly hurt in the past.

INTEGRATING ROMANCE

The journey through stage 1 that Nikolai and Katia made came to a point of integration when they went to live in the crystal palace. All the family prophecies, all the lovemaking, risk-taking, and relationship building came to fruition in that magical home. And they lived there, happily, for a time.

In the same way, we strive to come to a point of integration as the romance stage progresses. It is felt as "oneness," often acted out as a wedding, made sacred in church or at city hall. Our romance—its nervousness, then its lovemaking and risk-taking, build to a time of happy living. In that time, whether we know it or not, we are absorbing into the Lover's psychic body all the useful information and spiritual process we can.

Even as the new moment comes when we feel romance dying, we must never truly leave romance behind. Every stage of the Lover's Journey is integrated into later stages. We must keep practicing romance, keep saying "I love you," keep wearing sexy clothes, keep finding rituals of romance. Our biology and our maturing psyches need constant novelty and stimulation throughout our lifetime of love.

In integrating romance we never leave dependency behind completely. We will often be dependent on our lovers—we will get sick and need their care. Fate, crisis, an act of God, sudden unemployment, the death of a child—any of these can send us careening back into a time of utter dependency in which we need to see our partner as our savior, we need to trust utterly, we need to surrender. We are human, we are fragile, we have no choice, we need to depend.

But if we are adults, we need always to see dependency as a time of emotional recovery and physical convalescence, not as a permanent state. We must understand infatuation as only a first step toward mature love. In midlife, as our loved one's body gets older, so must our eyes. We cannot keep projecting a young body—or the dead princess who held the enchanted ring—onto her. In midlife, as our loved one faces disappointments and changes and seems sometimes to crumble before our eyes, we must move beyond our fear of our own life crumbling too, and see the spiritual journey he is trying to make. Finally, we must enter stage 2: become disillusioned with lovers, as with parents, religions or other things on which we have depended. We must fall from the garden. Our identities depend on it.

STAGE 2

THE FALL INTO DISILLUSIONMENT

You done me wrong
You done me wrong
Our love is gone
O Lord, our love is gone
—ANONYMOUS BLUES REFRAIN

And the eyes of both Adam and Eve were opened,
and they knew that they were naked.
—GENESIS 3:7 (KJV)

For Adam and Eve, everything went wonderfully as long as they kept up the illusion that everything was perfect. In the romance stage, keeping up this illusion is seemingly effortless.

Once, Adam and Eve ate from the tree of knowledge, however, they learned to see beyond the illusion. They became enlightened. They saw flaws—the smallness and imperfectness of their own bodies, the strangeness of their surroundings. They felt restlessness, they felt shame, and they felt fear. They had no choice but to leave the garden.

Who hasn't, at some time in life—like Adam and Eve in the garden—felt the perfection, ecstasy, and seeming permanence of infatuation, and then felt it crumble?

THE ENCHANTED RING: PART TWO

Katia and Nikolai lived happily for a time in the crystal palace. Then cracks began to show in its walls. Nikolai looked at Katia but yearned for the visage of the dead princess. He had, without realizing it, projected that illusion—that visage—onto Katia. When the living Katia disappointed, he distanced himself by going on prolonged hunting trips.

Katia, for her part, recalled her mother's admonition: "Find the source of his power." She knew she loved Nikolai, but without knowing the source of his power, she did not believe she really knew him. In her early projections, she had assumed that after marriage, she'd learn his inner world. Marriage has not made that happen. She sits in gloomy silences of her own.

Like Nikolai and Katia, we often create a crystal palace for romantic love, then find cracks in it. First we are connected with another person's life energy in a way that feels like mystical union. But we've actually accomplished this connection—this embrace of another's life energy—through a web of our own illusions about him or her and ourselves.

So we often begin stage 2 with the discovery that our partner is a stranger, and even that we ourselves are strangers. "I don't really know you after all," we say. "I can't really trust you after all. I don't know who I am either." We respond to our discovery of the cracking crystal palace by distancing ourselves, becoming depressed, becoming angry. We seek solutions. Sometimes we turn to support systems, parents, for advice and solace. Often, we think our relationship is doomed. Katia's father and Nikolai's mother look on and try to help, but they can't do much. The story shows great wisdom here. It says: these two lovers have to fix this on their own. Going back into their parents' vision of love isn't the right course right now. They need to work this out for themselves.

Then, as so often happens, moments of joy reenter Katia's and Nikolai's relationship. They fall madly in love again. The story doesn't tell us exactly how this occurs, but we know there are a thousand ways romance can get rekindled—flowers, a sexual breakthrough, the decision to have a child.

Katia sees her mother in a dream. Her mother gives her advice—"Promise him eternal love in return for his secret." So the parent's vision comes back in after all! Katia's unconscious, feeling desperate, turns to the best source it has known for advice, and that advice, like Eve's eating the apple, forces the couple into power struggle. They share secrets and feel liberated and drink and dance and fall asleep.

The telling of secrets in the disillusionment stage is ultimately an attempt to regain romance. We believe that if we open our hearts utterly again, practice absolute, boundaryless honesty again, our awesome love will return. We forget, though, that that awesome love was built on illusion. The telling of secrets is the stripping away of illusions. Once the illusions are stripped away completely, the stage will be set for stage 3.

LEARNING WE CAN'T TRUST LOVERS
WITH OUR IDENTITY

When I was a boy in India I heard this little tale, "The Girl by the Water," from a woman who helped raise me. In this story is an essential piece of wisdom about why first Katia's mother, then Katia herself, felt compelled to gain her lover's power at all costs.

A girl gives a boy jewelry, promises, and kisses. She finds out, however, that he is in love with another girl. Feeling betrayed, she sits by a lake in gloomy silence. An old woman comes to sit next to her.

"Why do you look so sad?" the wise woman asks.

The girl tells her story. "I think I will die," she says.

"So," the old woman says, "that boy's love is so powerful it can take away your life?"

"I gave myself to him, and he didn't want me. I am worthless. I am like the dirt. Why should I live?"

The old woman says, "Perhaps you are like dirt. How wise of you." The old woman instructs the girl to dig her hands into the lake and see what she pulls up. She does so, pulling up sediment in her cupped palm, and on top of the sediment, some water. The water, quite quickly, leaks away, leaving the sediment.

Pointing to the sediment the old woman says, "That is you. You are made of water and of sand. You gave him the water, but you did not give him the sand. In your watery tears, that dirt and that sand are ugly indeed. But your tears will pass. When they do, you will see more clearly the solid part of who you are."

In stage 2 Katia, quite unconsciously, touches her own very fragile, very fragmented self. Nikolai built the crystal palace; she did not. She did compel it to be built—but she can't see her power in this right now. All she can see is that *he* controls who she is. She needs to gain control over her self. In stage 2, we are growing up; we are striving to realize that dependency is not in itself a cure-all. We do not know what our full identity is yet, but at least we realize something is *ours*. We are individuating. What is ours? Katia wants the ring because, in the unfolding life of the story, she feels the ring will give her power, self, identity. Had she been the Indian girl at the lake's edge, she would have learned that she is part water, part sand. She has not in fact given her whole self to her husband's power; she has a self, especially a core self (the sand), which no one can destroy. But she doesn't quite realize this yet.

DISCOVERING THE STRANGER WITHIN: FEAR OF YOUR OWN INADEQUACY

In the Indian story, the old woman turns around the girl's statement, "I am like dirt," from something negative to something positive. "How wise," she says. "Yes, you are like dirt." And she shows the girl how.

What the girl meant when she compared herself to dirt is what we mean when, after romance ends, we fall face down into the mud and grime of our own inadequacy. "I feel like shit," someone will say. "I feel like dirt." "I feel lower than low." These metaphors are very appropriate—losing romance is a very grounding experience. Among our first reactions are to feel victimized by him or by her, to feel self-hating toward ourselves, and to strive outside ourselves toward someone else's power—someone else's self—to fill in our own inadequacy.

Nikolai, you'll recall, cleaved to his illusion of the second princess. Could one of the reasons he did this be that she was dead, and loving her was very easy? She could not judge him. She could not peer into him and discover any inadequacies. Dead, she was a perfect mate. Loving the fantasy lover is one of the most powerful ways we can avoid our own sense of worthlessness. The fantasy lover always loves us for exactly who we want to think we are.

As human beings, we experience two kinds of fears. First, we experience instinctual survival fears. These fears are based in our instinctual fear of physical death. We are alive; we experience ourselves as a *living self*; we do everything we can to stay alive; we spend much of life energy "making a living," "learning how to live," "living in a better neighborhood," "fighting to live," so that we protect the existence of that living self, our very body.

Our second kind of fear—psychological fear—is based in something more subtle: our fear of losing our *adequate self*. All psychological fears—fears of rejection, abandonment, disapproval, insecurity—can be traced back to our root fear of being inadequate. For years now I have been asking participants in workshops to think of any psychological fear that is not, at root, based in the fear of inadequacy. So far, we've thought of none, for all psychological fears gain their energy from the living self's fear that it will be found inadequate to face the huge world, the changing relationship, the lost job, the divorce, the children moving away, the romance dying into disenchantment.

In stage 1, we go to an enchanted garden and let biology and psychological projections keep us safe in our crystal palace where adequacy is actually defined as perfection. Once we eat from the tree of knowledge, once we learn all the secrets, we see clearly our partner's inadequacies, and worst of all, our partner sees ours. Sometimes, in this stage, our partners leave us, and like the girl in the Indian story, we feel so inadequate we want to die. "I've made a bad choice," we rage at ourselves. In resignation we say, "I'll never find someone to love me." "I despise myself." "I'm not worth loving." This feeling of inadequacy is, quite simply, awful.

What do you do when you get to the point of pressing

your finger into the wound of your own inadequacy? It's a question worth answering before you leave stage 2. Many of us self-destruct when we touch our own inadequacy; many of us seek to destroy others, destroy relationships; many of us simply drift, waiting for the next person, place, thing or process to enchant us.

Often I've asked clients to record in their journal how they've handled their own stage 2. Mark wrote, "I didn't like myself much, I remember that. I wanted Carolyn to tell me 'I love you' a lot. It's embarassing now to think about. I wanted her to go places with me, like me, listen to me. Early on, she was always saying 'I love you.' She was a tag-along, hanging on my every word. But pretty soon she got sick of me, I guess. I suppose I was selfish, always talking. Or I was just too needy. I don't know. When she got sick of me she left, and I felt like my world caved in. It's taking me a long time to trust again, to decide I'm okay."

The story of "The Girl by the Water" teaches us to attend not to our lover's secrets but to ourselves when disillusionment occurs. This is what Mark learned he had to do. Many of us don't truly pay attention to ourselves—we don't notice that we are part water, part sand. We don't see the sand that is left after the tears dry. Often we don't let ourselves cry at all during disillusionment. Just as often, we cry until we fall into soothing sleep, hoping never to awaken. Often we see the water and the sand in the lake in front of us but receive no mentoring about how to face the darkness, so we never learn to dip our hands in, and give rise to personal wisdom and spiritual progress. We don't learn some important things about ourselves that we can only learn here, in stage 2, in those moments of life when romance dies and we feel naked and ugly, those hours Adam and Eve lived after they realized their shameful nakedness but before they confronted God, left the garden, and made rich, fertile human lives for themselves.

DISCOVERING THE STRANGERS
IN YOUR LIFE

Here is a list of the ways disenchantment manifests in stage 2. See if these activities and experiences sound familiar.

• There is a disturbance in our garden, a broken illusion. We say things like, "You're not the woman/man I married." "S/he is so ugly/mean. How could I have missed it before?"

• We go into denial. "Everything will be fine." "S/he is just going through a phase." "S/he isn't really changing. We aren't really changing."

• We get depressed, angry, afraid, distant. This early sense of fear is usually fear about the other—fear of losing him/her. It is not yet fear of our own inadequacy as a lover/being. We go on long hunting trips, or sit brooding.

• We make an *overt* effort to gain reassurance from our lover. Sometimes we make a conscious attempt to dialogue specifically about the fall into disillusionment we are experiencing. "Are you going through something weird too?" Sometimes we come out and ask the other to love us more, tell us what to do to bring back the romance.

• Meanwhile, we make a *covert* effort for reassurance. We constantly question our partner's behavior. We "act better," hoping illusions will stand up again. We might chatter a lot, fill up silences. We buy our lover things. We are very watchful of our lover's behavior, where s/he looks and at whom. Like Katia, we are in that time when we want to know the secrets.

• When our partner does something surprisingly sweet, we become elated; we are now able to reproject the illusions. "Thank God, things are back to normal. He really is what I thought. She really is what I thought. I really am okay. We're okay."

• But then another disturbance in the illusions occurs. We react with depression, anger, withdrawal—again, grounded in fear. This time we begin to notice that we dislike ourselves, don't trust ourselves, feel terrible about ourselves— "How could I have loved this person?" or "If I were a better person, s/he wouldn't fall out of love with me."

• We generate fantasies of escape from this inadequacy. We might act on these fantasies, perhaps by sleeping with someone else. The fantasies are not in themselves "right" or "wrong." They are coping responses to our deep sense of loss and inadequacy.

• Either unilaterally, or in conjunction with our partner who is also experiencing disillusionment, we dissolve the intimacy system we had seemingly made during our time of infatuation and courtship. This means that either we leave each other, or we remain together and move into the next stage of relationship—power struggle.

We have all failed at love, all been betrayed. If we sit with the pain in stage 2 that comes with feelings of having failed at love, we gain the kind of growth that only suffering can give. As we need to, we reach out for the support of friends, therapists, mentors, and spiritual processes to help "make sense" and "make soul" of our pain.

THE SECOND SACRED TASK

Stage 2 of the Lover's spiritual discipline teaches us the second lesson of trust: *imperishability.*

No matter what happens to relationship, no matter how terrible I think I am, some part of me will survive. To move forward in my spiritual path, to trust one step more, I must begin now to learn who I am—not just the illusions.

Often I do not get a chance to know my core self as an adult until faced with stage 2. Often it is after losing the person I thought would save me that I see who I really am and feel ready to face life with the courage of seeing that there is sand in me no one can take away.

In an ideal framework of human development, this lesson of trust, this stage 2, would be well taught during our teenage years, even young adulthood. The longer I wait into my adulthood to move through stage 2, to discover in my guts my imperishability and nurture in response my sense of self, the less fulfilled I'll be in adult relationships. The less I am guided by parents and mentors to become comfortable with and learn from the pain of stage 2 in my adolescence and young adulthood, the more harshly I will awaken in middle age to discover how little I understand of who I am, and how perishable I feel.

Many of us come to middle age feeling very perishable. Until then we have not, for all intents and purposes, left Season One, especially a stage 1/stage 2 cycle. We have not really learned who we are; we keep romantically projecting fragments of ourselves onto others, only to have others disappoint us and hurt us.

Most tribal cultures teach stage 2 early in the second decade of a person's life. While we can never go back to being tribal, still those cultures provide some good modeling.

In the ideal stage 2, with the help of mentors, friends, parents, lovers, I push through the web of illusions I projected during stage 1; I discover that I am no longer a child, I cannot ask anyone else to hold my self—my sand and water—in the palm of his or her hand. I must hold it myself. And I begin, very consciously and maturely *and with guidance*, to explore my own feelings of inadequacy. These are part of my core too, after all.

Stage 2 of the Lover's Journey also provides the second element of focus for the lover's spiritual discipline: *acceptance of the imperfect world and self.*

To practice love as a spiritual discipline, I must accept that in love I will suffer constantly, and that my own limits, my own inadequacies, will hound that suffering.

I am not perfect nor will I ever be. Spiritual teachers have long taught us that we must feel disenchantment all through us. We must not find a numbing agent; we must go through this stage 2 of sadness, pain, anger, and fear with openness and clear consciousness. The poet Robinson Jeffers wrote, "The destruction that brings an eagle from heaven is better than mercy." People who have been damaged during childhood by parents and others they trusted often try to put themselves to sleep as stage 2 takes hold of their relationship. They just want the mercy. They don't notice that on the wings of suffering comes that eagle from heaven.

How have you handled your hurt, your disillusionment? What coping mechanisms do you use?

When you notice your own inadequacy, do you stay with it, dive into it, plumb it, until you notice that it does have a bottom, that it is not endless, that you can rebuild yourself?

In pursuing the sacred task of stage 2, we must be able to say, "I sit in *my* hurt and get used to hurting." I am like Jesus who must be hurt and betrayed to be free. I am like the Buddha who, as a boy, was sheltered in his castle; he could not move into the later stages of enlightenment without, as a maturing young man, living a life of pain and deprivation and only then learning compassion for himself and others.

The wound I feel when illusions crumble gives me power. Touching the wound—my own inadequacy, life's unfairness, love's betrayal—makes soul in me.

INTEGRATING DISILLUSIONMENT

Like Nikolai and Katia, in stage 2 we strip away illusions about our partner. The secrets come out. We hurt and cope as we can. We strip ourselves down to our worst self-image—though often unconsciously, aware of this process only by our awareness of our fantasies. We cope with our commitments as we can.

A person who integrates disillusionment into his/her quest for joy is a person who can say, "I'm hurting, but I'm feeling free"; "I'm in pain, but I'm growing"; "I feel lost, but I know I'm moving into something"; "I'm getting ready to be tested."

As we integrate disillusionment, we are indeed getting prepared for one of the Lover's great tests: power struggle.

STAGE 3

POWER STRUGGLE

That's why most relationships eventually turn into power struggles. Humans link up energy and then fight over who is going to control it.
    —James Redfield, *The Celestine Prophecy*

The wildish nature knows that [sometimes being] "sweet" only makes the predator smile. When the soulful life is being threatened, it is not only acceptable to draw the line and mean it, it is required.
    —Clarissa Pinkola Estés,
    Women Who Run with the Wolves

Sandra and Alan came to see me for marital counseling. They had been together twenty years, married for fifteen. They were in their mid- to late forties. They had two children, a girl, eight years old, and a boy, ten. They were middle-class inhabitants of a midsize American city.

ALAN: "We don't really have a relationship except through the kids. I'm ready to end this marriage. All our fighting is finally getting to me. I'm not sure it's good for the kids.

SANDRA: Alan was brought up by quiet, well-organized people. My family was always a free-for-all. My style makes him nervous. A lot of what he calls fighting, I just call talking.

ALAN: Sandra competes with me, especially in public. She says we have a style problem, but the truth is, she's insecure—even now that she's working, and successful, she has to bash me whenever she can.

SANDRA: Alan likes to say he's Mr. Nice Guy, but he's a lot meaner than I am. An example? Whenever he can't think what else to say, he threatens divorce. Since he makes most of the living, that's the most hurtful threat he can make, and he knows it.

ALAN: No one compares to Sandra in judgmentalness. I can't do anything right in her eyes. Anyone would want to get out from under her.

SANDRA: Alan is the most judgmental person I know, bar none.

ALAN: Sandra does not appreciate who I am and what I do. She wants me to change into some image or her father, or to become a feminist man, or a better lover. Who knows? She's always got a plan for me.

SANDRA: Alan has been looking in the mirror, I think. Nothing I do is right to him. He wants me to be his mother, or maybe the mother he never had. I can't keep up.

ALAN: I feel like I've given the best years of my life to this woman and what have I gotten back?"

SANDRA: I gave him my soul and he twisted it and now I'm afraid if I don't rescue myself from him, I'll die.

Doing therapy is a lot like being a detective. Something has been reported missing or misused; someone has been reported murdered, betrayed, or abused; somebody is in crisis and needs help finding the cause, and a solution. The therapist, like the detective, searches for clues. But unlike the detective, he does not do the surveillance himself, nor does he give much advice; he helps his clients dig into their families for secrets they've long forgotten, into their lives for clues, and into themselves for solutions. Yet in the end, to do his job, the therapist, like the detective, must have skill and training at hearing what is not quite being said, reading on bodies what the soul is trying to sing, and recognizing when danger is imminent.

In my work helping people understand power struggle I have come to a conclusion which, at first, amazed me: the vast majority of marriages and intimate partnerships in our culture become locked in power struggle early on *and remain in some form of power struggle throughout their existence.* Most of us do not get much beyond stage 3. Many people think they've gotten beyond it, and maybe do get beyond it now and then, but they fall back into it in the face of crisis or stress. It is the way of relating we know best. It was what our parents knew best. Often, we do not have a felt sense that anything safe or challenging lies beyond our struggle to personally control life energy.

ADAM AND EVE AND THEIR SONS

The story of Adam and Eve is a story of the first season of life. If you look back at the Bible you'll see that it is a three-stage story. In the first stage, Eve and Adam experience romance in the garden. In the second, they experience the fall of disillusionment. In the third, they experience power struggle. Adam and Eve leave the garden under duress, disillusioned, wandering. God sends them out in order to learn good and evil—the most basic rudiments of power struggle. These rudiments are symbolized in their two sons, Cain and Abel. Their power struggle ends tragically. This occurs after God, the teacher, the story maker and soul tester, accepts Abel's offerings but scorns Cain's. God's acceptance of Abel's offering is equal to spiritual power for Abel; his denial of Cain's offering is equal to spiritual powerlessness for Cain.

Cain, scorned and in a rage, kills his brother. Exiled, he sets up his own family, his own lineage, his own power base separated from God's. So, as the story of Adam and Eve ends, a culture is left with a legacy of power struggle. It is as if the tellers of the myth that would later guide our culture wanted us to see clearly how important it is that we be conscious of and come to grips with power struggle. There are contradictory forces in the world, we must learn to deal with their challenges.

The questions facing us as we understand power struggle in the Lover's Journey are these:

1. What kind of power struggle is necessary and how can we navigate it?

2. How do we wrestle ourselves out of the vast, unnecessary power struggles we so often fall into?

Answering these questions brings joy to stage 3.

THE ENCHANTED RING: PART THREE

When we left Katia and Nikolai, they lay together after disillusionment in a fleeting moment of resurgent, drunken romance. Katia wakes up before her husband. She takes the ring—the source of his power—off his finger. She twirls it, making his power her own. Fairies and witches appear to her. They give her what she wants—a new prince, who will never leave her, a castle *she* has created.

Katia represents the part of us that begins stage 3, power struggle. Whether we are male or female, we do what she has done. We see in our partner a kind of power we want. Throughout our present social system, this is going on: women want the power men have, men want the power women have; poor people want riches, rich people want freedom from wealth; ethnic groups want what other groups have. Our desire for the power of another is grounded in our long personal history, as Katia's is grounded in her mother's prophecy and admonition to get her husband's power when she can. Many fathers tell sons to make sure to control their wives; many mothers tell daughters to make sure to control their husbands. When parents are locked in stage 3 themselves, they'll give their children stage 3 advice.

Our desire for our partner's power is often grounded in our own sense of powerlessness, our sense of being caged. We feel trapped, lonely; getting hold of another's power seems the easiest way out. Once we get the other's power, we experiment with it—we twirl the ring. We try to get our fantasies met through that power. Perhaps we leave a spouse and pursue a fantasy. Often we do grave damage to ourselves and our families in this pursuit, but often, too, we find a new lease on life. This is power struggle. It is not without its destructiveness, nor without its joys.

Katia takes the ring and feels the ego strength to make a new life for herself. Nikolai wakes up in the barren meadow, realizing what's happened, realizing some of his own culpability and, down in the dungeon, cries to deaf human ears his solution—"Find the ring!" His natural instinct is to solve the schism that power struggle has created by regaining control of his power. He wants the ring back. He wants his power back.

Nikolai represents that same part of ourselves. When disillusionment sets in, we struggle to make things romantic again, but at some point, deep in the unconscious, it becomes clear to us that in fact we never did completely surrender to our partner. Like Nikolai, we always withheld some commitment through fantasy or, like Katia, through envy. Some crisis from the external world—the unplanned coming of a child, a job change or loss—or some crisis from the internal world of the relationship—Katia steals the ring—shows our conscious mind that all is not well, that this relationship is in deep trouble. Nikolai sends the dog and cat out to find the ring and bring it back.

There's little joy in this part of the struggle. There's just the constant fight between ourselves and our partner over who will control whom. Katia will hold on to the power she's gained and keep it away from Nikolai. Nikolai will fight to get it back, using his secret allies. Many—perhaps most—couples get locked here, in this struggle. Alan and Sandra were locked here.

In "The Enchanted Ring," however, the dog and the cat are not just allies of one side, Nikolai's. They are magical figures, entities whose job it is to serve the cause of joy, not just the cause of a single person's power. Not only are animals very often this kind of joy-based magical figure in Russian tales, but these two in particular prove their magic by the tricks they do to ingratiate themselves with Katia and her new husband. And they discover as they ply their magic that Katia misses Nikolai. They get to work stealing the ring from Katia's new husband. They reunite Katia and Nikolai. Nikolai does a smart thing—he sends the ring back to the old peasant, via the dog and cat.

Doesn't it feel as if these two have been tested and have tested each other, and now they sense they need to move on? Katia has had her moment of absolute power over the relationship—relegating her husband to a dungeon—but she didn't find it to be the joy she sought. Before her experiment with this power, Nikolai had possessed the ring, even winning his lover's hand with it, but now he too can see that it should no longer be the focus of power in the relationship—he sends it back to its source. What a great moment.

Katia has fulfilled her mother's prophecy and found that that prophecy was not, in fact, the whole guiding truth she thought it was. Nikolai has fulfilled his father's prophecy and found the same thing. These two are ready for stage 4, the awakening into the pursuit of their own truth, their own full selves. They don't realize this. They just experience the joy of having moved through power struggle—they live happily.

The power struggle they faced is the power struggle we face. It is a necessary stage of personal growth. And it must be navigated with such profound care that we do not lose ourselves and our lives in its electrical ego charges of energy, control, and abuse.

We've finished the story of "The Enchanted Ring," but let's go deeper into it still. Let's go deep into what's happening inside ourselves as we play out its drama. We will build toward an understanding of the key to stage 3—the enchanted ring. For before we leave this stage, we must understand what has been so lacking in ourselves that we needed an enchanted ring to fill the lack. Stage 2 started pointing this out to us. We cannot leave stage 3 without knowing it consciously, and being ready to find another way besides enchantment to become who we are.

NECESSARY POWER STRUGGLE

What do we mean by *power?* In stage 3, what we mean by power is control of energy. We must learn to control energy to survive in relationship—learning control of energy is about learning boundaries.

Someone who avoids noticing that many energies around us need to be controlled is a person who never truly learns to encounter the life-threatening and self-threatening eco- and social systems we live in. For us to develop a self, we must learn how to responsibly manage our own energy and attach it to energies around us, how to assert our needs and hold our boundaries in joyful ways. Stage 3, power struggle, is the stage in which we learn these skills by trial and error, by experimentation. By asserting needs and having them quashed or fed, by holding boundaries and having them respected or denied, we learn a great deal about how to live, and who we are.

While many of us have overemphasized power struggle, getting locked into it throughout our lives, others among us have sought to avoid power struggle as spiritual process. We have sought theologies and practices that would shoot us, as if out of a cannon, directly into mysticism and harmonious initiation into cosmic consciousness. We have forgotten that before the Buddha reached enlightenment, he had done the hard work of becoming altogether human; he had become a strong, compassionate self before he could come to represent a strong, compassionate soul. Stage 3 calls us to fight hard for our place in the world.

74

During the disillusionment of stage 2, we get a glimpse of our own independent identity; we glimpse it in fragments, but we're proud of a lot of those fragments. Maybe we were bad lovers during adolescence, but we were good at school. Maybe we are social misfits, but we have the character to pursue a rebellious dream that sustains us. Many people experience this kind of bifurcation between home and work, relationships and vocation. "I feel strong at work, like I really know what I'm doing," someone might say, "but in my relationship I stink."

For us to move to the next stage of individuation and spiritual growth—for our self to develop so that it is strong enough to make soul of our lives—we must accept challenges to our early, fragmented identity. Power struggle is our way of accepting challenge. Through our battles with others external to us, usually parents, lovers, authority figures, competitors, and children—even falling flat on our face or being bested by them—we experiment with our own identities. In power struggle we develop personally responsible strategies for how to win and how to lose in life. We receive challenge to who we think we are, and face (or avoid) that challenge.

Here is a way of understanding the activities and process of power struggle in our love relationships. There is a kind of progression:

1. We recognize (consciously or unconsciously) our powerlessness to recover the infatuation we had for our partner, to get our fantasy love needs met, and/or to feel good about ourselves without exploiting our partner's secrets.

2. We initiate a control system. Both partners usually try at this point to create a control system in the relation-

ship that gets them what they want. Usually, after a few months, it becomes clear that one partner's control system is stronger. Often the other complies with it, developing a strategy of passive aggression.

3. We try to modify each other. After initiation of the control system, both partners go through intense and consistent attempts to change their partner (and sometimes themselves) to match the objectives of the control system in place. "Change this—change that about yourself."

4. We decide (often unconsciously) to modify the strategies of our control system as we discover new weapons and tactics, new powers within ourselves and our partner. The power struggle and the fight for control in the control system are changing us, and we have new expectations of our partners. "I thought I wanted this from you, but now I've decided I want something very different." Often the new wanting is a fantasy want. When we're in power struggle, we generate a great deal of joy-fantasy as a way of coping with the pain of the struggle.

5. Throughout power struggle, we have interludes of *apparent* control-system dissolution. This dissolving of the struggle is usually caused by energy surges from giving birth to a new child or other external source of joy, or an internal resolve "to change things between us."

6. We watch our intimacy develop along the standards of the control system but can't seem to do anything about it. We test partners by how well they respond to our own threats of abandonment or domination, all the while feeling guilty for doing so. We feel powerless

against these behaviors but hide that powerlessness as much as we can.

7. We distill our wants and needs to one heroic ideal. During power struggle, we tend to distill our efforts to change our partner to one archetypal element we believe our partner should develop in order for him/her "to get better." "Everything would be fine if you were just more assertive." "You want to save this marriage? It's all up to you—express your feelings more!" We bully and nag our partners and ourselves in our tunnel vision around this singular ideal.

8. We move through interludes of despair and rage. We experiment with the possibility of leaving our partner or forcing our partner to leave us. We abuse our partner, get abused. In extreme cases, we kill or get killed by our partner. The withdrawer learns quite quickly that s/he does not escape the control system by seeming to withdraw from it. Most domestic violence occurs in this step of stage 3, in which one partner acts out on the other partner physical rage at his/her own powerlessness. The partner who acts out rage usually feels that his/her victim is the controller of the intimacy system.

9. We come to know that our own power struggle has caged us by noticing that we do not feel free to be ourselves in the system. This consciousness, if nurtured, supported, mentored, and acted upon, will begin our journey out of power struggle.

LONG-TERM PATTERNS OF POWER STRUGGLE

Most committed individuals drift within the first year of relationship into one or more of the following four power struggle patterns. Usually, each partner participates in each pattern to varying degrees during the course of the relationship, however long the relationship lasts.

1. *Direct control.* Each partner controls a lion's share of the relationship's spiritual process by controlling money or resources, sexual activity, children's loyalties, or emotional activity—sometimes through physical force.

2. *Compliance.* Each partner chooses a strategy of complying with the controller in order to appease. Usually, this compliance behavior finds a compensatory way of controlling—passive-aggressiveness, neediness.

3. *Rebellion.* One or both partners rebel against the relationship's control-based rules and structures. Partners often have sexual and romantic affairs as ways of rebelling.

4. *Withdrawal.* One or both partners withdraw emotionally, physically, or financially. S/he does this through distancing behavior or even divorce.

Every individual and couple will wrestle with these patterns. As we see a little bit of self emerging out of stage 2, we try to protect it. So it's normal to have this kind of protective power struggle.

Unfortunately, most committed individuals in our culture get locked into one or more of the four patterns throughout their lives. He controls, she complies. She controls, he rebels. Both control for a while, both comply for a while, both withdraw for the rest of the marriage.

I once worked with a couple, Louise and Herman, married twenty-two years, who could pinpoint when they had both withdrawn from the marriage. They had had one child in their second year of marriage. Looking back, they could see that power struggle had set in at that point. Herman, whose father had been emotionally distant, had felt pushed out of caring for his own child. His response was to try to control the way Louise raised the child, especially to change her protective style. Louise, whose mother had died when she was four, felt watched as a mother; she constantly worried about whether she was doing the right things with her child. She didn't like Herman's child-raising techniques and told him so. She pushed him away. The two of them brought their baggage to the relationship. For them, the child was the key that unlocked all the shadows from the bags.

Relational power struggle is not a condition limited to married people or parents. Often, uncoupled individuals have chosen not to commit or have been unable to commit because they were psychologically damaged by power struggles they witnessed in their childhoods, damage they cannot get free of. Their inability to commit is a power struggle in itself.

Many people divorce to escape destructive power struggles. For most of these couples, divorce does not end the power struggle. Divorced couples who have children often keep it alive through their children; many divorced couples who don't have children nonetheless remain enmeshed with the former spouse, still wanting his/her love. Childless individuals who divorce and don't remain enmeshed nonetheless all too often bring to new relationships the roots of their own power struggle, or decide to remain unattached the rest of their lives, a decision that leads most of them into a long struggle to retain personal power and self-image against the terrible force of loneliness.

POWER STRUGGLE PATTERNS

Ground yourself in your own life by answering these questions about how power struggle might work in your own relationship. You'll see that the questions are also applicable to any sort of relationship or community, even though we're focusing here on marriage and love relationships.

Do I tend to set up a direct control system in my relationships?

• Do I need to control family process and resources to feel things are going well?

• Do I get immediately angry with people who don't do what I say to do?

• Do others I am attached to call me rigid, unyielding, controlling, or narcissistic?

• If I let go of control of a system around me, do I believe it would fall apart? Do I believe I'm irreplaceable?

• Is talking more important to me than listening?

• Is being right more important than being there?

• Do I make a judgment on what my partner says before s/he has developed it with any depth?

• Do I judge my partner's *feelings* based on standards set by an ideological stance? This stance can be religiously, ethnically, sexually, or politically grounded.

• Do I tend to set up a compliance system?

• Do I generally perceive myself to be the victim or martyr in my partnership?

• Do I feel fear or rage immediately or soon after I or my partner try to have a close moment but repress those feelings, often covering them with sweetness and cooperation?

• Do I involve myself in constant verbal analysis of my partner's motivations, but often not to his/her face, often in others' company?

• Do I exert a lot of energy "making sure my relationship is okay" by not expressing my needs in effective ways?

Do I tend to set up a rebellion system?

• Do I make sure I have resources set aside "in case something goes wrong" in my relationship and/or "so I can always get my needs met somewhere else"?

• Do I act out sexually when my marriage or partnership has gotten boring or stultifying or for no other reason except that I want someone else?

• Do I often, and quite purposely, do things, enjoy things, involve myself in things my lover won't like?

• Do I enjoy fantasizing myself a rebel against not only my lover's authority, but also society's?

Do I tend to set up a withdrawal system?

• Do I pull away emotionally immediately or soon after I or my partner have a close moment?

• Do I experience revulsion toward my partner before, during, or after sex and other times of intense intimacy?

• Do I avoid speaking to my partner whenever I can?

• Do I avoid coming home to or spending time with him/her?

Do I avoid trying to change the power struggle in my relationship because:

• I'm afraid to be alone?

• I don't want to hurt my kids by putting them through a divorce?

- My spouse needs me; it would be selfish for me to leave?

- I'm afraid of what others will think?

- I don't want to admit I'm a failure at this marriage?

- I like the power I get in the power struggle; I wouldn't have it in a mutually developed intimacy system?

- I'm afraid that if we get out of the power struggle I'll discover I don't love my partner after all, or s/he will discover the same lack of love for me?

- confronting the power struggle won't do any good?

- confronting the power struggle results in violence against me?

- I am afraid of confrontation?

- my father/mother (or other powerful life model) lived with this, so why shouldn't I?

Your answers to these questions will give you a hard look at the power struggle you are facing in your relationship. You may need to be in it right now; you may not have yet learned valuable lessons about how to win and how to lose, how to protect yourself and how to assert yourself, how to commit to another without fearing you will lose love, and lose yourself.

YOUR ENCHANTED RING

The bottom line for us as we face our own power struggle is to identify what the enchanted ring is for us and to face it. Ask yourself: What has it been for *me*? What have *I* thought I did not have? What did I feel was so lacking in myself that I saw it in my partner and envied it and would do almost anything for it? Think about this for a moment as you work to understand what kind of control system you're in.

When children come, often we think it is our partner, not us, who holds the key to the child's power. We think our partner holds the enchanted ring that can best love a child. We become jealous, we nag, we control, we want to take control ourselves of the child's energy—we don't want our spouse to have it.

Career and financial ambitions can be forms of the enchanted ring; they can spiral into power struggle. Jealously, angrily we think, "He can go out and work, I'm stuck at home. He has more power than I do." Or "I'm stuck at work, I wish I had her freedom. She has more power than I do." Or "If he just did such-and-such, worked harder at such-and-such, our lives would be better." Or "She knows the secret that would mend and revitalize our lives. It's just revenge and laziness that she won't act on the secret."

These feelings are, deep down, about our own sense of inadequacy. We feel unmagical. We feel empty. We want to be filled up, and we think our partner is the one who can do it. We try to steal the ring in an effort to get filled up as much as we can.

Often the gender war—the political battle over male/female energies that is currently raging—can amplify a couple's power struggle, making it far worse than it need be. Often women and men truly believe that the other sex holds the enchanted ring hostage and thus that sex is the enemy. When they leave power struggle behind, they often find the actual enemy has been within themselves. This is not to say that we are not often quite right in saying, "He has more power" or "She has more power." Often a woman (or man) does get trapped at home, financially controlled by her (his) spouse.

Often a man (or woman) does get trapped at work, financially controlled by his (her) spouse's need for material things. And often community intervention is needed to help this couple resolve their differences. These facts about male/female power do not negate the fact that, still, during the power struggle stage, each partner must gain glimpses of himself or herself as empowered, needing no enchanted ring to feel whole.

The fragments of our identity—the sand of self, you might say—that we saw in stage 2 are tested in stage 3. Confidence is built by how well those fragments survive the tests. In stage 3, we steal our partner's ring whenever possible, but hopefully we are also meeting the challenges of love in such a way that we are noticing we have had a ring of our own all along.

If I marry a verbally incisive mate and learn to compete well with that verbal energy, my tools and skills as a person advance, as does my confidence. If by partnering with a mate more socially adept than myself, I can learn social confidence through competing, I am using power struggle as spiritual growth. I may be in that stage of life when my confidence needs building more by friction than by fusion. I am growing because I have mated with someone who has something I need to learn, some important secrets about power. I am most agile in this stage if I key in on those secrets, notice how I lacked them, and learn from interaction with this other how to control the energies the other is better at controlling. If I am brave enough to engage in this conflict, I face a risk— the risk of losing my partner. For competition is a process based utterly on the risk of winning one thing but losing another: winning a game, but perhaps losing a friend; winning a war, but taking a life; winning empowerment, but losing the old way I used to live, which, though insecure, weak, and pathological still feels like home to me. The more consciously we engage in the power struggle, the more conscious we are of what we are seeking in it—what the enchanted rings are that we're trying to steal—and the more enlivening and empowering the power struggle will be for us and our partners.

This is not to say power struggle is a safe place to be. Going through all the years of pain and friction, in one relationship or in many, begging for the power others have, competing for it, climbing corporate ladders for it, fighting with spouses for it, overreacting, involving ourselves in gender war and political combats—the whole process is a dangerous one. Spouses get beaten to death, spouses commit suicide. Children of power struggle grow up damaged and damaging—especially children of divorce, who knew nothing else but parents' power struggle, lost one or more parents to the divorce, and then, because extended families are basically gone and few institutions exist to substitute for parents or extended family, did not have community mentors to fill parental gaps. More than two-thirds of crime is committed by children of divorce and of single parents. These children of power struggle hurt themselves, their community, their own families, and the earth. The power struggle stage is so volatile that tribal cultures usually monitor and mentor it closely and constantly. Our culture gives us lots of help in feeding the fires of power struggles, but little help in dealing with their heat. It dangles the enchanted ring in front of us and says, "See, s/he has it, go get it, even if it takes a lifetime and ruins your life." Dealing consciously with power struggle takes incredible spiritual courage and, often, a spiritual withdrawal from the friction-addicted culture around us.

THE THIRD SACRED TASK

Stage 3 of the Lover's spiritual discipline teaches us the third key lesson of trust: *competition.*

To love and be loved, I must learn through experience the amount of damage I do and damage I can sustain. To survive as a self, I must be able to compete.

During stage 3, we are learning how to use the Warrior within us to protect boundaries and assert needs. We need to learn this experientially, by trial and error. We make more mistakes in this stage than we would like.

We also notice in this stage that the Warrior and the Lover seem constantly at odds. For example, people in power struggle will say, "I love her, but I hate her," "I want him, but I could strangle him sometimes."

This is where we need to be (for a while and with guidance!). It is the trial-and-error period that sets within us the foundation for true independence by showing us how desperately we need to become a self that is not dependent on another for its spiritual centering.

Stage 3 also provides us with the fourth element of focus for the Lover's spiritual discipline: *the assertion of our needs and protection of our boundaries.* Our discipline, our prayer, our meditation, our daily life, and our stories focus in this stage on how better to assert needs and better protect boundaries.

As participants in power struggle, our mission is to learn how to assert needs and protect boundaries here, in this stage, so that we don't have to spend the rest of our lives searching for these skills. We must guide ourselves and others toward a deep understanding of how dependent we still are on other(s) for Self, and how important it is now to move forward into stage 4, to awaken into the long, hard search for a solid, personality identity.

INTEGRATING POWER STRUGGLE

Often people will say, "How can we find joy in this terrible struggle for power? It's impossible." Yet it isn't. There is great joy here. We must be very conscious, however, of the obstacles we face in finding that joy.

It is not surprising that most of us get locked into lifelong, joyless power struggle with our mates, living as we do in a culture as spiritually troubled as ours, in family systems as broken as ours, in gender relationships as power-obsessed as ours, in partnerships as ignorant of basic male/female differences as ours, in workplaces as stressful as ours, and in physical environments so dominated by our technological power. Our inability to manage and then replace necessary power struggle is a primary cause of our need for therapists. Incessant, joyless power struggle is causing us to wake up and notice something essential missing from our lives. It is causing us to abuse, to renege on commitments to loved ones, to murder. It is causing our relationships to go into crisis.

Often the difference between the detective and the therapist is the therapist's insistence on helping his clients ask, "Why? Why is this happening to you? Why are you creating this?" The therapist, in asking why, is a spiritual agent, an agent of joy. To integrate power struggle into your quest for joy, you must do the detective work of understanding your relationship to the enchanted ring, looking back at the prophecies that inculcated that relationship in you, and committing to a deep journey of awakening out of them, into your Self.

Clients like Alan and Sandra transform their lives by going back through the power struggle to its reasons, tracking those reasons to their sources, and making a new life for themselves. Alan learns to cut back on judgment as he realizes how judgmental his father was, and he yearns to become someone different. Sandra learns how afraid of intimacy she is—and why. They discover that here, in stage 3, they possess only a *fragmented*, soft identity. They awaken into a journey of Self and soul that reveals to them a solid, *established* identity. They give each other space and permission to grow and remain married. In stage 3, we have been projecting fragments of our soft identity onto others and the world; sometimes we get them back, sometimes we lose them. Most often, all we can do is just try to stay *in control*; we can't really flourish. In the final analysis, leaving power struggle behind is a personal responsibility. Integrating it into the quest for joy is a personal responsibility. Specifically, as we seek this integration, we move into the season of independence, we seek to find out who *we* are—what our full identity is—and learning that, to feel safe to exist and flourish in a new way.

As we move toward stage 4, we must see power struggles as separate and discernable moments. We must leave behind the state of spiritual being in which our whole life is about the struggle for power, and our beloved relationship never leaves a state of tacit war.

Part Two

THE SEASON OF AWAKENING

Story: The Big People at the Bottom of the World

This story was told to me by villagers just outside the town of Van in Eastern Turkey. Initially, an old woman started telling it, than her husband got involved. A small group added bits to it here and there, while all of us drank tea. I, too, have added bits of my own. The story involves figures common to Turkish culture. Keloglan is the "bald boy," the wise youth known throughout Turkish folklore. Serpil, less known, is an amalgam of folklore women. In trade for the story, the old couple took my Seiko watch. I thought it a fair trade.

Once upon a time there was a woman, Serpil, who had been abandoned by her parents at a young age, was brought up in an impoverished orphanage, and later married very young. She had been married for five years. She lived in a house in a village with her husband. He spent his days working as a blacksmith. He spent his nights sitting and dozing. She was not happy, and her husband was not happy either. The two of them lived together in various states of momentary attraction, then disappointment and misery, then power struggle, then distance.

One day, Serpil went out walking. The woods had always been a place of refuge for her, but she never traveled to the woods across the river. On this particular day, in late summer, the river water was very low. "Don't cross," her husband had always warned her, "don't cross." But on this day she raised up her skirt and crossed. When she got to the other side, she felt dizzy. She walked a few steps, and fell asleep.

While asleep, she dreamed about an old woman who, in a cave, labored over a fire. The old woman threw herbs into a pot, then vegetables, then parts of animals, making a soup. The old woman talked to Serpil, something that had never happened for Serpil in any dream before.

"Walk until you get to the forked road," said the old woman.

With that comment, Serpil woke up. She stood up immediately and began walking. She walked and walked through the forest. Who knows how long? She met many people. She asked each one where the forked road was. Getting directions from many people, she came to many forked roads. They were not, after all, an uncommon occurrence. But none of them seemed like the right one.

Finally, just on the outskirts of a village, a young girl said to her, "Of course I know where it is. Let me show you." Hand in hand they walked until they came to a place in the road where two directions were quite clear, one heading southeast toward the ocean, one heading southwest toward the mountains. The young girl said, "Wait here." She entered a cave. The old wise woman from the dream came out.

"Just in time," the wise woman said, "just in time to eat some soup with me."

"Where did the girl go?" Serpil asked.

The wise woman said, "She and you and I are all one woman. We are one with the mystery too. Come, eat with me, then you will choose a road."

They ate together. The old woman gave Serpil magic herbs. "When you need these, you will use them. To some, they are poison; to others, they are treasure. Watch out. If you use them mistakenly as poison, you must have many apples about. Apples are the antidote."

After they had eaten, the wise woman took Serpil back to the fork in the road. The wise woman asked, "Now, which road shall you choose?"

"What awaits me on each road?" Serpil asked.

"No one knows but you. Take as long as you wish, then pick a road."

Serpil said, "But I don't know what awaits me."

"Of course you do," the wise woman said, "you just don't realize yet what you know and who you are. One day you will." She walked back into her cave and left Serpil standing at the forked road. Closing her eyes, Serpil made her choice. She walked down the road toward the ocean.

As it happened, she did not make it to the ocean. After walking for a time, she met a giantess, a huge woman as big as a tree, who peered out over the treetops toward the ocean.

Serpil hid, being frightened of the giantess, but of course she made noise. The giantess walked to her hiding place behind a boulder. She lifted the boulder and smiled at the trembling woman. "Don't be afraid," she said, "I'm your friend. Are you heading to the ocean?"

Serpil nodded.

"Then I'll accompany you, and I'll show you a shortcut. You need a friend out here. There are many bandits."

Serpil warmed to the huge creature and went with her. The giantess told her stories of her own life in the woods. Serpil talked about where she had come from, her husband, her boring life. Soon they came to a huge hole in the ground. "I live down there," the giantess said. "Come down for a moment so I can pick up some things." Serpil lost sight of the giantess as the huge being slid down the slippery slope of the well, laughing gleefully. Serpil liked the wild sound of the laugh. She hitched up her skirts and slid down on her butt too.

At the bottom, she found a huge cavern and a lair. The giantess said, "I'm afraid I did trick you a bit. What I really need is someone to cook for me. You're that someone now. I ate my last one. Sorry." Serpil saw that she was trapped. She could slide down the hole, but there was no way to climb up.

For a year (who knows how long a year really is in our time?) she served the giantess. The huge being went off and came back with Serpil's husband's jewelry and tools. "I've killed him and eaten him for you," the giantess said. "Why should you have to live with a boring man?" Even in her shock and grief, Serpil saw that the giantess had done this with good intentions. Serpil suddenly did not understand anything about the world.

It was at this moment she decided to poison the giantess. As she cooked and cleaned for her mistress, she put the wise woman's herbs in the food, on the pillow, in the air. Slowly, the giantess lost strength. "What has happened to me?" she asked. "Did your husband have sorcery in him? Should I not have eaten him?" The giantess clearly did not see her tiny and captured companion as any sort of threat. "Maybe I'm feeling sick with the loss of my own husband," the giantess moaned, as her stomach knifed her with pain. "I wish he would come back." This was the first Serpil had heard of a giant. Suddenly, she wished she had not poisoned the giant-ess. What if the giant came back and took revenge? But it was too late. Serpil had no apples to use as the antidote the wise woman had told her about. And the giantess died.

As if he had felt the death, the giant returned to his lair at the bottom of the world. He found Serpil and his dead wife. He sniffed and he ate. "You have poisoned my wife," he raged, beating Serpil and chaining her to the cave wall. "I will eat you myself." Why the herbs did not kill the giant, or even weaken him, she did not know. To save her life she cried, "You must get apples, feed her lots of apples. That's the antidote."

She won a reprieve. "You will stay alive long enough for me to see if you are telling the truth," the giant declared. The giant went out every night and returned with apples, hundreds of them. He forced these down his wife's throat. He laid them all over and around his wife. They did not immediately revive her, but they did somehow keep her from decomposing.

Where did the giant get these apples? Serpil, chained and wan, could not know. Nor could the giant know that the apples he stole would bring about the next part of our story. Let us leave Serpil and the giant for a moment. We will return to them.

Once upon this same time, there was a great apple orchard situated a few miles from town, tended by five brothers who had never married. They made a good living from their famous orchard, and they protected it and prized it like a child, but they had few friends in the nearby villages, mainly because their own parents had been difficult people, mean and with few friends. So the brothers kept to themselves, working their land, taking pride in their crop, and living in isolation.

One day, one of the brothers came running back from the periphery of the domain. "In the night, something ate all the apples on one of our trees," he cried. All the brothers ran out to see. Sure enough, one apple tree was stripped of plump, juicy apples. Nothing quite like this had ever happened before. That night they all stayed out near the ruined tree, weapons at ready. No one showed up, though. The next night, too, nothing happened. Now they were becoming very tried, and losing their workday. Maybe the threat was gone, they thought. But to be safe, they decided that the eldest brother would hide behind thick trees and watch that night. If he saw trouble, he'd come back to the house and wake his sleeping brothers, and together they'd confront the enemy.

As it happened, the eldest brother fell asleep, awoke remembering nothing, and found a second three completely stripped. Sheepishly, he reported his failure. The next eldest brother stayed out the next night. He too fell asleep and lost a tree. So all the brothers stayed out again, but without incident. So the next oldest stayed out and lost a tree, and then the next. Exasperated, the brothers did not know what to do. The youngest brother, little Keloglan, stepped forward. "It's my turn," he said. His brothers laughed a little, but then figured they had nothing to lose. He was of manhood age. Though small, he was sometimes wise. They let him go.

As Keloglan hid behind a tree, he felt himself falling asleep. To stay awake, he took out his sword and cut his own palm. The pain kept him awake. As he sucked at his hand, he heard and felt a horrible thumping, thump, thump, the earth shaking. A giant came to a full tree and very quickly stripped it of apples. Keloglan had no time to run back to house for his brothers. The giant moved swiftly away with his treasure.

Keloglan intrepidly followed. The giant kept moving farther ahead, taking his huge steps. In desperation, Keloglan threw his sword. It hit the giant in the back of his foot, the place called the Achilles' heel. The giant cried out but did not stop. The sword fell out of him. Keloghan scooped it up and saw the giant drop down into a huge hole. Keloglan followed, sliding downward. He thought two quick thoughts: why didn't that giant stop and confront me when I'm so tiny? How the hell am I going to get back up this hole?

He hit bottom. He had dropped into the cavern where Serpil was chained. He saw her and, as happens in fairy tales, they immediately fell in love with each other. As also happens, giants take advantage of the young. The giant laughed. "Now I have you, you intrepid little bald boy. You're just at that juicy age of manhood. I'll eat you with this woman here." Keloglan saw that he was completely trapped. He could not get out of the hole. He watched as the giant placed the apples gingerly around the giantess, who lay immobile up on a huge table.

While the giant did his ritual, Keloglan went over to Serpil, who said, "I have had time to understand how to kill this giant. First, you must approach him from behind, and when he is distracted. That time will come soon, for the giantess will revive soon and her mate will pay attention only to her new breath. Second, you must cut off the giant's head. You cannot do that with your small size, so you must cut his ankles off, then cut his knees, then his hips. Each severing will drop him closer to the ground. When he is small and low enough, you'll reach his head."

The giantess began to revive, and, as Serpil predicted, the giant bent over her, encouraging her breath. Keloglan ran up behind, cut off the giant's feet, then his knees, then his hips, and then, just as the screaming giant began to turn, Keloglan cut off his head. The giantess, bare of strength, could not get off the table except to fall. Once she hit ground, Serpil cried, "You must cut off her head too." Keloghan ran to her and made the cut. Both these huge beings who lived at the bottom of the world were now dead.

Exhausted and covered with blood, Keloghan found the keys to the chains and freed Serpil.

"I am Keloglan," he said.

"I am Serpil," she said.

And they told their stories. Keloglan, with Serpil's help, cleaned himself at an underground spring. Serpil, who had not eaten in days, ate the only food she could find, Keloglan's apples.

After a time they felt revived and searched for an escape route. They searched especially for a hole through which the spring came, but found only holes too small for a body to pass through. The more desperate they felt, the angrier they grew with each other, as if all their love had disappeared through the tiny holes of desperation. Trapped and hungry, they ate all the apples and then began cutting off pieces of the huge beings and eating them. This meat seemed to make them even more angry with each other, more irritable.

But then, after they had eaten all but the heads of the giant and giantess (who knows how many years have passed by now?), something started to happen to them. A calmness came. Without knowing how it happened, Keloglan and Serpil found themselves feeling at home down in the dark cave. Once they started feeling at home and resigned themselves to being there, in that place, forever, they began to get along again. Their love was renewed and matured. They divided up tasks, built separate places for themselves in the cave, felt satisfied with each other, and even felt the urge to dance.

It was at this very time that they heard a sound from the top of the hole, that hole by which each had separately descended to this shared fate.

They ran to the hole's bottom and saw the shadow of a stork flying above. They called up, "Help, help us, stork." Storks, they knew, as every Turk knows, are magical birds.

The stork heard them and flew down to them. "We are trapped down here," they explained. "Can you carry us upward on your back? We will be heavy, but we are ready to rise, and we will do whatever you ask."

The stork saw the situation of these people—now no longer young—and agreed to the task. "I ask only that you give me sustenance to carry your weight," it said. "When, as we fly upward, I say 'Gaaak,' you will feed meat into my mouth. When I say 'Geeek,' you will feed me water." Keloglan skinned the remaining meat off the heads of the huge beings while Serpil found a skin canteen and filled it with spring water. The two climbed onto the stork's back, and the stork began his ascent.

Serpil and Keloglan had expected the stork to ask for sustenance, but not every few seconds! They found themselves pushing meat and drink into its mouth constantly. Then, as they neared the top and smelled the sweet smell of freedom, they realized there was no water or meat left. The stork said "Gaaak," and Keloglan cut a piece of his own thigh to give the stork. After taking it into its mouth, the stork said "Geeek." Serpil grabbed Keloglan's sword, cut her arm, drew blood into her palm, and quenched the stork's thirst with that.

When they arrived on the surface, the stork said. "You have done well, you have given of yourself for the common good." It pulled the piece of Keloglan's thigh from under his tongue and returned it to Keloglan's leg. It kissed Serpil's arm, returning her blood to her.

Keloglan said, "My people live near here. Please come with Serpil and me, and we will treat you like a god."

The stork said, "My work here is done. Allah bless you," and their ally flew off.

Keloglan and Serpil went to the orchard, where they married. Not only did they marry and have children, but all the brothers married, and all the couples had children. Friendships developed, and the village and the orchard joined. Although the apples now were not as perfectly tended and as pretty, there were more of them, and they fed more people. And all the land lived happily.

STAGE 4

AWAKENING

I woke up one morning. I didn't know where I was. I was in my own house, sleeping next to my husband, but I didn't know where I was. It was like my whole life, my whole marriage, I'd been asleep and suddenly I had woken up. I was scared, I was terrified. But I was more excited than I'd ever been.

—LOUISE, CLIENT IN MARITAL THERAPY

In my mid-twenties, I walked on the cliffs of Masada in Israel. I stood out at the cliff's edge, slightly removed from a group of French tourists, looking at the Dead Sea and Jordan. I felt as if I were in some sort of trance. I had felt that way on and off for months during my travels through Europe and the Middle East. I had the sense that I did not know who I was, as if I had been asleep for most of my life. I wrote often in my journal about how shameful, bad, and worthless I was to feel so sleepy, as if my life were being wasted. I did not know yet that it is a rare person who does not feel like he's been asleep; it is a rare person who can wake up without first losing himself in the misery of power struggle, or the despair of emotional isolation, or the sleep of addiction.

The air on Masada was a dry heat graced by a breeze. As I stood there, the history of the place swept through me—a small band of Jews withstanding Roman hordes. In my hand I held the brochure explaining the story. The empty air below me, stretching thousands of feet down the cliff, seemed to embrace me, even pull me downward. It felt to me, quite literally, like a welcome cradle. At this moment I did not have thoughts of suicide; rather, I felt a last-ditch desire to be utterly cared for.

Part of my ancestral heritage is Jewish, so I have no doubt that I felt, too, at some indefinable level, a freedom to feel on that cliff that I was one with Jewish heroes. I stood in a country that had awakened and become heroic for the sake of all Jews. I could not know all this at the time; I was living it. But there are no accidents in life, and it was no accident that I felt, on the high plateau of Masada, that I could look out at the Dead Sea and at Jordan, with whom this country was in power struggle, and by looking there see what was dead in my life and what was lost in power struggle in my relationships.

I did not realize it consciously at the time, but I had been in a sleep of dependency for twenty-five years, a sleep marked by romances, disappointments, and power struggles, a sleep from which awakening would be heroic. I was ready to awaken. I was ready to stop seeking cradles. I was ready to be independent, to find out who I was. I did not realize anything about new stages of life at that time. I just knew something had happened inside me because, as dusk spread out around me, I began to cry. My tears dropped over my eyelids and down my cheeks, my chin curled up as it does when I cry. My wet eyes, the inside of my mouth, the tears on my cheeks became slightly cool with the evening breeze. From somewhere inside me, a voice rose up and out, saying, at first in a whisper, "I need to be free," then a little louder, then a little louder, "I . . . need . . . to . . . be . . . free!" I paused a second, laughing a little, the thought shooting through me that people were watching my back, but nothing mattered in that moment of epiphany except my own free voice. I raised my arms up slightly to the Dead Sea and cried out, "I need to be free."

There I was, a tall, gangly young searcher, awakening.

THE STORIES OF AWAKENING

On the cliffs of Masada, I did not call it awakening. I had studied Buddhism but did not call it enlightenment. I recalled in my journal a month or so later, after I had left Israel and come back to the United States, that Moses had cried for a people's freedom somewhere near where I'd been—"Let my people go!"—and this made me feel connected to larger purpose. Yet I did not see my epiphany as a whole people's cry. In my journal I called my epiphany on Masada "a timeless moment," a term I had learned in college from studying the poetry of T. S. Eliot.

Years later I would hear the Unitarian minister Roger Kuhrt talk about stages of faith and life. He used the term *awakening*. I went back to my books and memories and work and saw how wonderfully appropriate the term is. Awakenings occur in myths and stories with the frequency of raindrops, or discovered treasures. People are constantly asleep, cursed by witches or demons, evil fairies or sorcerers. When we study their sleep times, we notice many sleeps of dependency, and we see that each awakening is an awakening into new freedom, new independence.

"Sleeping Beauty" comes to mind. In that fairy tale, Princess Aurora sleeps under layers and layers of dependency—dependency on her father, on the three good fairies, then on the prince. King Stefan, her father, forgets to invite the evil

Maleficent to her christening. Maleficent shows up anyway and lays a curse on the baby girl—"She will be pricked by a needle and die." The fairy Merryweather is able to alter the curse of death to a curse of sleep. And she adds, "From this slumber you shall awake, when true love's kiss the spell shall break."

King Stefan and the good fairies try to protect Aurora from both death and the long sleep, but Maleficent manages to set up the prick of the needle. Aurora and the whole castle go to sleep. Aurora's life, which depended on father and fairies, now depends on the prince. Of course, as you know, the prince does find and kiss her. She and the whole realm awaken. Unfortunately for her, her awakening, so dependent on the prince, moves quickly into a sleep of marriage with him. It's no accident that we tell children fairy tales before bed, as sleep inducers. By the time our kids hear, "And they live happily ever after," they're asleep!

Many young women have felt like Sleeping Beauty, forced to remain dependent, given a hint of independence usually through the promise of a prince's energy and domain, then finding their moment's independence quickly turned into marriage and new dependency. Many young men, too, have felt a hint of independence only to find themselves "trapped" quickly in marriage.

In John Keats's poem "La Belle Dame Sans Merci," a mournful knight tells his story. He did everything he could for the Lady in the Meads, whose "hair was long" and "eyes were wild." He made a garland for her head, and bracelets and many other things. They loved each other, and, thought the knight, they gave their love to each other for life. And then:

There she lulled me asleep,
   And there I dreamed, ah woe betide!
The latest dream I ever dreamt,
   On the cold hill side.
I saw pale Kings, and Princes too,
   Pale warriors, death pale were they all;
They cried, "La belle dame sans merci
   Hath thee in thrall!"
I saw their starv'd lips in the gloam
   With horrid warning gaped wide—
And I awoke, and found me here,
   On the cold hill's side.
And this is why I sojourn here,
   Alone and palely loitering;
Though the sedge is withered from the Lake,
   And no birds sing.

A sadder tale, at least on the surface, than "Sleeping Beauty," in "La Belle Dame Sans Merci" the knight, who has been betrayed by dependency, awakens into loss, pain, and despair. This poem is about a jilted man. It could just as well be about a jilted woman. Dependency is, after all, dependency, no matter your gender.

Many of our awakenings contain moments like these, when we taste the spirit of freedom only to find it transitory; moments when we awaken out of dependency but do not know what to do except to despair over the loss of what we previously felt made us whole. The knight awakens, but then falls back into stage 2 disappointment and remains there. Aurora awakens, but then because she enters stage 1 romance again, never fully awakens into her own journey.

In the story of "The Big People at the Bottom of the World," awakening leads to more. It leads to independence, and beyond.

INDEPENDENCE: THE REASON TO AWAKEN

To learn true *independence,* the guiding psychospiritual task of the second season of life, is to learn to care for our adult selves, both physically and psychologically. To be independent is "not to depend." This does not mean the severing of all dependencies—nothing in life is ever so clear-cut. But it does mean that we have emotionally separated from caregivers and objects of dependency in order to discover who we are. We are able to say with authenticity: "This is who I am."

Independence is a profound state of self-trust that we must experience if we are to be successful at fulfilling, interdependent relationships. As Sam Keen once put it, "We have to find out who we are *before* we find someone to journey with us through life." If we don't separate from caregivers and go through the long process of finding out who we are, we make mates, children, religion, nature, and work into dependency objects. We remain in power struggle with them for the rest of our lives.

Using the word *soul* instead of *self,* Thomas Moore writes, "Individuality rises out of soul as water rises out of the depths of the earth. We are who we are because of the special mix that makes up our soul. In spite of its archetypal, universal contents, for each individual the soul is highly idiosyncratic. Power begins in knowing this special soul, which may be entirely different from our fantasies about who we are or who we want to be." When we awaken, we see much of this individuality already in place within us, noticing and honoring it as we never have before; we also see what false selves we've had to create—we move out of them as much as possible, as if working our way out of a shell; and we seek to develop new ways of being individuals. Unless we awaken, these won't take place. Just adding more years to life doesn't necessarily do it, even though, as children growing up, we are constantly seeking independence, and even though with each pull away from parents toward independence, we move further and further away from caregivers. We still need to awaken, to finally discover that our self-esteem, physical survival, and emotional maturity need no longer be primarily dependent on any one object or person. Ideally, our communities are ever watchful over our journey to independence. During childhood, our parents are usually our immediate mirror of self-image. As we grow into adolescence and young adulthood, our society, our community (for teens it is often, for a while, peer group) mirror our growth, initiating us into adulthood. Then, if society accepts us fully as men and women, we see that we have become truly independent.

Independence is not just about rebellion, then, or personal isolation. By independent, we do not mean alone or uncaring. We mean that we are solid in our own identity as a person, a self. Always, the independent self fits into the larger whole of community, family, and spirituality.

In many societies, especially in a society like ours—nontribal, polycultural, with extended family broken down and even the nuclear family in tatters—the ideal time for the journey to independence is *before* marriage and children, for mating and marriage require us to give up a great deal of independence and become interdependent; our children especially require us to become utterly absorbed in interdependence. We better have a pretty good sense of who we are before we have kids. If we're still dependent, we'll end up teaching them to take care of us, to develop false selves so they can meet our emotional needs. A primary reason family systems in our culture are so destructible is that so many of us mate and have children before we develop independent selves.

THE STRUGGLE FOR INDEPENDENCE
IN TRIBAL CULTURES

In many tribal cultures, kids have kids, but it works. Why? Because they have extended families to help them. The whole family raises the children. Grandparents care for kids and constantly mentor young parents, and interdependence is spiritually grounded throughout the tribe. In our culture, psychological children have children without intergenerational support. We suffer.

In extended-family cultures, independence is defined differently than in ours. In India, for instance, some children marry at eleven, twelve, thirteen, the beginning of adolescence—still dependent on caregivers. Some people say, when looking at many extended-family cultures like these, "They don't know what independence is." Women, especially, remain tied to power and family dynamics in which, by our definition, they never seem to develop an independent self. At the same time, in these cultures, an independent self is nurtured and honored through adolescent initation processes such as vision quests, fertility ceremonies, and tests and trials that often last for years. Independent self is also honored, in every tribal system, through role. A child becomes an adult by developing him- or herself into the female or male role, and modifying him/herself to gain social acceptance and personal growth within the role. These young people learn to be loving, wise, and powerful adults, and they learn that to get along in community and with a spouse, they must understand they are separate beings who have come together for three primary purposes, in this order:

1. To support the community, its children, and the earth
2. To raise their own children
3. To find romantic satisfaction

Our culture, of course, does things differently. We switch the three purposes around, moving 3 to the top, leaving 2 the same, and moving 1 to the bottom position. Our purposes look like this:

1. To find romantic satisfaction
2. To raise their own children
3. To support community, its children, and the earth

And our culture has substituted *individual* for *role*. We still teach gender roles—though we like to think we will one day get to the point where we don't need them—but we seek to find selves that are independent even of role. "I can be myself," we say in all seriousness, "without really being a man or woman, a father or mother, a grandfather or grandmother," and so on. It is our cultural destiny to fight a battle for personal freedom that we are convinced shall give us an advanced kind of independence but in which we sacrifice the emotional safety of role and family structure.

This, then, is some of the cultural context for awakening. Now let's return to the story.

THE BIG PEOPLE AT THE BOTTOM
OF THE WORLD: PART ONE

In the first part of the wonderful Turkish story, all of us, male or female, can sense the stirrings of the awakened self. Let's look at how it happens for Serpil, then Keloglan.

Serpil is coexisting with her husband, but is not happy, nor he with her. He is part of what has confined her, as any spouse can be—"Don't cross to the other side of the river," he says, "don't cross." He is unhappy, but he doesn't want to lose what little he has. He may even be afraid for his spouse, the woman he loves, afraid that she will discover danger. He may also feel that if he can control where she goes, one day things might become better. There are a million reasons we try to control each other. Serpil and her husband begin the story in their own form of that power struggle.

But one day, Serpil crosses the river. This is an act of independence. Serpil falls asleep, dreams, then wakes up with purpose. This kind of waking up takes a lot of courage. Whether it's our adolescent self awakening into an adult self or role, or our midlife self awakening into a mature self, the awakening needs to be "en-couraged" by visions, dreams, mentors. In this story, the wise woman comes to Serpil in a dream and gives her a vision of the forked road.

The dream and the vision are not the same thing. The dream is the large and fluid archetypal container for the very specific, very vivid vision of the new place we need to go. We dream of "finally becoming a woman" or "finally becoming a man" or "finally finding myself"—that's the large, amorphous dream. Within it, we have more exact visions of what we must do, where we must go, what peace we must make with parents and children, what mentors and teachers we must find, what part of life needs to be cleaned out, what relationship needs to end, what new work needs developing.

Following the vision in the dream, Serpil walks and walks in search. After our own awakenings, we take up this task through reading, talking to friends, journaling, praying, meditating, experimenting with new lifestyles, new gurus, new systems and models. We walk and we walk. No one, at first, is able to help Serpil find the forked road. Most people don't know what she's talking about. They just send her down the road to the next fork. In the same way, not everyone can guide us to the forked road we need to find. That road is deep inside us. Only very particular magicians and wise ones can show us the way. We learn much just through the process of seeking it, yet finding it remains our goal.

Then Serpil meets the young girl who knows where the wise woman is. That girl represents Serpil in her innocence, in her early awakening, coming back to teach her again, now, in her adulthood. The girl disappears and the wise woman appears. She's a wise woman who lives in a cave, the wise woman whom Serpil saw, in her dream, cooking a tasty soup that contained all things.

This particular wise woman has a lot of magic. She holds a key to Serpil's future. She cooks food for the inner journey; she gives Serpil the herb; she is egoless enough to be able to show Serpil how she is innocence (girl), adult activity (Serpil), and wise direction (old woman) all at once. All are parts of herself. This wise woman knows her role as mentor but makes sure Serpil learns that the magic is all her own. In stories, food often represents courage; the old woman feeds Serpil to help nourish her for the journey ahead.

At the forked road, Serpil feels the normal fear of the future, fear of the journey, fear of picking a road. The wise woman—who is truly a symbol of the wise voice in all of us—says Serpil knows what is down each road, she just doesn't realize it yet. What is this about? Could this be about Serpil's need to stand now at the road and cry for a vision, a vision that will rise from within herself to tell her where she needs to go, which road she needs to take? I think so. Serpil must decide which road to take based on feelings and instincts that rise from within *her,* independent of others. The wise woman knows that Serpil will be empowered by the experience of making her own choice. Therapists understand the same thing when they say, "Where do you want to start today?" or "What do you need?" or "What work should we do today?" They use their magic to help guide us to our own magic of choosing. They know that if we've been locked in power struggle and dependency, we need to make our own choices and to honor them.

Serpil, who was bored, or miserable, or just felt shapeless and personless both in herself and in her relationship, takes the risk, awakens, and sets out toward the ocean.

Meanwhile there's Keloglan, the youngest of five brothers who all live in a kind of sleep. They have little contact with the village except to sell those perfect apples. Their lack of contact indicates their isolation. And though we are dealing with five brothers here, we can assume that the five indicate one person psychologically. The "man" in this story is emotionally isolated and good at his task, relating to community through the task, not through intrinsic vitality of his own.

He is forced to awaken when something starts eating away at the one thing he holds dear—his orchard. Men and women both experience this kind of awakening. We are focused on our work, family, or dream; things are going fine for a while, our needs seem to be getting met; then we lose our job, or a child goes astray, or a spouse leaves us: crisis catalyzes awakening. We hurt, we try small solutions, but finally, if we're on a path of spiritual growth, we realize we must send that fifth brother in us out into danger, emotional and spiritual reckoning, so that we can find a real self—our Self—the goals and needs that will ultimately make us whole.

And our awakening sometimes requires wounding. Keloglan can't quite stay awake, so he cuts a wound into his own palm. The pain keeps him awake. So many times we awaken, then hit a hard time, and drink ourselves back to sleep, or overwork again to distract ourselves from our vulnerability. Some external or internal challenge—some friend or therapist saying, "Hey, you're just getting back into your old mold. Wake up!"—cuts us like a wound. "You're right," we say, "yes, okay," and we get back to the hurt of being awake, the pain of not drinking, not overworking, the arduous task of looking inward and not always liking what we see.

Keloglan's wakefulness is rewarded by the coming of the giant. The giant in Turkish stories, like the dragon in European or the evil sorcerer in Persian, represents the Shadow side, *our* shadow side. It is one of the primary elements of ourselves we must confront in stage 5, the Conscious Descent. We cannot find our*selves* unless we find, confront, pass through, and integrate our own Shadow—our own dark side, our worst fears and nightmares, our most painful and enervating wounds. In stage 4, Keloglan is introduced to his Shadow. He must decide whether to pursue it or let it get away. He pursues his Shadow.

Again we see wonderful direct correlation to our own lives. So many times we awaken, surviving the initial urges to go back to sleep, but then once we actually see our own Shadow—once we see that we are physically abusive, that we have a terrible inferiority complex, that we are an alcoholic, that we don't know any other way to live except to control, that we are scared of life—once we see our own Shadow (and it has many component parts), we run. We run and run, back to our safe, isolated house in the middle of the

113

orchard. We sit back there and don't confront the Shadow again until the giant has eaten all our apple trees and has begun, like the wolf, to blow our house down.

Keloglan makes his choice, as Serpil did. He too stands at a fork in the road. He goes down the road that the giant knows better than he does, along which the giant moves faster than he can. Keloglan, a courageous searcher, throws his sword into the giant's Achilles' heel to slow the huge being down. He follows all the way down the huge hole— the hole of our beings, the hole in the center of us that we must plumb to discover who we are, the hole that awaits us in stage 5.

The wounding of the giant is a foreshadowing act of insight and wisdom on Keloglan's part. It is unconscious, but we know that later he will learn to cut the giant down by cutting at that same spot at each ankle, that place of vulnerability.

Your Shadow has its place of vulnerability. Your own insight, along with the wisdom of therapists and mentors, helps you find that place of vulnerability. "Working on yourself" is about performing that critical surgical procedure. Maybe you come to realize that the key to your growth lies in working through your fear of being humiliated. Maybe you find that the key is your fear of showing anger. Maybe your key is your fear of vulnerability and trust.

When we find the fear that controls our own Shadow, we often notice how we have accepted it as prophecy and destiny. "My God," we say, realizing our deep fear, "I guess I've just always believed I'd be this way. You mean I can change?" Or, more specifically, "My God, my mother/father did it this way/always felt like this, so I just assumed I would too."

How wonderful it is to feel the sword enter our own

Achilles' heel, and yet see we don't die, It was not destiny; we just have to keep pushing forward to fight through the Shadow even more.

Serpil and Keloglan both awaken in their own way. We gain by seeing them as a woman and a man in stage 4, and we gain by seeing their whole story as Self. Every part of the story is a part of us. How is each of them a part of you?

YOUR OWN AWAKENING

Have you awakened? Answer these questions to get a sense of how you have navigated this stage, or are doing so, or might need to. Have you, through outside guidance, internal process, or surprising epiphany, come to the realizations that:

• Power struggle in my intimate relationships is a place I am no longer happy to be in?

• In struggling for power, I have tried to collect and control other people's power—I have not really found my own? I am ready to discover true personal power, which is, by definition, dependent on no one else?

• I have asked others to mirror back my identity to me, but now I'm ready to find my own identity?

• I have created false selves by which to love others, function in my parents' family, function at work, and so on—am I ready to give up the false selves?

• I have not been properly initiated into womanhood or manhood—am I ready to discover what a full adult is?

• Have I come to a point in life where I need either to break down a role I've been locked into or find a role for my life that gives me useful limits?

• Have I tried to be spiritual—to mystically delve into the life of the soul—without having a clear sense of Self?

• Has it come time now for me to develop a personal spirituality? It may be a spirituality that is completely nontraditional. It may be one composed of elements from traditional religion. It may be a particular religion. Am I ready to accept a spirituality as my own?

• In my search for power, I have not been of service to others and the planet—am I ready to seek out a way of servant leadership that best fits who I am?

These questions naturally arise out of the awakenings that must occur in us in order for us to move forward in our spiritual quest. Though they are listed here under stage 4 as if they get asked all at once, we know we can awaken into each question over a period of years. Yet wouldn't it be wonderful to live in a culture that understood their worth and place in stage 4 and guided us to them in adolescence and early adulthood, *before* we had kids, *before* we became overworked adults, *before* the conditions of life forced us to take on false selves just to survive?

As we build an ideal vision for the new millennium of how our culture can move its children through the stages of growth and partnership, we will probably find that this stage 4 must happen not at middle age, as it does for so many of us—often *after* our kids are grown!—but in adolescence and young adulthood, when it is already naturally occurring through hormonal changes and social pressures. Waiting to awaken until we enter midlife crises and passages is dangerous. When we are mentored to become independent selves in the second decade of life, we learn a process at that crucial stage by which not only to develop as free beings, but also by which to awaken ourselves again and again as we need to, in our journey through the problems and joys that fate and crisis will bring us.

How have the realizations, the epiphanies, the awakenings happened for you? Take a moment to recall, even journal them. They are a valuable part of your life story.

One client of mine awakened into the realization that she had brought a false self to her marriage. "I woke up one day," she said, "and simply knew I was in the wrong marriage. I never looked back."

Another had this experience: "I felt I had 'woken up' but my wife hadn't. I resented the fact that I was on a path now and she wasn't. But I have to give her credit. She let me do my thing, my men's groups, my meditation, and then one day—oh, it must have been a year later—she seemed to wake up. She started taking *her* journey. Wow, it was great. We're still together."

I have had many clients who recalled awakenings from adolescence and early adulthood. Almost to a person, these people report having awakened for a while, but then having felt alone, unguided, unmentored, undirected, confused. They drifted from their awakenings into overwork, power struggle, romantic dependency. As one workshop participant put it, "I vividly remember waking up one day when I was at camp, at seventeen years old, and thinking, 'I'm not a child anymore.' But then I just kind of lost it, and married and had kids, and didn't wake up again until I was forty-five." In that workshop room filled with people, there were more nods of agreement and mutual remembrance than I could count.

Sometimes we awaken, we have "realizations" intellectually, but not in our deep heart's core, our "guts." Have you had them in such a way that your whole body has vibrated with them, in a kind of mystical empowerment? When you have them that way, the old stories teach us, you know you've woken up, and you'll never be the same again.

Here is a psychological framework for what the process of stage 4 often feels like.

• We have an epiphany or other awakening moment in which we realize the worth of searching for an independent Self. We know it's time to cross the river, and we cross. We cut our own hand to be awake.

• We feel a wonderful infatuation with being awake, with planning our independence.

• We begin to explore and through experience possible paths for our independence. As adolescents we do this through rebellion and future planning. As people in middle age we do it similarly, though we tend to emphasize exploration of new spiritual paths, relationship paths, new books, new guides.

• We come to like one or more mentors and paths. We find our wise woman at the forked road.

• During self-examination, we admit, at least intellectually, the power of our own Shadow, our own dark side. We see it right there, that giant, that giantess as clear as day. We know we're in for some deep work.

• During self-examination, we make a promise to ourselves to develop a healthy distance from our partner's (or, in adolescence, parent's) Shadow.

• We become suspicious of our own new empowerment and even fall backward for a while into unhealthy appeasements, self-doubts. This is a valuable time to fully explore whether our path of awakening is the right and necessary one for us. Have we found *the* forked road, or are we standing at just any forked road and thinking it's the one we need?

• We disturb the universe—quit a job, leave home for a while, rebel in some overt way. We destroy a dependency structure that has enchanted and disempowered us. In our own way, we do not turn back to get the other four brothers. We set out on our own.

• We cry for vision, for a deep, happy new life, and we prepare for a personal journey into the darkness of our woundedness, addiction, conflict, pain (even joy, grace). These preparations are our source of joy.

Take time to recall your awakenings. Did you go through these moments in your awakening?

If you can recall none of them, nor any awakenings for yourself, take time to dream of what an awakening might be like for you. This is *your* moment. Grab it.

THE FOURTH SACRED TASK

Stage 4 of the Lover's spiritual discipline teaches us the fourth lesson of trust: *emancipation.*

To progress further now into spiritual depth, we must commit to unfettered self-discovery. I must learn who I am, with mentoring but without dependency on caregivers, so that I can trust who I am.

From self-discovery will come self-trust, from self-trust will come trust of others and life and spirit. As we awaken, we glimpse this continuum. We are not self-trusting beings yet, but we do *commit* to becoming self-trusting beings—we commit to the descent, stage 5. Joy, we realize, comes to those who emancipate themselves from dependency and seek independence.

In stage 4 people often get confused about *self* and *soul.* People often say, "To me the key to being a soulful (joyful) person is to get rid of my self." They say, "To trust myself, I need to focus on how I'm not really here at all, I'm an illusion."

This confusion between self and soul is partly the limitation of words, but it also comes from our efforts during awakening to blend Eastern philosophy and Western traditions. Western psychological and religious traditions tell us to build up a Self—whether a "personality" in psychology or "character" in religious–moral teaching. Eastern traditions tend to tell us to break ourselves down. When in our Hindu–Buddhist practice we hear the word *Self,* we hear "ego" and "illusion." When in our Judeo-Christian-based practice we hear the word *No-self,* we hear "escape, avoidance of Being, fear of living." Because we are now, as we enter the next millennium, creatures of both East and West, we often find in stage 4 that we must come to grips with this theological/psychological dichotomy. And, more practically, we find that both goals are good ones—both to build a Self and to break it down—but first and foremost, we have to build one up *before* we can break it down. We have to be Somebody before we can be Nobody.

Steven Hedlin, a clinical psychologist and student of the soul/self conflict, made his point at a recent conference at the Kuroda Institute in Los Angeles: "Too often people try to lose their 'ego,' or sense of self, before they have actually worked through their own personal psychological material, and established a healthy sense of self." Hedlin calls this "premature disidentification."

A strong ego gives us the ability to function well in the world. We need to have this functioning well established be-

fore we go off into the mystical search for oneness. We must
have a Self in order to do the work of the soul. If we don't,
we will be like a spaceship drifting in the cosmos, meditating
every day and seeking awakening and enlightenment without
any grounding in a journey of purpose.

We realize this in stage 4, or later in our second season. If
we don't, we try to learn self-trust by denying ourselves. We
often find that this works for a while, but then we notice the
same old dysfunctions and fears. We have tried to become
holy—in Hebrew, "separate"—without first becoming
human.

Stage 4 also provides us with the fourth element of focus
for the Lover's spiritual discipline: *emptying.*

*To practice love as a spiritual discipline, I must empty my internal
and external life of notions and baggage that weigh me down unnec-
essarily.*

We do much of this automatically after the moment of
awakening, as if our brain chemicals pull us to it. We discard
material things we no longer need, we clean house, we leave
jobs, leave lovers, leave religions.

Good spiritual models for this stage of our discipline come
from the Native American vision quest and from Buddhist,
especially Zen, practices of sitting in long meditations that
empty the body and brain of needless things.

The vision quest, like many tribal traditions around the
world, exists to awaken young people into stage 4 and help
adults find spiritual renewal and new awakenings throughout
their lives. A youth is quite literally told by parents and mentors, "You've been in the sleep of childhood. It's time to
wake up." The youth, of course, has probably been awake
for a few months, even years already, or has yearned to come

into a spiritual container or adult process that would make the awakening occur.

In some tribes, vision quests last three days, in others fourteen. Many quests are done during a youth's adolescence. The vision quests are part and parcel of the longer—years long—process of initiation into adulthood (stages 4 through 6 in the Lover's Journey model). Early in the vision quest, when the youth or questing adult is "at the threshold," he or she is guided to "empty."

Catholics empty by confessing; Jews empty every Yom Kippur as part of the atonement process; some native Australian tribes teach youths that before entering dreamtime, they must empty themselves of their previous lives and chatter. Buddhism and Taoism have made emptying a primary principle at the essence of their religion. When the Buddhists teach us to find No-self, they are teaching the art of emptying. The *Tao Te Ching* advises that the sage go about doing nothing.

In stage 4 discipline, joy rises in us as we learn to lose for awhile. We commit to learning how to release fears, empty out desire, clear out old, unhealthy patterns and ways of being. As we focus on this in our prayer, meditation, and daily practice, we sense things differently, think about things differently, love things differently.

We become more able to distill what we need to its essence because we are emptying ourselves of distractions, false selves; emptying our lives of dangers in our relationships; emptying our vision of the kind of pride that says, "I am greater than what I face," but really means, "I feel inferior to what I face."

Through our spiritual practice in this stage, we commit to a kind of joyful life in which we will trust ourselves not by what we consume, but by "making a journey," "trusting a process," "discovering who we are," "becoming a searcher." Joy, in stage 4, is experienced through emancipation from the past and commitment to the future.

INTEGRATING AWAKENING

Sometimes we awaken and say, "I'm getting out of this relationship, this religion, this family, this job," yet we do not move on to stage 5—rather, we return to the same old power struggles that bound us in stage 3. We move into a hatred of our spouse, religion, family, workplace, life. "I'm so glad I'm awake now; I can see how it was all his/her fault." Brought up in power struggle, we easily slip into its rhythms of aggression, revenge, bitterness. Sometimes we remarry without making the whole journey of the second season, and thus remarry into the same dysfunctions we divorced.

Often we awaken into a new political consciousness, like feminism or antigovernment activism or environmental activism or the men's movement, and move into gender war or socioeconomic war as a way of facilitating change. And we often do facilitate deep, piercing changes. But still, we will awaken later on and seek something other than power grappling.

Sometimes we enjoy the moment of awakening so much we decide to do it over and over again. We join a religion or cult, feel "saved" or "enlightened," forge a new relationship, find a new job. But soon, the fervor wears off and we wake up to the need for a *new* religion, a *new* relationship, a *new* job. We replay, after awakening, the romance/disappointment cycle of stages 1 and 2, endlessly awakening, going to sleep, awakening again.

Just being awake is not always enough to push us through

the awakening stage into stage 5, the First Conscious Descent. But an awakening that involves substantial emancipation and substantial emptying can lead to great joy.

We could say the "Me decade," so often mentioned in our culture, was about a whole group of people seeking and often getting lost in awakening. Those of us who went through it recall how wonderful and necessary it felt to wake up, leave behind traps and baggage and people and jobs and, often, commitments, promises, and duties we had sworn to fulfill. Locked for so many generations in old rigidities and endless power struggles, we were a whole culture seeking freedom.

We are leaving that behind these days as we approach the beginning of a new millennium. We continue to gain from rampant awakenings; but we also see how clearly they can destroy families and communities if they are not well guided and disciplined; and we sense in ourselves a moving forward into something else. We are starting to leave the mass consciousness of awakening behind for the next stages of life and love.

As with all other stages, individuals never leave awakening behind completely. We integrate awakening. We carry its energy forward; we have awakenings throughout our lives. To make the First Conscious Descent, however—the individual journey that takes us deep into our own darkness and ends with our ability to stand up and be counted as a Self—we do need to cry for vision. We do need to recognize that our lives have been, thus far, a tug-of-war between our needs for dependency and independence; we do need to realize that now it is time to find a Self that is strong enough to guide our personal journey of soul.

That journey is where we go now.

STAGE 5

THE FIRST
CONSCIOUS
DESCENT

I asked myself, "What is the myth you are living?"
and did not know. So I took it upon myself to get to
know my myth, and regarded this as the task of tasks.
—C. G. JUNG

Only after painfully experiencing and accepting our
own truth can we be free.
—ALICE MILLER

The author Gabriele Rico tells this story from her own life:
"When I was small, I read a fairy tale about a princess who
was born with a glass heart. One early spring day, grown into
a lovely woman, she leaned far out the window sill in the
castle, feeling joy at the sight of the first crocuses in the palace
garden below. The pressure on her fragile heart proved too
much. There was a tiny sound, like glass breaking, and she
fell as if dead. When the confusion settled, the court doctor
discovered her heart was not broken after all but it had a
long, slender crack in it. The story evolves from there.

"What is most vivid in my memory is my childhood
amazement that she lived to be very old and, even more
amazing, that she continued to find deep pleasure in her life.

I remember puzzling, 'How can she run and play? How can she be happy and not be afraid every minute of every day?'

"My mother died in a bombing raid three weeks before the end of World War II. It left our family vulnerable, confused, afraid, and in great pain. I pictured a long, jagged crack across my small heart. I felt fragile as glass, and I wondered if glass could ever heal. Then I recalled the princess' words: 'What survives a crack and doesn't break on the spot will be all the stronger for it.'

"At seven, I did not believe it. Now I do. Although not a single one of us is exempt from pain—in fact, we are all damaged somehow, somewhere, somewhen—the real issue is not whether but *how* we learn to deal with our damage. That makes all the difference."

When I listen to Gabriele Rico tell this story, I'm struck by its deep truth about how anyone at all—even someone with a crack in their heart (like all of us) can experience joy. I'm impressed by the deep pleasure she describes, not from avoiding the crack, but from confronting it. That confrontation, built on a foundational belief that joy is possible no matter what obstacles we face, is the subject of stage 5 in our quest.

Do you agree that all of us are damaged? If you don't, stage 5 will not make sense to you at a visceral level, for it is primarily about confronting our damage and the forces that damage or potentially damage. It is about confronting the experiential sources of those fears we isolated in our Shadow in stage 4. In the many years of work of stage 5, we heal our woundedness (carrying always our scars) and feel the empowerment of having gained a personal, independent identity through a long journey of heroic self-challenge, spiritual conflict, risk-taking, and inner growth.

A man in his fifties spoke of his journey at a recent work-shop. "When you put it in this language of stages, I get it," he said. "I get this stage 5. I'm in it. I 'awakened' to it when I got a small heart attack. It was nothing really, not much anyway, but I was only forty-six, so it scared me. I had to change my diet, eliminate my drinking, had to work less. I got into reading. It's hard to say when I actually committed myself to making a 'journey,' but I guess I did, because in the past I never admitted when I was hurting, or my weak-nesses—no way would I admit those. It just wasn't some-thing I did. My ex-wife and I talk some these days. She says it's one of the reasons she left me. I just wouldn't be vulner-able. Nowadays, I feel like I'm always on the edge of crying. I'm so deep into changing myself I can't ever go back. I just know that I'm becoming someone, someone I think I'll be proud of, and I just don't ever want to go back."

"I am in stage 5," a woman said at a workshop. "I'm still struggling for power a lot. I still get enamored with things and people and then discard them. There's a lot of the first season still in me, a lot of dependency work, but also I re-member my awakening very well. It happened about eigh-teen months ago, with the birth of my little boy—or really just after, when I hit him, and I knew that was wrong. I used to be ashamed to admit I hit him, but I can admit it. It changed me for the better. Now I'm in therapy. I'm seeing my own past through my son's eyes. I'm not in a relationship, just working on myself. I'm in pain a lot. I have moments of joy when I confront something then think, 'Aha, I'm done with all this pain! I've done it!' but then the next day or so I know I'm back in the hard journey again, working again, still trying to understand."

THE FIRST CONSCIOUS DESCENT

Most cultures and traditions include somewhere in their mythology an epic journey into the underground, the dark cave, the dark center of human life and the psyche. Something essential to human experience hides in the dark, and we yearn to know it intimately. We sense that our greatest powers come from there, and that to know them we must return there as we make our way through life.

The First Conscious Descent is something beyond Adam and Eve's "fall" we explored in stage 2, for now we are consciously descending rather than involuntarily falling. This descent is a pursuit of en*darken*ment. This conscious, heroic journey is a confrontation with our own underworld, our own unconscious, the place of our deepest fears, our wounds, our shadows; in it we will find demons, dragons, giants. Myths and stories speak of the dark place toward which the psyche descends as a cave, a labyrinth, a well bottom, a deep hole, Hades, Hell. In our personal lives we experience the descent as depression, sadness, grief, "pushing through dark fear," "trying to get myself together." While we're in this stage, we often feel as if we're locked in a basement, a bogeyman closet, the bottom of the sea, a prison cell, a dark tower, a long tunnel. It is the primal darkness of Judeo-Christian–Muslim tradition in which out of the darkness came the light. It is Saint John's Dark Night of the Soul. "Without darkness," May Sarton wrote, "nothing comes to birth."

Of this process the Catholic philosopher Pierre Teilhard de Chardin wrote, "I became aware that I was losing contact with myself. At each step of the descent a new persona was disclosed within me of whose name I was no longer sure and who no longer obeyed me. And when I had to stop my exploration because the path faded beneath my steps, I found a bottomless abyss at my feet, and out of it comes—arising I know not from where—the current which I dare to call my life."

As we descend, we have assistance. In *Women Who Run with the Wolves,* Clarissa Pinkola Estés writes, "As we descend to the primary nature, the old automatic ways of nourishing ourselves are eliminated. Things of the world that used to be food for us lose their taste. Our goals no longer excite us. Our achievements no longer hold interest. Everywhere we look in the topside world, there is no food for us. So, it is one of the purest miracles of the psyche that when we are so defenseless help comes, and right on time." As we emancipate and empty ourselves, as we wander into darkness, we find new hungers in ourselves for new foods. Therapists, grandparents, friends, books, teachers, mentors, all help us find the new food that will sustain us through the journey and give us new life.

OUR POSTMODERN DARK PLACE:
FAMILY WOUNDS

We descend *toward* many things, many wounds, many sources of insight and growth. For most of us, the First Conscious Descent—which can be, in practical terms, an amalgam over a period of years of many life crises and painful challenges—involves a descent into the darkness in which our family past awaits us. Some people call this "inner child" work. The psychologist Joan Borysenko writes, "As Carl Jung and John Bradshaw have said, we can't find the light in our lives until we've gone back through the darkness and transformed the 'original pain' of childhood. Until we do,

we are covertly ruled by the wounded, emotionally immature child within, who searches for the unconditional love it
needed but did not receive from its family of origin."

Every tribe, every culture, has its own Shadow place.
Among the Shavante of Brazil, the Shadow place is called the
Bush. The young people move through stages 4 and 5 via
initiation rituals that involve surviving out in the bush, wrestling the anger of the bush and gaining its power. Tribes elsewhere in Native America sent initiates into the wilderness for
three or ten or fourteen days, and many times over, to do
vision quests. In the dark and wild of the wilderness, the initiates survived, learned who they were. Among the Hopis
the underground kiva was the dark place. Initiates all over
the world have been led into dark places—physical and very
real—in order for them to gain access to energies within
them, psychological and very real.

For many of us today, the process of going back to acknowledge the wounds imposed by our families of origin
seems to fulfill much of the function of the dark place. We
don't have external ritual structures built into our tribal life
in which to access the world of the dark. A sauna is hardly a
kiva. Our wilderness has been tamed; it's littered with trash
and spotted with campers. It certainly does wound us and
hurt us—people die every year in river accidents or lost on
mountain trails—but this isn't a ritualized Conscious Descent.

No, though we have stripped the stage 5 journey of its
tribal ritual structures—and in doing so robbed ourselves of
much of its sacredness, depth, and joy—we have by no
means lost the crisis of the journey. We don't need the Shavante Bush to wound us; our families wound us. We don't
need to go into the darkness of the bush to confront the dark,

mysterious forces of nature and our own inner nature. We go deep into our families of origin for this work.

In tribal cultures in which family systems provide emotional safety, doing "inner child work" would be ludicrous. In fact, for most of human history—in which the unsafe components in life were climate, earth changes, warring enemies outside the tribe, sickness and early death, pugnacious leaders, starvation and poverty—spiritual teachers led young people to descend into developing personal identity against these external odds. As we have done much to curb poverty, control climate, modernize and distance ourselves from war, treat medical problems, democratize the election of leaders, and so on, we have (at least we like to think) created more external-cultural safety for ourselves. We've taken much of the intimate Shadow out of leaders, climate, sickness. To make these gains of invention and personal freedom, we had to break down traditions, tribal systems, and families. We created our own peculiar place of Shadow to replace the shadows on which our inventions shed brilliant light.

For our ancestors, the searcher gained the gift of independent Self after the journey into understanding the power of fate, crisis, earth power, worlds of the gods, and evil spirits. "In the sweat lodge," an Indian elder would explain to participants in a vision quest, "where it is darker than dark, you will meet evil spirits and you will feel all your life's troubles openly. Where it is darker than dark you will descend into the seventh direction, the Within Direction, and feel from your heart. Inside your deepest self, where it is darker than dark, you will need to be the strongest and the most steadfast, or you will perish." For us, the gift of independent Self often awaits us after such a journey through our own wounding at the hands of those who most loved us. They are the "evil spirits" who live in our hearts. To gain the gift of Self, we often refeel the pain of being the child we were, reopen the wounds, then heal them. We often face our sense of inadequacy as we lose a job, or face a divorce, or have a heart attack, or destroy relationships, or abuse our children, or face our own suicide, then follow that inadequacy all the way back into the great pain of feeling unloved as children. We have a lot of work to do in stage 5, for we have not escaped from fate, crisis or evil, and we must descend into them as our ancestors did. Yet we must descend into our families as well.

In this is the great curse and blessing of our lives. It is a curse because it means we are brought up with no real place of psychological safety. We are set up by our families and culture to feel alone, isolated, worthless, valueless. Yet it is a blessing, for without the traumatic changes to family and tribal systems our culture is vanguarding, human society would not make the next step in its psychosocial evolution—a step toward joy unimaginable to most of our ancestors, for whom restrictive gender roles, culturally exclusive religions, and tribal xenophobia were the norms. As each of us descends consciously into our own deepest fears and wounds, and develops through that descent a solid, authentic Self, we live out the larger allegory of our times.

THE BIG PEOPLE AT THE BOTTOM
OF THE WORLD: PART TWO

Serpil and Keloglan, you'll remember, were involved in a descent of their own. Their story is rich in wisdom for each of us as we descend, as we make the Hero's/Heroine's Journey, for truly that is what we're doing when we make this First Conscious Descent: we are becoming heroines and heroes.

Serpil meets her Shadow as a giantess, a huge woman as big as a tree, who peered out over the treetops toward the ocean. Wisely, Serpil is afraid and hides. The giantess hears her, discovers her, and smiles away her terror. I'm your friend, the giantess says, I'll protect you from the bandits, and we'll travel together to the ocean.

The three earlier parts of the Self—innocent girl, woman in search, wise crone—have now found their fourth: the Shadow Self. Innocence took the searcher to the wise woman, the wise woman put the searcher on a path, the path has now led to the Shadow. The message of this story, like every story of the hero's/heroine's quest, is simple: you cannot get to your destination—an integrated Self, an independent identity—without passing through the Shadow. No one can. And watch for the Shadow's tricks. They'll lead to revelations, but they can be lethal.

The giantess, like so many Shadow figures, presents herself as the protector. To do this, she must point out other shadows and make us afraid of them. The bandits, she says, are the real shadows. I'm your friend, I'll protect you. This trick sits in the very nature of our psyches. We often align ourselves with the worst part of ourselves (usually without consciously seeing the alignment at first) to protect ourselves against what we think will be a much worse fate. We live in a life-destroying addiction, all the time crying, "I *need* this. Without it I'd collapse, I'd lose my sanity." We align ourselves in dependency with the very parent who is most hurtful to our growth. "Yes, okay, my mother is overbearing, but what would I do without her?" A client of mine had come in his therapy to the time when he had to confront the rage he felt toward his wife of twenty years. Every time he and I got close to working with it, he defended himself and expressed his anger at his parents, the world, himself—never at her. He made bandits out of everything else to avoid dealing with how he really felt about the woman he loved. The Shadow walked with him all the way to the ocean, but he didn't let himself know that rage was the Shadow he needed to work with now.

We spend years walking toward the ocean in the protection of the Shadow. We tell the Shadow our secrets, our past, the small part of our Shadow we are conscious of at this early point in our Descent. The Shadow stores these details for later. "You think you're an addict because your father was distant. That's good to know. I'm going to keep hurting you with that thought of yours later on, and as long as you'll let me."

One day the Shadow decides it's time to take you deep into the pit, where it can enslave you and then eat you. It does this *after* it has learned your secrets. "Come down with me," it cries gleefully, sliding down the hole, and by now you are dependent on your Shadow and follow. Down at the bottom of the pit, after you're trapped, the Shadow says, "Oh, well, I tricked you." Stuck there, you become your Shadow's servant; you wait to be eaten.

So often we see this in our attitudes, lives, behavior. We are stuck, we are caged, we are in a darkness and can't get out. We're in the bottom of the pit. We don't really understand how we got there, for we've been living the life we thought we were supposed to be living. Who tricked us into this pain, this sorrow we feel, this lost relationship, these suicidal urges, this monotonous existence, this endless pattern of sexual acting out, this addiction, this depression? If we could just find out who did it, everything would be fine.

But of course it won't be fine. We are down here and we've given our secrets to this giantess, and now she is going to destroy something we value. The giantess eats Serpil's husband. The giantess brings his valuables as trophies. "You shouldn't have to live with that boring man," the giantess says, and Serpil sees good intentions even in the Shadow's actions.

This is the confusing world of the Shadow. It is an amoral world that we seek to control through moral teaching. Yet our shadows have their own moral compass. The best a culture can do is provide worthwhile guidelines. In the end, each of us must determine how to handle the destruction each of us is capable of. This is our personal responsibility. Many people, unlike Serpil, enjoy the giantess's ability to eat up past husbands/wives, children, jobs; in enjoying this kind of Shadow power, many of us serve the giantess until she enjoys all the destruction we create ourselves, then eats us too.

But Serpil has had the advantage of being well mentored. She chooses another course. She has the herbs the crone gave her and uses them now to poison the Shadow.

This moment in each of our lives when we *choose* personal growth is one of the most defining moments in our journey to a solid Self. We *choose* to change our Shadow patterns. We *choose* to change our lives. We directly confront the Shadow—the addiction, the depression, the rages, the sexual acting out, the love addiction, the spiritual emptiness—and it feels very much as if we are risking our lives. By *life,* we do not just mean the kind of "disturbing the universe" we did in stage 4, where we left a job or relationship or attitude behind. We mean we disturb our whole way of doing things, our whole way of being.

And so often, as happens to Serpil, we take this risk only to find another Shadow waiting in the wings. The giant comes back, as if he sensed his wife's dying. "Tell me the antidote this second!" he orders, beating Serpil, chaining her, threatening her. He is unaffected by eating the herbs. Why? Serpil can't understand it. She has taken all the risks, found the empowerment, challenged the Shadow, and now it seems as if for naught. "Get apples," she cries, lost in her battle with the Shadow, seemingly defeated. "Apples will save her." The giant keeps her alive long enough to see if the apples will work.

Often, like Serpil, we take the risk and poison the giantess, but we feel even more lost than before, for now we are trapped by a seemingly new Shadow, equally as powerful. Often at this next defining moment, we give up. We return to the old patterns of destroying relationships, acting out, self-destruction. We align ourselves with a new Shadow, more violent, more terrible than the first. Our own level of cruelty to ourselves increases, and the amount of cruelty we get back from others increases. We are more cruel to spouses and children and they to us. We are more cruel to enemies. They, in turn, become more cruel to us. We are more cruel to friends, destroying friendships, feeling destroyed. It feels as if our psychic body is being completely broken. We become bitter, isolated.

We know that if we help the giant find the antidote, the giantess will be cured, and we'll have both of them to torture us. Yet we speak up. At the time, it seems like our desperation speaking, or our simple need to live a few more days, months. We do not realize yet that in speaking the antidote aloud, we begin a whole new cycle of growth. And we don't realize yet that we are not alone in our fight with the Shadow—we have an ally we have perhaps not met yet. This ally is equipped to fight the giant. This ally is Keloglan.

Masculine and feminine are equally necessary at a joyful story's end. Male and female unite at a story's end to live "happily ever after." Given their common necessity at the story's end, it stands to reason both are equally necessary in the life-defining confrontation with Shadow that constitutes the middle of the story. Our own inner story is as finely woven as Serpil's and Keloglan's. The herbs that poison the giantess bring the giant. The apples that will cure her bring Keloglan. Masculine and feminine do indeed confront the Shadow together, within the psyche. The idea here is that while we are descending, we must realize how our wounds come from both masculine and feminine Shadows and require heroism from both feminine and masculine to be healed.

This lesson has been a terribly difficult one throughout human history. Integration of masculine and feminine once meant that men and women worked and lived together while occupying very distinct gender roles, compensating for the lack of romantic love for each other by sacrificing romantic love for communal survival. This state of affairs was adaptive for quite a long time, but then, as we sought more romantic love and built civilizations around that pursuit, it broke down. More recently, male/female integration has been taken to mean androgyny, resulting in a push to destroy the structures of male society and the structures of female society. This push has led to the modern gender war. In the last few years, some of us have been rethinking that course. It is my sense that we are just becoming capable of joyful love—love that honors separateness but begins in romance and promises at least twelve stages of joyful interaction. This is a kind of love we cannot have without rich integration of female and male power. As always, stories and fairy tales like that of Serpil and Keloglan—stories that have, for millennia, tried to point us toward joyful love—have a lot to teach.

As each of us confronts our own Shadow, we notice that one single part of us can't do the battle alone. A man might more easily be able to confront the abusive shadow father he carries within himself than the devouring shadow mother he can barely discern. Many men tell me their "father work" is—though terrifying—clearer to them, and easier to do, than their "mother work." They are male, they live in a male culture; they can more easily come to internally (and sometimes externally) challenge their father's masculine authority than challenge their mother's feminine. To do this work—to understand their mothers—they must delve deeply into her world, the world of the feminine, exploring the feminine within themselves so that they learn what medicine will finally finish their unfinished business with Mother.

Many women, too, speak honestly throughout our culture of their need to develop the masculine within themselves in order to confront the shadows they face. One woman at a workshop voiced it this way: "I've had to confront many shadows from the masculine—my father who sexually abused me, two ex-husbands who left me, a son who betrayed me and went with one of my husbands. Before I really began developing my own understanding of the masculine world and my own sense of power there, I always saw the shadows as masculine, and 'out there'—father, husbands, sons. I had a therapist—he was a man—who said, 'Stop being the victim; take control.' To me, this was a very masculine approach. I started taking aikido. I developed my body in ways I never had. I lifted weights. By paying attention to how I could take control of my life, I was developing the part of me that was masculine, integrating it. Maybe for others your masculine is something else, but for me this is what it was. As I developed this part of myself, I stopped being a victim. My whole life changed. I didn't see 'them' doing it to me anymore."

Keloglan is now that other part of Self that emerges to confront the Shadow. He has followed the giant down into the cave because the giant has been stealing his sustenance— the apples. It is no accident that Keloglan's sustenance and the Shadow's sustenance are the same food. Keloglan is like those of us who must become conscious that what is keeping us going in life is Shadow energy. Keloglan and his brothers have been tending an orchard but have little activated Lover in them. Their lack of children indicates lack of creativity or fertility in the language of stories, as does their lack of contact with the world except through sales of their product. With the giant's theft, their apples become the conscious fruit of the Shadow.

When Keloglan gets to the bottom of the hole, he realizes that the giant has trapped him. The giant, whose primary goal is to revive his wife, laughs at Keloglan. "I'll eat you and this woman soon," he says, then proceeds to his ritual with his wife. Keloglan, like Serpil, is now in the position of having to confront the Shadow. He must find a way to destroy the giant. He is trapped. He has no choice; circumstances have conspired to put him here. It has become destiny.

The giant, like the giantess, and like all shadows, can be bested with endurance, intelligence, courage, and wisdom. Its energy can be challenged, destroyed in its present form, then integrated into the Self. Keloglan must find the way to do it. Unlike Serpil, he had not been given herbs. But Serpil has already been in this cave awhile. She knows now the secret to the giant's destruction. She has been observant. "Cut his ankles first," she whispers, "then his knees, then his hips, then when he's down to size, you can cut off his head." She even tells Keloglan when the best moment would be—when the giant bends over the reviving giantess. Keloglan takes her advice. As the giant bends, distracted, Keloglan cuts him. The giant puts up a fight, but he is quickly brought down to size. Keloglan cuts off his head. "Cut hers off too," Serpil cries, for the giantess is awakening. Keloglan decapitates the weakened giantess as well.

Serpil alone could not destroy the Shadow, nor could Keloglan. Together, they accomplished it. Each held a secret—whether a piece of knowledge, magic, or prowess—that was essential for the confrontation with the Shadow. As always, the individual's journey to Self is an allegory of the culture's journey to society. As each of us seeks to learn what is masculine and feminine within ourselves and confront and integrate these forces, we live out and aid our society's attempt to bridge the shadowy gorge between male and female. And we unite as men and women to confront the shadows that face our culture.

When the group of Turks was telling me this story in their village, I said, "Wouldn't it be interesting if the giantess, who was now destroyed, had had the face of Serpil's mother, and the giant had had the face of Keloglan's father?" I explained how in so many of the lives of people I knew, the face of the human Shadow is composed of parents' faces. The shadow's arms, legs, torso, genitals, and so on might be other people or forces in our lives, but so often, when we get down into the pit and really do the hard work of confronting our fears, our pain, our wounds, we find our mother's face on the giantess, our father's face on the giant, even if from the grave.

When I explained this, there were nods in the storytelling circle. "Why not?" one old man said. "Let the faces be the parents' faces." He smiled a blessing smile. And that was that. For all I know, when these particular people tell the story these days, long after I've left Turkey to live in the United States again, they've added that detail.

To me it's an important detail, for if this story is to speak to us in our culture, it must speak about the faces we see on the giant and the giantess. For you it may not be a parent's face, but some face will be there. It will perhaps be the face of someone or even some deity who you feel has hurt you utterly. When you cut off the head, the face gets cut off from the body. You finish your work with this person. You destroy this person's power over you—the mother who beat you or could not adequately bond with you, the father who was absent.

The cutting off of the head is about mature confrontation with those who have power over you. It involves direct confrontations—if the person is alive, speaking to him/her—but even more often it involves therapeutic confrontations with the energies of this person as they live within you. A person who has been sexually abused often does not have the perpetrator available. The victim must do the confronting, the head cutting, within. And, even when an abuser is available, the head does not normally get cut off by a victim's raging and blaming of the perpetrator. The Self develops because of the work it does within its own cave. That is where the story really takes place.

Keloglan and Serpil are images of the parts of ourselves that do this work. They destroy the huge beings at the bottom of their world who have power over them. They integrate the power, changing it from power *over* to power *with,* by eating the Shadow. Our task is the same. Our discovery of who we are—our discovery of that Self we know as a combination of core self and identity; our discovery of connection to soul; and our stripping away of false selves are all inseparably linked to correcting the balance of power within us.

Somewhere toward the end of stage 5, sometime after the head is cut off and we realize the powers we've discovered in ourselves, sometime around when we are going to eat the Shadow and say, "All right now, this business is done, I'm ready for a new life"—at just about this time we find ourselves saying, "Oh, my God, so that's who I am," or "I have found myself, I know who I am, this is what I have to offer," or more simply, "I am alive, I'm free, I've come through." While we are saying this, Keloglan is saying his name to Serpil and Serpil to Keloglan. In stories, the moment of Self is often captured in the process of naming. When Keloglan and Serpil say, "I am Keloglan," "I am Serpil," they have said, this is my identity, this is who I am.

YOUR OWN DESCENT

Have you been through stage 5? Are you going through it now? Did you go through it for a while and find a way to come back up to the surface too early, before the descent toward confrontation with your Shadow and discovery of your identity was finished?

In tribal cultures, much of stage 5 is accomplished in the second decade of life. The vision quests and sun dances, the mentoring and trials and challenges, the supervised emotional growth that we spoke of in chapter 4 continue in a young person's life as stage 5, lasting for many years of adolescent and young adult challenges and spiritual renewals. When that young person leaves the First Conscious Descent, s/he is ready for what fate and crisis can muster, ready for the pains of life, prepared by a strong sense of personal identity, spiritual mission, and communal role.

Most of us did not have this supervised quest, so those of us who go through stage 5 usually do so later in life. It takes us many years. It gets interrupted, but we get back to it. Many of us, of course, never get this far. We get locked into power struggles or pursue eternal awakening without ever confronting our deepest fears, our great shames, our lack of identity.

Do you feel you know who you are? Do you feel you have integrated your Shadow? I have found it helpful for people to discover where they are in relation to stage 5 by answering the following questions.

• Do my parents still hook me with verbal or nonverbal signals that send me into inner turmoil?

• Is my self-image primarily dependent on a job, other people's treatment of me, social success, professional accomplishment, material acquisition, or personal stereotype?

• Is aiding others in building their own spiritual discipline an unimportant goal for me?

• Do I need to control the responses of people with whom I'm intimate (whether at home or at work)?

• Is it fair to say I have never had an epiphany that showed me how small I was and how little I really knew?

• Do I only feel happy when I'm obsessed or addicted?

• Do I have trouble with authority figures?

• Do I lack deep knowledge of how to care for myself spiritually? Do I lack sacred personal rituals?

• Do I feel that my life is often empty? Do I feel that my life is often out of control?

• Am I often afraid of living or of dying?

If you answered yes to one or more of the questions, you may be able to feel how there are still places in you that need your stage 5 journey. When you make it, here is what it often feels like. If you have already made it, you've felt much of this already.

• We stand, awakened, preparing to be truly tested. Our "dabblings" in a heroic journey have not been enough. Awakening has not been enough. We must now descend into terrible pain, woundedness, confrontation with demons and giants.

• We dive into what feels like a bottomless pit in the center of our being. Things seem to fall apart around us; we feel like we're falling apart. Things are dark. We prefer basements to meadows.

• We develop survival coping mechanisms down in the land of Shadow. We feel tricked, victimized, lost, unable to find a way out.

• At some point, shifts occur. We have gotten so accustomed to the dim light down there, we can now see all of what's under there for us. Faces from the past start to become clearer; painful memories emerge. We listen to criticism of us as we haven't before. We feel wounds we hadn't before.

• We realize we are gaining, have gained, and will continue to gain personal powers, even magic, in our descent.

144

• We identify the key elements of our Shadow—our personal sources of (1) our fears of inadequacy and (2) our sense of valuelessness. We know what we must confront.

• We confront those elements. Many of us confront and separate from the mother. Many of us confront and separate from the father. We confront our fears, our powers over others, our past victimizations.

• This confrontation is still not enough. We confront our darkest Shadow again, so that it seems we will be endlessly confronting, endlessly in the pit.

• We come to a place where we can do nothing but trust good allies. We trust them, and new ways of confrontation open up. Often we become spiritual here in a way we never have before, making a deep connection with a source of power we had not known before.

• We emerge from descent with our Shadow eaten and a Self system (a clear identity, separate from expectation and role) in place. This realization of Self leads us, toward the end of stage 5, into an overwhelming sense of joy at simply being alive.

In an ideal framework, most of the season of independence—and the foundational work of this descent—takes place in the second decade of life or near it, so that most of the rest of life can be spent in interdependence with family, community, spirit, and earth. Since, for most of us, this ideal process did not occur, our adult heroic journey involves new, adult experiences of who we are, but forces us to move in midlife through experiences of separation from parents, modes of self-exploration, initiation experiences, role and responsibility learning, development of spiritual practice, and expression of joyful vision that should have been taught to us in the second decade of our lives.

How wonderful it would be if we did not have to live so much of our lives feeling as if we don't know who we are. How wonderful it would be to live in a culture that does not ask us to wait until middle age (if we're lucky) to fully awaken and make our descent, but instead understands spiritual growth and guides it from early on. How wonderful it would be to awaken to the hard descent into self-discovery and healing *before* we had to spend half an adulthood feeling lost in the war between our dependencies and our need to be independent. How wonderful if we could change the way we do this in our children's lives!

THE FIFTH SACRED TASK

Stage 5 of the Lover's spiritual discipline teaches us the fifth lesson of trust: *self-trust.*

The Hero and the Heroine make their journeys into the depths of darkness and fear and risk destroying themselves and many of their relationships, so that when they survive and flourish they are able to say, "I am I, I am solid, trustworthy; I have intrinsic value; I am worth loving. I am in charge of my own happiness."

Self-trust and *self-love* can be used interchangeably here. We do not experience them until we've gone down into the pit, been wounded, taken unimaginable risks, altered dependencies, changed our own lives, and discovered, in the end, a Self, independent, loving, wise, and powerful.

The trust in ourselves we discover in stage 5 is nurtured throughout our lives through relationships, faith, work, conscious love, and disciplined spiritual practice. Whenever we face self-doubt later in life, we will always have the trough of stage 5 to drink from. Our memory of the years we spent descending will give us the faith in ourselves to meet any psychological fear. People who have not gone through stage 5 do not have a foundation for pushing through self-doubt. They tend to seek external agents to help them assuage their doubts—dependency on religions, dependency on relationships, dependency on material things or substances.

Stage 5 provides us with the fifth element of focus for the Lover's spiritual discipline: *the Great Confrontation.*

To practice love as a spiritual discipline I must confront my demons, my Shadow. Having done so, I have access to every recess or crevasse of my own psychological power. I do not need others anymore to fill my identity up, to make me solid, to conceal the dark hole my Shadow had been hiding in.

I will know how to relate to others, especially intimates, without power over them or powerlessness in relationship to them. My need for control, most manifest during power struggle, grew in large part because I had to keep my Shadow hidden, unloved. I have now confronted my Shadow. I don't have to hide it from myself or others anymore. I have integrated it into my very being—taken its powers and made them my own.

Accomplishing stage 5 of the Lover's spiritual discipline requires vulnerability, courage, help from allies, a certain trust in the ultimate safety of my own psyche, and personal endurance. Stage 5 takes time. We have to be tough and resilient to make it through the dark tunnels, the underground forests, the dungeon cells of the psyche. And somehow we have to be tough without ever losing our compassion. Because while we're involved internally in the Great Confrontation, we are working, raising kids, seeking love and loving others, and living everyday lives.

INTEGRATING THE DESCENT

Ingrid Bengis writes, "The real questions are the ones that obtrude upon your consciousness whether you like it or not, the ones that make your mind start vibrating like a jackhammer, the ones that you 'come to terms with' only to discover that they are still there. The real questions refuse to be placated. . . . They are the ones that reveal their true natures slowly, reluctantly, most often against your will."

As you move to integrate stage 5 work into your journey, you know that stage 5 is not a static, discardable thing. It is an experience that has given you the creative force to withstand, now, any obstacle; to be a worthy Self no matter what fate or crisis throws at you; and to relate to others with equal parts vulnerability and self-protection.

The great questions will always remain, however; the obstacles will always be there; your own shadow will not go away; the giant will reappear in the orchard; you'll suffer new wounds that need healing; your hands will get cut off and need rebuilding; you'll need to be a hero again in your life.

The process of integrating stage 5 and moving forward is a process of deep acceptance of life's randomness, death's closeness, and pain's appropriateness, as well as your ability to respond without losing yourself. As you integrate stage 5, you give to yourself and the world a whole new being, an independent one, who has gained courage he or she never had before, insight and wisdom that were not possible without years of work, and new energy other people will come to admire.

This new courage, wisdom, and energy cry out for new skills by which to exercise them. That is the mission of stage 6.

STAGE 6

REFINED
INTIMACY

For one human being to love another, that is the work
for which all other work is but preparation.
—RAINER MARIA RILKE

When my daughter was younger, I used to read her a children's book by Jack Kent called *The Caterpillar and the Polliwog*. I joked with her that since it was about a caterpillar
and a tadpole, it was about a pillar and a pole. Seeing how
entertained I was by my own pun, my daughter would say at
bedtime, "Daddy, read the 'tory 'bout the pillar and the
pole." Here it is.

There was once a youthful caterpillar who went around
bragging, "When I grow up, I'm going to turn into something else." She bragged to the snail about this, then to the
turtle, then to the polliwog. The polliwog in turn felt sad. "I
won't turn into anything," he mourned. He didn't understand his true nature yet.

Encountering a fish, he expressed his sadness. The fish
smiled at his consternation. "Don't worry," said the fish.
"You too will be transformed into something else!"

When he next saw the caterpillar the polliwog cried happily, "I'll become something else too!" The caterpillar, surprised by this, couldn't quite see the polliwog as a butterfly.
All the caterpillar knew was that when you turned into

something else, it was a butterfly. The polliwog knew nothing to contradict this. The two of them decided the polliwog would turn into a butterfly, but the caterpillar said, as if winning a great victory, "Okay. But I get to go first." The polliwog agreed. He wanted to watch how it happened. In truth, he hadn't a clue about how to do it himself.

So the caterpillar set out making a cocoon. She spun and spun till only her head remained unwrapped. "I have to close the lid," she said, "and when I come out, I'll be a butterfly." The polliwog, delighted, watched the process. Soon the caterpillar was out of sight in the cocoon. The polliwog waited patiently for the transformation to occur. Days and weeks went by.

Suddenly one day, the cocoon stirred. The end of it opened. Out came a beautiful butterly. The polliwog, excited, jumped up and down like a frog. A frog! When had this occurred? He looked himself over. He had become transformed into a frog. "I was so busy watching *you*," he said, "I didn't notice what was happening to *me!*"

And so it was that a polliwog who had expected to become a butterfly became a frog, and a caterpillar who had expected to become a butterfly became just that.

And so it is with lovers. The refined intimacy that stage 6 promises cannot occur unless two partners have transformed themselves—through their romance, their disillusionment, their power struggle, their awakening, and then, especially, the long heroic descent into new selves, solid, unmistakable, confident selves. Sometimes we call this new self our "true self," "adult self," "mature self." These abstract adjectives are attempts to express in metaphor our sense that we are *real* now in a way that makes the past all look like preparation. We have become butterfly, we have become frog.

Often, as in the caterpillar's case, the identity into which we are transformed will be the one we had envisaged years before, perhaps in our childhood or youth. We become, basically, who we, with the help of visionary mentors, planned to be. Just as often, as in the case of the polliwog, we become a new self, utterly surprising. Whichever transformation or combination of transformations we experience, we are now capable of refined intimacy, though we will need to work very hard to learn its techniques. Refined intimacy is a skillful way of doing love. Some people call it "mature love." What is meant by these phrases? What are the skills we seek in stage 6? The Big People at the Bottom of the World have some wisdom for us.

THE BIG PEOPLE AT THE BOTTOM
OF THE WORLD: PART THREE

Serpil and Keloglan, you may recall, had just successfully wrestled from the giant and giantess their power. Serpil had provided the "medicine" needed to do it and Keloglan the action of doing it. Keloglan, bloodied, freed Serpil and, with her help, cleaned himself at an underground spring. Famished, Serpil ate the apples. The two set out looking for a hole through which to escape from the cave at the bottom of the world. They found no escape route and began to feel desperate, irritable. Much time passed. Hungry, they ate the rest of the apples, then started eating the giant and giantess. At first, the food from the bodies of the huge beings seemed to make them even more angry at each other, but after a time they felt something happening to them. It was a kind of resignation. They realized they might be down there together forever. This realization tempered them. They got

along again, their love renewed. They divided up tasks, as-
serted places for themselves as individuals in the cave, felt
satisfied, and danced together.

In this transition between finishing the battle with the
Shadow and coming to the beginnings of comfortable intimacy
with each other, a lot of eating gets done. First, Serpil eats Keloglan's apples. She accomplishes many things—she feeds her
own hunger from Keloglan's orchard, connecting with him;
she eats the antidote to the poisonous herb she brought into the
cave, tying up this loose end; she consumes the apples that gave
her Shadow life, taking into herself the power of the ritual on
which the existence of her Shadow depends.

And Keloglan and Serpil eat the Shadow beings themselves. As we said earlier, they gain power and Self from this
eating, but also, as regards their intimate relationship with
each other, they gain irritability. Wisely, the story points out
what most of us experience as we make our transition from
our heroic Conscious Descent to the refined intimacy of
stage 6. Eating our own Shadow brings up anger, irritability,
moments of old pains rising up, days and even weeks during
which power struggle begins again. It is not easy to fully confront and then eat our Shadow. We sometimes act out the
hard time with our partner. One might even say that while
we are eating our Shadow, we are also trying, in a last gasp,
to reject it, to push it onto our partner. We get mopey and
want him/her to rescue us. We get irritated easily and want
him/her to calm us down. We are imperfect beings and respond to the intensity of the descent in myriad ways that seek
last-ditch dependent responses.

But at some point, something clicks and we push out of
the transition. The shadow is digested. We have the realization that *we have become who we are* and that *the relationship we*

are in is the relationship we need. This is a liberating, emotional insight that makes us realize four practical things in its wake:

1. If this relationship is going to work, I have to apply more than projection and fantasy to it, more than romantic idealization, more than disillusionment and power struggle, more than awakened search and my independent journey. I must become truly intimate. I don't really know yet what that true intimacy is, but I can learn, my partner by my side.

2. If this relationship is going to grow, the intimacy system I develop, this new way of loving I find, must be one in which I apply *mature skill* to relationship, not just fragmented skills but real *spiritual discipline.* Unless I give my new, independent Self the skills to be intimate, I cannot be intimate; I am not fully committed, the relationship may not last.

3. I was not born knowing these skills, this discipline, this refined intimacy. I was born knowing how to be dependent.

4. I did not learn much about refined intimacy from my parents, for they were most likely locked in a form of power struggle—a struggle between their need for dependency and their need for independence—that my partner and I are now ready to grow beyond.

Keloglan and Serpil have these realizations and develop an intimacy system. They learn the dance of intimacy. They divide up tasks—that is, they come to a working arrangement about day-to-day action and labor so that they need not struggle for power there. They discover and honor their differences, building separate "nests" for themselves to retreat to, places of separate ritual and activity that honor each person's independent Self.

Not surprisingly, once they've learned the dance of intimacy—once they've spent the long, hard time learning skills and discipline so that they can flourish in close-quarters co-existence—a new liberation presents itself. "Help!" they cry to the stork, that magical bird. They ask the stork to carry them upward, out of the cave. The stork agrees to it but tells them they must feed it and give it drink as it travels.

Stories teach us how impossible it is to learn refined intimacy—in fact, to fully appreciate any of the stages of life and love—without some form of mentoring. How can we, who were not born knowing the skills of adult love, nor had many early models for it, learn how to refine our intimacy without the magical help of wise ones?

The stork represents that mentor. The stork's mentoring liberates the lovers from the cave. Many couples report having worked on their own to refine their intimacy, but ultimately needing the help of a book-and-video program, a series of workshops, a specific teacher, marriage encounter, a therapist, an older family member, or a combination of all these. The help couples seek and find is the stork. That stork, with its magical energy to teach refinement, brings the couple together in a way that liberates them, pushes them upward and forward in their life journey together.

This particular stork accomplishes this by giving the couple a task: "When, as we fly upward, I say 'Gaaak,' you will feed meat into my mouth. When I say 'Geeek,' you will feed me water." Keloglan and Serpil know how to divide tasks. Keloglan gets meat out of the heads of the giant and giantess, and Serpil fills the canteen. They take upward into their lives the last piece of the Shadow, and they take the waters the

Shadow has lived on. They don't balk at having to give the stork something back for its efforts on their behalf. Climbing aboard the stork, rising upward on its back, they respond to its straining by providing the meat and drink. Toward the very end of their ascent, they run out of meat and drink. They sacrifice pieces of their own bodies in order to continue the ascent.

It is important here to see deep inside the story. For now Serpil and Keloglan are not merely giving up to their mentor something they value. The stork and the two lovers are, of course, each part of one Self—your Self. When Serpil gives her blood and Keloglan his flesh, it is symbolic of interior sacrifice. Each of us will experience such a time in refined intimacy when we must sacrifice of ourselves, without any argument, because the life of our relationship depends on it. This is a different kind of sacrifice than we experienced in stage 1 when we exclaimed, "I'll give you my very heart, I'll give you anything I have!" This is a refined sacrifice. It is a piece of the flesh, a drop of blood, the giving of *some* of our life essence—not the whole body, but nonetheless a giving of a piece of the Self.

The stork gives the essence back once the ascent is complete, in the same way that there is, in a relationship that has become refined, the activity of receiving back what you give, either in direct quid pro quo, or in varying kind. The balance of sacrifice does not weigh down too heavily on his side of the scale or hers. The partners expect to give and get back, without watchfulness—for Keloglan and Serpil are not watchfully waiting for the flesh and blood to return to them—yet with a certain magic that only people in refined, mature intimacy experience.

Keloglan invites the stork to come to his home, where he

promises to treat the stork like a deity. But like every good magical agent, and like every fine mentor, the stork knows when it's time to move on.

Keloglan and Serpil have come through stages 3, 4, and 5 together. They are ready to experience the kind of joy that only two *independent* selves, who have united in love, can experience. They return to the orchard and make a life together. They promise to love each other, be there for each other, live with each other, perform sacred tasks of living together. Serpil, who was orphaned, finds a home. Keloglan, who was always the small one, becomes big in the eyes of his people. Their joy emanates into all the world. All the brothers marry and have children; the village and orchard merge. Love and joy grow in this community in tandem with the new imperfections of the apples, and in tandem with the new prosperity of the apples. There are more people to tend them now. The story ends with the perennial statement of joy's quest: "They lived happily ever after."

This, then, is the story of Keloglan, Serpil, and the Big People at the Bottom of the World. When what is underneath is, through painful and joyful effort, brought up to the surface, the world of the people discovers fertility, an end to isolation, and a refinement of spirit. Let's not be done with the story yet, though. Let's move from its metaphorical realm, in which magic moves in the rhythms of story, to our own practical realm, in which, if we are to experience the magic of refined intimacy, we must elevate the level of our intimacy skills through our own hard efforts.

PRACTICING REFINED INTIMACY
WITH YOUR PARTNER

Stages 4–6 are stages of initiation into mature adulthood. By the time we reach stage 6, we feel initiated—we feel like we've been through a refining fire and have come out re-molded. Now we are ready to act with the skill of one who has been initiated into adulthood—initiated not only separately from a mate but, quite often, initiated into adulthood *with* a mate. In a tribal culture, many of the skills of loving, the spiritual discipline of relationship, are taught in the second decade of life. In our own culture, most of us find we learn them when we are already with someone—either married quite a while, or in a series of relationships that each provide us a romantic crucible in which to forge new skills.

Here are some elements that are foundational to our practical application of refined intimacy skills. Answer these questions, and see where you are in relation to stage 6.

• Do you know who you are, and, knowing that, can you verbalize your identity to your partner? Even if you are not a very verbal person, or feel it is arrogant to talk about your identity, you still have the responsibility in this stage to verbalize your identity's *boundaries*. Not to do at least that is to keep them secret—power struggle—and sabotage your relationship. Can you say, "I am the kind of person who needs . . ."?

• Have you created a code of conduct for intimacy with your partner and committed yourselves to it? Its covenants will be primarily verbal, so they can be clarified and confirmed. You and your partner have to have gone through a process much more detailed than "Do you take this man/ woman to be your lawfully wedded . . . ?" Marriage covenants are inspirational models, not practical commitments to act in a disciplined way with a partner.

• Have you learned good communication/conflict skills, and do you practice them in your relationship?

• Do you acknowledge your own imperfections and accept those of your partners? Are you able to practice the art of apology with dignity and integrity?

• Do you acknowledge that your partner's personality and most of his/her foibles will not change? All that can change are specific behaviors, evolving values, and day-to-day attitudes. Do you encourage coevolution of change in these rather than change in personality and "being"?

• Are you able to articulate your family wounds and cultural disappointments without depending on others to heal them?

• Can you intelligently explore your own and your partner's primary fears without shaming either yourself or your partner?

"Primary fears" usually get inculcated because of systematic childhood trauma, or systematic trauma experienced elsewhere in intimate social relationships. Fear of abandonment, fear of loneliness, fear of rejection, fear of domination, fear of emasculation—these are ways we express primary fears. As we refine our intimacy, we must be able to articualte our deepest fears, fears we confronted and learned a language for in stage 5; and we must be able to notice them at work in stressful times in our relationships. Noticing them at work, we must be able to say something like, "Oh, yes, that was my fear of abandonment. That wasn't about you. Sorry. Let's start again."

There is an old saying that comes from the Ninja school of martial arts: "Your worst enemy is not your opponent, but yourself." Our primary fear becomes, as we move into later stages of life, our emotional "worst enemy." We will usually find that our primary emotional fear and primary emotional need occupy two sides of the same coin: if my primary fear is a fear of being dominated, my primary need will be to dominate; if my primary fear is a fear of abandonment, my primary need will be to control others, cutting off their power to abandon me; if my primary fear is a fear of humiliation, my primary need will be to punish and humiliate others.

We must absorb our knowledge of our own imperfections (I use the word *primary* but don't mean to say we don't have more than one very deep fear) into our quest for joy. We must be able to articulate the ways in which our apples are imperfect, yet still flourish. We must be able to vibrate with the knowledge of each other's deep fears, yet never take advantage; rather, we must make the world safe for moments of those fears. This is deep nurturance.

• Am I able to honor others for their differences from me? Especially, if I'm a man, do I honor women as different but equal? If I'm a woman, do I honor men as different but equal?

• Have I finished my deep work with my parents and family past? Do I now feel that I deserve to be loved?

We know we have done much of our stage 6 work when we are able to answer "Yes!" to these questions, and then to cocreate rituals, practices, and covenants that nurture our answers.

Here is one such couple's ritual that has been very useful as I've taught it in workshops. Its framework was inspired by the teachings of Al Turtle, a couples counselor trained in Harville Hendrix's Imago training. Some people use it as a kind of guided imagery process within themselves, imagining they are interacting with someone else who is not there or does not know the skills. You may want to use it that way, especially if you're not in an intimate relationship right now.

If you are partnered and can use it with your partner, it will alter the way you do conflict together.

The exercise involves couples in doing therapy for and with each other during times of anger. Couples need to be well advanced in their communication and conflict skills for this exercise to be absorbed, as a ritual, into their spiritual discipline. The danger in this exercise is that one partner will be emotionally engaged and the other detached, which can feel like patronizing, judgment, even shaming. Both partners need to agree at some point ahead of time that they will use it in their relationship.

The key to making this exercise work is the detachment of one partner. When one of you instigates direct conflict, the other does immediate self-counseling to detach. The one who detaches we will call the *receiver*. The one who instigates the direct conflict we will call the *conflictor*. In this exercise, it is essential to see that the conflictor is in primary conflict with *inner* issues—not with *you*. The world must be made safe, by the receiver, for the conflictor to do his/her spiritual work; thus, the receiver's nonverbal communication must show openness and absence of judgment. Here is an example.

Step 1. The receiver receives the conflictor's immediate feelings of anger and mirrors them. Then the receiver asks what hurt the conflictor.

CONFLICTOR: I'm angry at you, dammit. You're too busy for me—at least that's how it seems. You're working at your computer. I come for some communication with you, and you can't break free from that damn keyboard. How dare you?

RECEIVER: You're angry at me because it just felt a few minutes ago like my computer was more important to me than you are. Can you talk more about the hurt?

Step 2. The receiver receives the conflictor's answer and mirrors it. Then the receiver asks the conflictor what deep, primary fear lay under the anger and hurt.

CONFLICTOR: It hurt me to feel second best, second to a machine. It's a hurt like at other times when you're doing something and I ask for affection, and you just keep on with what you're doing.

RECEIVER: It hurt you to feel inferior, especially to a machine. There's an accumulated hurt, too, because this same thing has happened before. Can you tell me what you are most afraid will happen, deep down most afraid of, when you're feeling this hurt?

Step 3. The receiver receives the conflictor's answer and mirrors it. Then the receiver asks the conflictor who in the conflictor's past did something to him/her that provoked this fear.

CONFLICTOR: I'm afraid you don't love me, deep down. I'm afraid you'll abandon me, leave me. That's always under my hurt when you don't give me the affection I want. And I'm afraid you won't think I'm worth loving.

RECEIVER: You're afraid I don't love you, that I'll leave you. You've felt that before, often, in similar circumstances. Deep down, you're afraid I won't think you're worthy of loving. Who in your past did you not feel loved you? Who in your past did you feel abandoned you this way?

Step 4. The receiver receives the conflictor's answer and mirrors it. Then the receiver asks the conflictor what huge thing the receiver could change about him/herself so this hurt and fear won't be generated again.

161

CONFLICTOR: My father. So much of this goes back to him. I would go to him while he was working out in the yard, or at his office, and he was busy. I wanted to work with him, be with him. He wanted his privacy.

RECEIVER: It felt to you like your father abandoned you emotionally. He was too busy for you. Is there something pretty major I could do to change my behavior so that in our relationship this stuff wouldn't come back up for you?

Step 5. The conflictor expresses what s/he wants changed. Conflictor and receiver discuss whether it is possible for the receiver to change in the way requested. A pact is made to insitute the change. If the change is too big to be accomplished, receiver and conflictor decide through dialogue on one smaller behavior the receiver could change.

For example, perhaps the conflictor wants the receiver always to disengage from the task at hand in order to fill the need for affection the conflictor has. Upon discussion, it becomes obvious this is impossible and, perhaps, not spiritually healthy anyway for either conflictor or receiver. The receiver suggests that s/he concentrate on disengaging from the computer when the conflictor engages emotionally. The two make an agreement to pursue this course.

All through this ritual, the conflictor corrects the receiver when s/he feels the receiver has not heard correctly or mirrored correctly. And, while the above example involved a family-of-origin issue—Dad—the ritual works for issues involving previous spouses, children, coworkers, and others with whom the conflictor has been intimate.

Rituals like these become a part of stage 6 relationships. For some people, this kind of ritual appears patronizing and artificial. Once people make its structure their own, however, changing the language and using nonverbal and verbal skills that an exercise on a page can't display, the ritual becomes powerful.

Refined intimacy is a stage of life and love that rewards us beyond imagination, but it requires rigorous discipline. In a culture that does not teach us much about spiritual discipline, a culture that not only neglects spiritual teaching about the stages of intimacy but also neglects teaching us the primacy of spiritual discipline for joyful life, it should come as no surprise that most of us don't get to stage 6. When we do get here, though, we can feel an immense pride. Even if we aren't yet here, it is empowering to realize the kind of refinement that can be ours.

THE SIXTH TASK

Stage 6 of the Lover's spiritual discipline teaches us the sixth lesson of trust: *commitment to another from the position of confident autonomy.*

In order to trust, I must refine my loving separateness from my partner and give him/her permission to do the same with me. Deep down, this means forgiving my partner for not being me and loving him/her, with full commitment in that separateness. I must trust myself so confidently and forgive myself so completely for my own Shadow and imperfections that I no longer need to see my partner as the primary sacred object of my dependency needs, the missing key part of myself.

Therapist Terry Trueman puts it this way: "You can't respect anyone else any more than you respect yourself. You can't love anyone else any more than you love yourself. You can't trust anyone else any more than you trust yourself. What you feel for yourself is what you'll be able to feel for someone else."

The feeling of confident autonomy is wonderful; even more wonderful are the feelings we experience as we learn to commit to and give to another love comparable in quantity and quality to the love we feel for ourselves. Our spiritual discipline in this stage requires us to accept our autonomy and, simultaneously, covenant our lives to another. If we can do this, we can certainly learn the skills that refine the intimacy we have promised and been promised in stage 6.

Stage 6 also provides us, then, with the sixth element of focus for the Lover's spiritual discipline: *the dance of conflict.*

To practice love as a spiritual discipline, I must do the hard and fruitful "skills work" of learning how to appropriately communicate and do conflict. I must practice what I learn and adapt my practice as needed.

Throughout world mythology, we find a metaphor for doing healthy conflict: the Dance of Swords. The idea in this metaphor, as in a martial arts demonstration or fencing, for instance, is that the dance of the swordplay is as important as (and sometimes more important than) who wins. Conflict and even a lot of basic communication is assumed to have a basis in competition, but that competition is sublimated into a relationship dance.

It is this dance we refine in stage 6. We need incredible focus to learn this dance, for conflict easily falls into traps of overreaction, undervaluing our partner or self, distancing, passive aggression, and so on. Here are some specific ways to make the dance of conflict a part of the spiritual discipline you practice in your relationship.

• When communicating with your partner, agree on the

goal of a communication and stick to that goal. When you stray from it, return to it. After you've satisifed that goal, clarify another one. Conflict that is about the whole kitchen sink usually gravitates into a mess, rather than healthy communication.

• Understand your own and your partner's projective sources before, during, and after conflict. Be aware of who you're turning your partner into: Your mother? Your father? Someone you're angry with at work? Remember that during conflicts we often unknowingly transfer energy we feel toward one person onto our intimate partner. If you're doing this, stop! And even if you think you've figured out who your partner has transformed you into in his/her mind, don't force *your* understanding of your partner's transferrence onto him/her during the conflict. S/he will probably not want to be psychologized right at that moment.

• Validate what you can in each other, *then* confront. Give something before you take. For example: "What made sense to me in what you said was . . ." Or, "What I agree with in your statement was . . ." Then: "What didn't hit me right was . . ."

• Avoid universalizing: "You always . . ." "You never . . ." "I always . . ." "I never . . ." These kill the dance. So does excessive, disrespectful interrupting.

• Use "I" statements, paraphrasing, clarifying, always inviting your partner's perspective: "Here's what I heard you say. Is that what you said?"

• Develop a sense of humor in conflict. Make sure you both agree on what's funny in your conflicts. If you don't, the humor you use often feels like attack.

• Listen carefully and with an open mind, and dialogue whenever possible about the dance of conflict you are engaged in. Make it a *conscious* part of your intimacy. In listening, assess your own and your partner's power boundaries. Notice what you need to do to reach your partner. Tell your partner what s/he needs to do to reach you. Don't assume s/he understands what you need, nor that you understand what s/he needs.

• Agree on common ground at appropriate intervals during the conflict. "So here's what we agree on . . ."

• Avoid analysis of the other's projections, and avoid comparison of the other with self: "You were projecting your dad onto me; you do that all the time." Or, "Why can't you do such and such like I do?"

• Develop rituals to manage your anger. Go elsewhere if need be and use a towel or stick to get out anger. Remember that a lot of confrontation is about built-up stress and tension that has little to do with your partner; recognize that a lot of "now" conflict is unexpelled "then" conflict. Own your last one to twenty-four hours. See if you've expelled your previous tension. Relieve that stress and tension through physical rituals so you can come fresh to new conflict situations.

INTEGRATING REFINED INTIMACY

"The most beautiful thing we can experience," said Albert Einstein, "is the mysterious." In relationships that evolve to refined intimacy, this is an indisputable truth. For what was secret during power struggle becomes mystery in stage 6. What was imperfection during disillusionment now becomes an apple whose taste leads to new and eccentric realizations.

Our partners' foibles become things we like about them; they become the very things by which, if we embrace them, our partner will reveal on any given day a novel slant of self, a different piece of personal evolution than we expected.

Our own personal autonomy, and our skillful practice of the dances that relationships need of us, both give us joy because they lead us deeply into love. Now that we have a refined structure for loving, it becomes easier. Now that we have a strong sense of self, love becomes nurturant in ways that resemble romance but feel so much deeper, so much bigger.

As we move forward in our journey, we integrate refined intimacy by continuing its practice. We are ready to pursue the Great Sacred Task of our relationship, whatever that task may be (and there will be more than one), and we feel prepared—we feel, as we leave Season Two, that we have awakened to the great spiritual search; that we know who we are; and that we have learned skills of loving that protect *both* our autonomy (independence) and our intimacy (what was dependency and is now becoming stage 7, creative partnership), sacrificing the integrity of neither. Feeling these things, we feel connected to the cosmos. We need that deep, rich experience if we are to have the power to do what we now have to do. For now we must create new beings and new worlds out of our coupled relationship. Creation is the act of God and Goddess in concert.

We stand ready to join our energies with theirs.

Part Three

THE SEASON OF INTERDEPENDENT PARTNERSHIP

Story: Isis and Osiris

This story comes from ancient Egypt. It is the story of a Divine Couple on whose royal marriage the functioning and flourishing of the world depends. Such stories of divine marriages are found throughout the world. From ancient Assyria and Babylonia, we have Ishtar and Tammuz; from Phyrigia, Cybele and Attis; from Phoenicia, Adonis and Astarte. These divine couples serve as cultures' original beings whose love stories teach the wisdom of the season of interdependent partnership. From the Divine Couple come order, fertility, creative society, a balance of the masculine and the feminine. The Divine Couple has developed so generously that it grounds society in nature and nature in society.

We, of course, become that couple at some point in our lives. Our season of interdependence lasts, in the ideal, many decades of a human being's life; its models are divine.

Isis, the Great Goddess, and Osiris, the King of Kings, lived out a love story that has experienced a rebirth of interest, not just in Europe and the Americas, where Goddess literature and mythology have regained strength, but also in North Africa. Like the Nile, it still flows forth.

In Egypt I bought a papyrus painting of the Divine Couple. The surly gentleman who sold it to me cared little that I wanted to talk about the mythological meanings of the figures. But when my wife and I sat admiring the piece in our taxi, our driver talked at length about the annual celebration of the Mysteries that takes place in Abydos, a small town on the Nile. Isis and Osiris, he claimed, "are in the blood of

every Egyptian. We still hear their music through our veins."
Many scholars believe Isis became the Virgin Mary and
Osiris/Horus became Jesus in our own culture's mythology.
One could argue that the Divine Couple who guided the
Pharaohs now sings in the blood of hundreds of millions of
Jews, Christians, and Muslims too—your blood, my blood.

Ah well, but maybe that's going too far. It's just a story.
Let's listen.

Long ago, before there was a before, there were the Waters
of Life, called Nun, from whom all would come. Resting
motionless on the Waters was Atum. From the union of
Atum and Nun came a daughter, Tefnut, Moisture; and a
son, Shu, Air. For a time, there was happiness and rest on the
Waters, but then Tefnut and Shu both sank and vanished in
the dark waters, each in opposite directions. The eye of
Atum descended into the darkness and, after a long time,
found them and brought them back to the surface.

During their descent into the water, Tefnut and Shu had
become more than they were. Tefnut had become Order,
and Shu, Life. They gave birth to a son, Geb, and a daughter,
Nut. Geb was Earth and Nut, Sky. They in turn gave birth
to two sons, Osiris and Seth, and two daughters, Isis and
Nephthys. The world's activity got divided between these
divine offspring by the powers who brought them into the
world.

For her part, Isis carried the work of the rain and dew and
all the wet and moist places of the earth. Without her no
seed could sprout or grow. Her breath was life's breath, her
milk life's milk. She was the giver of life.

Osiris carried the work of soil, crop, vine, seed, flower,
and fruit. He carried the energy of the planted or moving

thing. His breath breathed the order of growth. His seed planted the world. He too, in his way, was giver of life.

As much as Osiris loved the winding Nile, his Isis, so did she adore the fertile land he worked, her Osiris. They were the Great Lovers whose marriage blessed all.

Seth, the red-haired one, had dominion over the desert. He sent scorching heat off the red desert toward the green lands. He loved the night that swallowed the sun.

Nephthys, his lover, belonged to the darkness. She hung the moon over the desert so the white sands, her Seth, glowed with her affection.

Nephthys and Isis were very close. Not so with Seth and Osiris. More on that later.

Isis and Osiris led the people with generosity and discipline. It is said that the people could not imagine life without the tutelage and protection of goddess and god, for when Osiris, for instance, was occupied with travel, Isis filled in; and when Isis was occupied with other things, Osiris filled in. Because of their care for their world, the night never encroached too much into the day nor the desert into the green domain. Children of all things grew, as did the children's children. Isis and Osiris were called the wise rulers, for they rarely forced submission by arms. Rather, they convinced by reason and passionate belief. Isis and Osiris were called spiritual teachers, for they taught the people how to worship the great cycles of life, how to revere the divinities, and how to hold families together with the energies of the Mysteries. Isis and Osiris were also called the civilized ones, for they taught laws and values and justice and the language of commerce.

And so it was that all went well for a time in the realm, stewarded by its divine servants, Isis and Osiris. But there were shadows about, creeping along the edges of life. What of these?

While Isis and Osiris were conceiving their child, Horus, the moon goddess, Nephthys, who was in love with Osiris and quite jealous of Isis's mate, tricked him into giving her his seed. She too conceived a child. And her husband, Seth, had a trick of his own. Jealous of Osiris's fertile lands, Seth plotted to take them. He got conspirators together. Secretly, he measured his brother's girth. He and his conspirators made a magic chest his brother's size and painted it with magnificent drawings. Seth threw a party. In the center of the celebration, Seth called for the magic box to be brought forth.

"To whoever fits this magic box exactly," he told his guests, "I shall bequeath it." Everyone in the room took their turn, but none fit until Osiris, always gracious, last to try, lay in it perfectly. The conspirators wasted not a second in crashing the top down, nailing it shut, and throwing the locked casket into the Nile, where the river swept it toward the open and endless sea.

Isis had not been at the party. When she heard the news of her husband's demise, her mourning was felt throughout the world. She cut off a braid of her hair, and the world felt its own ugliness. She set out to search for her mate. A group of children told her she must go to Byblos, in Phoenicia, across the sea. There the casket had become lodged in a tamarisk tree. The tree had grown around it to such a size that the king of Byblos had ordered the tree cut down and a pillar made of it for his house.

Isis went to Byblos, hiding her identity. She hid near a spring. She always liked water, for it was like her own blood. When the servants of the queen of Byblos came to the spring, Isis served them, plaiting their hair. When they returned to their queen, the lady smelled Isis's beautiful fragrance on her servants. She called Isis to her castle and, troubled in her own breasts, asked the full-breasted Isis to nurse her hungry child. It is said that Isis went a little mad, tossing this child into a fire (without harming it) and turning into a swallow every night to fly around Osiris's pillar.

Finally, Isis revealed who she was. At her request, the king cut the pillar down. Isis stripped its bark and found the casket and wept over it. She then commanded that it be lifted onto a boat. She sailed home with it, opening it and kissing her Osiris. She became a huge bird, and with the wind of her wings, she gave Osiris the breath of life. Soon after, they landed back in Egypt, their own realm, and while Osiris slowly recovered, Isis lay down to bear Horus, their son.

While Isis lay in the birth throes, Nephthys gave the realm a full moon. Under its brilliant light, Seth tore his still-weak brother into fourteen pieces, scattering him all over. Isis found out immediately and, with her great love, set out to search for Osiris again. Nephthys and her son, Annubis—of Osiris's blood—helped Isis search, for Nephthys felt remorse now.

Wherever Isis found a piece of her husband, she buried it in the loam of that place. She found thirteen pieces but could not find his penis, which had been eaten by a fish. She fashioned a penis from earthen clay and reassembled Osiris. Then, with Annubis's help, she performed a ceremony that gave Osiris back the breath of life.

In Osiris's time of death, he had not been wholly asleep. He had learned things he could not have known before. After a passionate reunion with Isis, he said, "I have learned of the Underworld that has no leader. Without one, it languishes, and its unrest harms our realm. I cannot spend all my days

with you, my darling. I must become king of the Underworld too."

And so he did. He and Isis continued their love and yet
led separate realms. And all was well enough.

Things went on this way for a time. Horus came of age,
both Osiris and Isis teaching him their gifts. As Horus grew,
he came to see that his destiny lay in righting his family's
wrongs. And, so, one day, his mother by his side, he challenged Seth, and won. It is said that on this day, there was
great joy throughout the world, a joy that increased manifold
as Osiris gained, after Seth's demise, the ability to be resur-
rected every year and return uninterrupted to his Isis's arms.
Horus and Isis were each heard calling, "Rise, Osiris, rise.
You went away, but now you have returned. You slept, but
now you awaken. You died, but now you live again!"

Osiris was heard calling, "Yes, I have risen!"

The divine chorus repeated itself for all to hear throughout
the realm. Even Atum and Nun, Geb and Nut, and all the
divinities who held the keys to the Mysteries looked on at
the reunion of Isis and Osiris with great joy.

And so the people became truly One with life. In the journey of the Divine Couple, they united the Underworld with
the world above. The drought in their dominion, which,
while Isis and Osiris had been gone, fell into Seth's hands,
faded into the rising of the Nile again, and the planting of
seed. The people celebrated the rich and unified nature of
their realm in ceremonies to Isis and Osiris. They learned
from the Divine Lovers a new religion and a new ardor for
life. They gained, in Osiris's descent, a way of salvation they
had never known. They learned from his rising a way of
personal renewal after death—they found the courage and
rituals by which to be eternally reborn. From Isis's journey

they learned compassion and endurance they had not known. They learned of medicine and miracles from her. Because the Divine Couple was reunited, the realm was blessed. Every year the cycle of life repeated. Above all else, the people learned that to love is to live in the interdependent web of all things, small within it, capable of losing everything, yet courageous upon it, and able to endure even the harshest winds together, in joy.

CREATIVE PARTNERSHIP

*We can learn that the essence of love is not to use the
other to make us happy but to serve and affirm the
ones we love. And we can discover, to our surprise,
that what we have needed more than anything was
not so much to be loved, as to love.*
—ROBERT A. JOHNSON

*As though in the blinking of an eye, the whole creation
was formed through love.*
—HILDEGARD OF BINGEN

The scene was a retreat center in the woods. Forty women
and men had come together to explore the Lover's Journey.
We had been together two days. We were exploring on this
particular afternoon what the creative partnership of stage 7
feels like. Everyone who had kids and everyone who knew
themselves as hard working and creative knew that at some
level they had become creative people. We saw this immediately, yet we knew there was something special in the psychology of human relationship, something we called creative
partnership, that occurs not just because we have the power
to create someone or something in tandem with another
human being, but because we have moved through the maturing process of the earlier stages of loving and find ourselves

ready for the kind of spiritual interdependence we were promised at the beginnings of our partnerships.

Riki, forty-five, spoke: "I felt we had gotten to creative partnership one night when we came home from a party, a party filled with people James and I couldn't quite relate to. Years before we would have loved the party, but now, with our kids four and seven, what we wanted to do was put the kids to bed and sit in the living room in our little 'cocoon' That's just what we did. We read awhile, we talked, we watched TV. It's hard to describe, but I remember that whole evening I was filled with a deep contentment. It wasn't just that I'd had some wine! It was very deep.

"I remember I said something to James like, 'We've arrived. We've struggled and now we've arrived. We have enough to live on. Our love has made two babies, and we'd die for them. We have a good relationship. We have this private world we love and nurture. You've never been more creative in your work, I've never felt more creative in mine. The kids drive us crazy, but we flow so well together. This is the marriage my parents never had.'

"James doesn't talk much. He usually lets me go on and on. Finally I said to him, 'Do you understand what I'm saying? Do you feel it too?' It was like I had a moment of panic, like he wouldn't feel it. But he hugged me and told me what it was like for him. We made love. I've never forgotten that feeling, all through me, filling me with love."

James forty-two, did not remember the night. "I don't remember these exact moments and conversations like Riki does, but I know what she means. I feel this creative partnership we're talking about when I'm playing with the kids or they're helping me with yard work. Being with them is what

I want most. I measure what I do in the world by the love Riki and I have for each other.

"Riki went through a real man-hating time; that's when I met her. I had been divorced about a year, separated two years. The whole time I was way down in the pit. Riki and I had lots of troubles, but we worked hard. Justin came along, and we just knew we had to work hard. I didn't want another divorce. Riki had had a miscarriage with a man before me. It took her deep into her pain. I had had an affair during my first marriage. Riki was afraid I'd do that again. We had our share of messes, and dependencies, and hurting each other for a few years.

"But Ashley came along, and we just kept working. Like Riki says, it must have been about then, about a year or so ago, when I knew everything was the way it's supposed to be. At least for now. We still have problems, but we've got our priorities straight, and we work hard at loving each other."

In some eyes there were tears as this couple talked about their experience of creative partnership. Their story inspired another, from Chris and Jerry, who had been married thirty-two years. Chris, with Jerry's blessing, spoke for both of them.

"When you asked us if we'd gotten to stage 7, both Jerry and I knew immediately when it happened for us. Our good friends' daughter was getting married. Jerry and I sat there during the ceremony, not knowing that the other was having this feeling. It was like Riki said, it was *physical*. It was this tingly, very spiritual feeling of being completely alive and unafraid, for the first time, together. We held hands and felt very young and very wise at once. We are different now than we were a few years ago. We have a kind of power in our

partnership now, a power that I think comes from two people finally becoming one without the tension of two people
really hating to be one, if that makes sense. The couple was
getting married, and the minister talked about 'becoming
one,' and I thought, Jesus, it took us thirty years to become
'one.' I'm glad for Riki and James their kids are young. Our
kids are long gone. How different their lives might have been
if we could have had that tingly feeling twenty-five years
ago."

I have often found that, like these two couples, one or
both of the partners recall a "moment" in which creative
partnership seemed to take over the relationship. This moment is often a physical sensation. The body feels as if it's
filled up. The container of Self feels tingly. For one person,
the moment occurs during prayer, for another while sitting
in traffic, for another during lovemaking, for another while
looking at a child sleeping. A warmth, a vulnerability, a solid-
ity encompass the body and want, immediately, to be shared
with the partner.

It's just as often the case that neither person recalls such a
moment. Yet both know, upon looking back, that they have
gone through the stages of romance, disillusionment, and
power struggle; that they have awakened, descended into
personal challenge and pain, fought through, resurfaced, and
learned the skills of loving. They have seen how nothing is
ever completely finished in life, the Shadow and the darkness
and the woundedness never wholly subdued, yet there's been
a molting in the two partners individually and in their relationship. Now they have come to years of life and love that
hold the promise of creative joy.

There is no one "right" lifestyle that gets us ready for stage
7. Some people get ready before they ever marry/partner for
life. Some people get ready through the gradual growth that

accompanies a series of divorces. Some people get ready while in one lifelong relationship. However it occurs in your life, when you get to stage 7 your relationship has, for its model, the relationships of Divine Couples, these couples who discover in the interdependence of this season a third source of power—a source undiscovered by two people who are in independent searches for personal freedom, a power that absorbs and transcends energies of personal dependency and independence. This third power—interdependence— arises from the commitment of two free Selves to each other and to sacred acts of creation and communal nurturance. This third power—the power of a true couple—blesses Self, children, community, the earth; it makes Soul.

INTERDEPENDENCE: THE CIRCLE OF LIFE

Interdependence is the condition of our needing, primarily, the *support* (not the *care*) of other people, spiritual systems, and environmental connections; interdependence is the condition of our feeling solid enough about our place in the universe to allow others to be *unconditionally* dependent on us. This means we will not require our dependents to create false selves for our sake, to take care of our needs. Human interdependence shows itself most profoundly in our connections with and sacrifices for mates, children, extended/tribal/ ethnic systems, workplaces, the earth, and spiritual practice/ religion.

Interdependent lovers feel "one with the great web of life."

An interdependent person knows his/her place in the world. S/he experiences self-doubts, of course, and myriad problems; yet the basic foundation of maturity is solid, and the purpose clear. In the Walt Disney movie *The Lion King,* Mufasa, the lord of the realm, explains to Simba, his son, the purpose of his life. Being king, he says, is not about being arrogant or ruling any way he wants; being king is about making sure his realm is one with the great cycle of life. Being king is about serving children, community, and earth while growing an even deeper, richer self.

"In giving ye shall receive," Jesus taught. When we are interdependent, we understand this wisdom. When pursuing dependencies, we feel that in giving ourselves to a dependency object, we will receive ourselves, cleaned and cared for, back; when pursuing independence, we feel that in giving, we will be taken, so we avoid deep giving. Becoming interdependent, we do not seek to receive, in the spiritual realm, any specific item or piece of self; we seek to receive *whatever comes back,* mysteriously, to us by our giving. And we do not fear losing ourselves, for we know we cannot be lost.

Those who discover the quality of interdependence in their lives are individuals and couples whose work becomes nurturant of community and earth, and who devote themselves to this work—which is often children—with the fervor of a soul that feels so connected to the cosmos that every act of creation and sacrifice and nurturance reverberates somehow throughout every tender line of life's vast web.

In most tribal systems, girls and boys are consciously initiated into interdependence through many years of education and adolescent initiation experiences. Only after their acceptance of their own adulthood are they allowed to seek a mate. Acceptance of adulthood means we consciously act on the basis of this idea: "While we have always, in earlier stages of life, sought to bless the earth and our community, we realize now that we are interdependent beings, so blessing earth and

183

community is not just *one* of our purposes in life, it is our *primary* purpose in life." Knowing this, young people mate.

Unfortunately, most of us mate while we are still in a tug-of-war between our need to be dependent and our need to be independent. We are children/adolescents who create children. We take on the responsibilities of interdependent partnership without having matured, psychologically, into a person who can fully meet the demands of interdependent partnership.

Specifically, the difference of our culture from tribal and premodern cultures looks like this. In those cultures, the patterns of the first two seasons were dealt with by the time a person was twenty years old or so. That is to say, dependency was honored as the primary system in which children matured in the extended families; then initiation awakened them to independence and to their roles, which in tribal cultures were most of identity. By the time they married, they were ready for interdependent partnership. The community knew this or, quite often, didn't let them marry, and/or wouldn't leave the marriage unsupervised. What we in our popular culture call true intimacy did not often happen till decades into the interdependent lives of these couples, if ever.

Our culture has chosen a different course. We want to be in love with each other *from the very beginning* of the partnership. Our culture has thrown out initiation; we learn independent self and identity mainly by rebellion, if at all. Our culture does not make Season Two into a *conscious* experience for its young people; our young people just wander through adolescence. As a rule, we don't tend to get to the Season of Interdependent Partnership until our unconscious pushes us toward it around midlife. Spiritually and psychologically, we grow up at between thirty-five and fifty-five. This pattern—

falling into romantic love, marrying, having kids and/or committing our marriage to other creative lifework, *then* perhaps learning how interdependence feels (or just remaining in power struggle, misery, or divorcing) when the kids are already half grown—causes terrible spiritual pain and emptiness. Especially once kids are produced in a marriage, the partners' dependence/independence tension, their inability to be truly interdependent, becomes dangerous to the children, and thus to the community and society.

Things become even more complicated when we who, in midlife, have the courage and wherewithal to journey out of power struggle into awakening, descent, and refined intimacy, and then into Season Three, discover that the models for intimacy and interdependence we have from our families of origin are not models many of us want to follow. We discover that very few people we know are in Season Three. Where are our models?

In addition, our longevity affects the picture. We have the luxury of not necessarily having to grow up psychologically and spiritually till we're in our forties or fifties. We live half again as long as our tribal ancestors did. Basking in this luxury, we discover that we have caused danger by not growing up—not just danger to our children, but danger to earth and to community. When we create products, systems, and technologies in the spirit of creative partnership yet without having solid Selves, nor a language for the making of soul, nor a sense of what true interdependence with society and nature implies, we create things and systems that consume others to feed our dependencies and manipulate others to preserve our independence. We create products to make profits rather than soul. We fight for causes, yet in our own everyday lives, or in our fanatical pursuit of the cause, we do as much destruction as what we struggle against. We think our creativity is grounded in the spirit of interdependence, what's best for all, yet in fact it is grounded in what we perceive as being best for us. And by "us" we really mean "me," and by "me" we really mean a half-developed self that has not done the inner work of identity. In the absence of this well-earned ontological security, we project onto the world around us countless images of our own inadequacy. We create that inadequacy around us, through our children, causes, products, and systems.

The myth of Isis and Osiris teaches another way, the way of interdependence. In this other way, we experience our life energy and our partnerships as essential to the spiritual (eternal) life of our world. We know our place, we know our purpose, we know which sacrifices are sacred and which are not; we know the cutting edges of personal responsibility; we seek not to blame but to grow; we strive to create, wherever we are needed, our offering to the great cycle of life.

ISIS AND OSIRIS: PART ONE

People who find role models report feeling filled up, made larger, more whole. People who find divine models—models whose existence is rooted in mythology about the sacred realm—are even more fortunate. They feel a kind of ontological certainty that divine models provide. In Europe in the Middle Ages, people often tried to model their behavior after that of Jesus and Mary. In Native America, Coyote and Raven Woman have been models. In India, people model themselves on different gods and goddesses at different times in their lives.

For anyone who chooses to see the partnership of Isis and

Osiris as divine, there are rewards, for when the people of ancient Egypt measured themselves in tune with Isis and Osiris, they learned the joys of interdependence. One thing they modeled was how to divide up sacred labor. For them, of course, this division implied a strict gender role. For us, it implies the roles we develop, in conscious dialogue, with our partner. When a couple decides to have children, for instance, and the wife, who has worked, decides to stay home, giving the husband more wage-earning responsibilities, these two adults are doing what Isis and Osiris did. One is going to care for creation in his way, the other in hers. The role of each is equally sacred. (For our world, the gender of the wage-earner and homemaker don't matter.) In the Isis/Osiris story, there is no superiority or inferiority, no imbalance, in the Divine Couple's sacred duties.

The Divine Couple gains its sacred tasks, and its interdependent camaraderie in fulfilling these tasks, through a family history that carries within it the energies of all creation and evidence of earlier stages in the Lover's Journey. Their great-grandmother and great-grandfather were Nun and Atum, the Waters of Life and the Action of Life. From their interdependent partnership Tefnut and Shu were born, first as Moisture and Air, then, after their descent, as Order and Life. From their partnership, Earth and Sky were born. From their partnership, Isis and Osiris were born, the two Givers of Life—Isis for the waters and Osiris for the land—yet neither water nor land were capable of bearing fruit without the other.

Couples who reach stage 7 will have integrated their family histories in earlier stages. They have tossed out primary dependency on the parts of those histories that have caused harm. They have made the self-defining descent, metaphorized in the descent of Tefnut and Shu into the dark waters and known in the Lover's Journey model as stage 5. They've risen again, individually, transformed into something more refined. From that effort, their interdependent partnership is born; they create progeny, and the life of the new world begins. Before Isis and Osiris were born, there were only abstractions—no concrete life yet, certainly no human life. So the myth teaches that in the same way our creative partnership is somehow not born until we have moved through dependency, independence, and identity-building into interdependence.

People over the years have told me myriad ways they felt this in their lives. Poets, writers, and artists have said, "I didn't really create with my whole heart until I had kids," or "I owe my mature work to the fact that so-and-so and I are together." People in all walks of life often feel spiritually aimless, confusingly hedonistic, lonely, numb, unable to deeply engage in life until they find their place in the web of life, or find their purpose. Often this means growing in marriage, or having kids, or devoting themselves to a religious community or other spiritually maturing work. While we are always creating, from our first spoken word in infancy, creative partnership is something unique, something requiring maturity, something we recognize when we have it and yearn for when we don't.

In return for providing us with a sense of purpose and destiny, creative partnership requires things from us—sacrifice, service, vigilance, duty, honor. It is fragile; there is always a crack in it, a flaw, because we are human. "I have found out why I'm here," someone will say. They'll also say, "The responsibilities of it scare me."

One man, Lynn, told me, "The night Clair and I had our first daughter, I dreamt I was on top of a mountain. I saw a whole rainforest under me, clouds above it. It was like Mac-chu Picchu, so beautiful. Clair came to me and held my arm. The mood was like the soft light you get in old forties mov-ies. Then Clair pointed downward. There was a hole in the forest ceiling, way, way down. Down inside that hole, lying down on the forest floor, was our newborn, Gretchen. She was so far away, so far down there. I remember panicking in the dream. I remember feeling like she was so far down there, how could I ever get to her, be there for her, protect her, care for her? I was terrified of being a father."

We become in creative partnership like Isis and Osiris, on whom the world of life depends. We have moved beyond our own dependencies into independence and integrated our independent identities into a creative partnership. We have become he and she upon whom others will depend, and from whose safe world other people, earth, systems, and things will launch into their own turning wheel in the great cycle.

On the boundaries of creative partnership are always to be found people who do not respect it, younger people who laugh rebelliously at the rigors of interdependence, peers and friends who area jealous of the successes our creative partner-ship is yielding us, elders who react against our particular generation's form of creative life. There is always a Seth, seeking to deny his brother; always a Nephthys, seeking to mate with Osiris. In Seth and his desert and Nephthys and her night we have metaphors for our own Shadow sides and the shadows lurking outside us. The greatest external ene-mies of creative partnership are those people and forces around us who still live in the logic of power struggle. The greatest internal enemies of creative partnership are our self-doubts and distrust of others and the world. Just because we have journeyed to stage 7 does not mean we have left all our shadows behind.

Isis and Osiris are highly advanced partners, but on each of their arms is the Shadow. This is represented by their shadows being their own flesh and blood, adjacent to each of their realms, always competing to conquer more of their sacred world with shadow kingdoms (Night and Desert). People in stage 7 trust themselves, the world, and the cosmos more than they ever had, but they are not naive. In all their humility and basic trust, they still watch for spooks and demons; they still peer within whenever they can so as to nurture their own humanity. If people, earth, systems, and things depend on us but we do not attend to the shadows, our nurturance will be permissive, even lax. Our progeny will grow up without spiritual discipline.

In earlier stages of our journey, the Shadow could consume us, so we confronted it. When we were creative in earlier stages, our creations were generally creations of our independence, our power struggle, our descent—many of them worthy creations, but few of them creations that grew from mature vision. Now, as in partnership we offer our creation to the world, the Shadow can consume not only us as individual searchers, but also our partnership and our creation. How shall we protect ourselves? Instinctively, we do it through physical and emotional vigilance. In this we are protective, as we've always been. But like Divine Couples before us, we must also learn a more subtle art of protection. We must practice spiritual discipline, and we must teach the discipline we practice. If we don't, the created beings will not know how to nurture themselves—how to move through the life cycle, protect themselves, and mature out of dependency.

It is crucial, then, that we and our partner become like Isis and Osiris, a Divine Couple: basically in agreement about values, ethics, and spiritual life; equally grounded in our personal power by dividing up role and labor and mutually respecting the other's being; and ontologically secure as individuals and as a couple. From this place, we teach children, others, earth, systems, and things how to be spiritually disciplined. In the myth, this activity is characterized by the way Isis and Osiris—in equal partnership and respected by their people—teach their realm how to worship the great cycles of life, how to revere the divinities, how to hold families together with the energies of the Mysteries, what laws to follow, values to believe in, justice to pursue, and language to use.

These are huge responsibilities, yet we meet them in the third season of life. Not to do so relegates what we create—the sacred part of ourselves we give to Mystery—to a world of isolation, valuelessness, insecurity, and inadequacy. In the *interdependent* web to which we have given our spiritual life, there is no such thing as an *independent* being, removed from the rigors of living. The independence we nurture in our growing children—or our evolving work—will one day become the strong but humble servant, as we ourselves have, of a cycle greater than themselves. We as creators/caregivers ("we" includes more than individuals or nuclear familys, of course; it includes mentors, community, extended family, friends) are most responsible for the future of the life cycle through our hands-on work with whatever children, people, piece of earth, system, or thing(s) we create through our conjunction of Isis's water and Osiris's seed and loam.

CREATIVE PARTNERSHIP, THE CHILD, AND SOUL MAKING

In exploring our commingling with the divine story, I've tended to stress children as the primary sacred project of creative partnership. I've done so because, biologically, as Darwin put it, "Children are the reason we're alive." It is important to honor—especially in a time and culture that has forgotten the primacy of children—that once a child enters a family *or even a community,* its care needs to become the primary purpose of its guardians' activities, if only for the period of the child's upbringing.

At the same time, we know there are many kinds of work that rise from creative partnership, sometimes in tandem with children, sometimes without them. There is a grave danger in judging people who do not have children. Their creative project may be something other than their own blood or adopted progeny. Throughout human history, cultures have battled with their own judgmentalism toward people without kids. Today's homophobia can be seen as a continuation of this judging tradition.

While creation can occur in any stage of life and result in just about any product, creative partnership exists when two or more people come together with the *intention* of making and nurturing a new *soul.* Artists in creative partnership put their souls into their work. Monks or nuns in creative partnership devote their souls to a divinity and shift energy in the world through prayer, which is a commingling with that divinity. Manual laborers, information specialists, businesspeople, merchants, and professionals in any field who practice creative partnership do their work with deep regard for its results. No matter what sacrifices they must make, they keep their eyes, as Martin Luther King said, "on the Prize." The prize for them is that their work amounts to a contribution essential to the great cycle of life, the making of soul.

In earlier stages we have focused mainly on developing a Self. We knew that we had to develop ourselves into an individual spiritual container—first by gaining a confident core self through the dependency process, then a clarified Self (identity) through the independence process—but we were not sure *why* we needed this container. In fact, many of us remain without this spiritual container throughout our lives, never knowing why, never having faith in ourselves or in life. But for those who do develop the container, through the joys and pains of the first two seasons of life, for those who answer the first ontological question of existence, "Who am I?" stage 7 begins answering the second one, "Why am I?" In stage 7, in our creative partnership, we give birth to life itself, we make a naked soul. In the first seasons of life we answered the question "Who am I?" with the word *Self*. In stage 7 and throughout the next two seasons, we answer the question, "Why am I?" with the word *soul*. Anyone who has experienced creative partnership has experienced that feeling of "growing in leaps and bounds once I had a child," "opening up vast parts of myself that were asleep when I found my creative calling," "knowing why I'm here," "learning how to feel real." And we don't just create "another soul" when we join to create a child, system, or thing: *we create our own soul*. We don't just "make something out there," we "make soul in here."

For this reason, the easiest way to judge whether our creation is "soul making" is the metaphor of the child. For people in creative partnership, the unconscious (and often the conscious) mind is always asking the question "Is what I/we are doing best—in both the short and long run—for a child?" People who use that question as their standard of moral judgment truly understand the rigors of creative partnership. They will often make mistakes. They will sometimes take the question too literally—as often happens with fanatical antiabortion proponents, who argue that protecting the *quantity* of newborns is the ultimate standard of a community's obligation to children. They will still face ancillary questions like, "What I'm doing hurts a child now, but helps later; is that all right?" or, "What I'm doing can save some children but harms the earth; is that all right?" Facing these questions, the questioner will face his/her own soul, and try to make the best decision. Like Isis and Osiris, questioners will, in creative partnership, have each other to share the questions with. This is the best life can do for us at this stage of growth—give us joy by giving us a companion with whom to take the risk of creating a new world and soul.

YOUR OWN CREATIVE PARTNERSHIP

To get a sense of your own connection with creative partnership, answer these questions. The first set concerns you as an individual. The second set concerns your intimate partnership. If you are not partnered with a lover/mate at this time, explore this section in the context of your relationship with your community, children, job, church, other entity, or even previous mate.

• Do I have some solid answers to the question "Why am I here?" I have felt and created things which mirror my life purpose to me.

• Do I have a value system that is flexible but basically solid? I am unsure of how to answer certain ethical questions, and I am always seeking to grow, but I have a value system I can articulate *and am willing to sacrifice comfort for.*

• Do I have a pretty clear sense of what my talents and skills are? I might change my job one day, but still I see, with self-guiding clarity, what abilities and potentials I have.

• Do I believe I'm as important to this world as just about anyone else? ("Just about anyone else" is meant to imply that humility always requires us to feel smaller than prophets, bodhisattvas, or others we feel have given us more than we can ever give them.)

• Am I a person of faith and spiritual practice? Have I committed myself to a spiritual system (not necessarily dogma or doctrine) greater than myself?

• Are my hurtful reactions to others nonetheless creative? For example, is my anger a creative force in my family life and working world? Does it grow from and lead to deepening spiritual discourse and discipline?

• Is there rich variety in my daily activities? If I am addicted to one or two activities, I am in some form of dependency that denies my growth to stage 7. While I may go through a week or two, even a month, of tireless, singular activity, it must give way again, after the child is born or deadline met, to variety.

• Am I capable of sacrifice for the sake of my creation, even if it means, upon my best judgment, sacrifice of myself?

• Have I learned a role for myself as a man or woman and settled into it comfortably? This does not mean I must have accepted a traditional role. Nor does it mean I have given myself over to a role completely, not knowing who I am except for being "a mom" or "a dad" or "an employee of such-and-such" or "a Christian" or "an artist."

• Have I come to a place in social life where, at least among a small community of peers, I am respected for my creation/work?

In this second set of questions is also a psychological framework for what we go through as a couple during stage 7.

• Have you and your partner come to a place where you've accepted each other's identities? "You are who you are, I am who I am, we're not going to change much, and that's more than okay."

• Have you and your partner divided up labor in your creative life together so that you both feel you are sharing successes and responsibilities equally? "We have joined forces." "We have become one in our intentions." "We share the garbage and the glory." "What s/he accomplishes is mine too, what I get in life is his/hers too."

• Are you and your partner, in equal proportion, sacrificing time and energy toward mutually agreed-upon creative goals? Equal sacrifice does not mean immediate *quid pro quo*. It does not mean one partner watching the other, suspicious: "I'm doing more than s/he is." It means that in the long term, as activities weave through the years of partnership, both partners are sacrificing the same quality and quantity of their independent energies to the cause of interdependent creativity.

• Are you and your partner willing to change earlier lifestyles to meet new creative goals together?

• Have you and your partner developed healthy relationship skills and rituals by which to resolve conflicts and solve family/couple dilemmas?

• Have you and your partner consciously agreed on primary values, beliefs, goals, and ethics for your partnership?

• Do you and your partner experience an infatuation-like sense of couple's (family) space? In this experience you feel that your home is the most sacred space available (a "co-coon"). You say things like, "We need only each other and our family. We have everything we want right here."

• Have you and your partner experienced the grief of letting go of old friends and communities who do not support your creative partnership and/or have become a drain on it?

• Is your partnership strong enough to withstand questions about its integrity and functioning, even questions from very powerful sources like parents, ex-spouses, employers, children?

In your own affirmative or negative answers to these questions, you'll get a sense of where you partnership stands. Is it in stage 7? If it is not, these questions may help you focus its energies so that it can develop into creative partnership.

THE SEVENTH SACRED TASK

Stage 7 of the Lover's spiritual discipline teaches us the seventh lesson of trust: *interconnectedness.*

To move more deeply into spiritual creativity, we must notice the ultimate and complete interconnectedness of ourselves with every atom, every planet, every person, every thing in the universe, and build relationship based on our participation in that connectedness.

"When you kill the deer," a native teacher might tell his pupil, "thank the deer." In his next breath he might say, "What you do affects the next seven generations." Animal or human, present now or still unknown in the future, you are connected to everything.

Lately an African saying has become popular: "It takes a whole village to raise a child." In this social thinking, community is one whole interconnected organism, not a mere physical place where individuals reside together.

197

Is it possible to be in creative partnership, to learn its layer of world trust, self-trust, and trust in being without having some sort of spiritual belief in interdependence? Perhaps, but I don't think so. Without this belief, we don't quite know where our creations—and therefore where we ourselves as creators—fit in the life process. The urge to create is biological. The discipline that spiritually grounds creativity, especially a couple's creativity, does not reveal itself unless we are willing to be the song, not the echo; willing to be connected to all things and thus create new life energy from our position as an embodied voice of the cosmos, rather than a disembodied franchise.

Stage 7 provides us with the seventh element of focus for the Lover's spiritual discipline: *creative sacrifice.*

While we make many sacrifices in all stages of our lives, we do not truly understand the creative nature of sacrifice until we mature into creative partnership. Once we focus our sacrifices along with a partner's, and in service of Sacred Tasks, we sense the development in ourselves of a new energy of spiritual discipline we could not discover before: (1) we united with another in sacrifice; and (2) we knew, without doubt, the sacredness of our task.

Coupled people who have not cooperated in interdependent creation have not journeyed to stage 7. They have not experienced yet the spiritual mystery and joy of sacrificing toward and serving a Sacred Task, a task of creation so complex and rich it humbles them.

There are those who come to the creative energy of this stage long before they ever join with a partner. Soldiers, for example, can be trained to bypass the development of a Self. They can be trained to join with others and make sacred sacrifice; they do not exactly create a new soul, but they make the world safe for others to do so. Anyone whose work grows out of the Warrior archetype can be trained to do this kind of soul bypass in his/her sacrifice and service. These people move to stage 7 temporarily. When the danger is over, they will revert back to whatever developmental stage of their spiritual discipline they were in before the specific soldier training. In the same way, many parents when they first have children will temporarily appear to be in stage 7—their partnership utterly united, their lives filled with interdependent sacredness. As the first months of the child's infancy pass, however, these parents will return to their earlier developmental stage.

It is essential, then, that we approach stage 7 focus and discipline with a long-term view, that we see beyond the electrifying surges of soul and sacrifice that creative crises can bring, and that we are sure in our own lives we are committed to the focus of stage 7 for the long haul.

INTEGRATING CREATIVE PARTNERSHIP

In stage 7, joy comes from the creative union of the goddess and god inside each of us. After long individual journeys of self-search and the hard work of learning to refine relationships with each other, they unite, like Isis and Osiris, in common creative purpose.

As we come to know stage 7 and yearn to integrate it into our continued journey, we develop conscious rituals, as did Isis and Osiris, and as they taught their people to do. We learn that creative spiritual discipline requires creative spiritual *practice*.

Here are some suggestions of specific things you can do as a couple to integrate your creative partnership.

• Cocreate as a couple a renewable and revisable covenant

of marriage. In that covenant write down what each person's role is going to be in the everyday life of the marriage. Since the culture doesn't do it well for us these days, and since we know standing at the wedding altar for ten minutes can't last a lifetime, write this covenant yourselves; renew it on every anniversary, revising as need be.

• If you didn't do it in the last stage, take a communications skills and conflict skills class together. In this class, workshop, seminar, or group, learn to fight fair, listen, and speak your truth. Unless Goddess and God know each other's languages, how to communicate with each other and how to do refined intimacy, there can be no lasting peace in the community and world.

• Develop rituals and ceremonies that honor both the Goddess and God. Amid all the wonderful co-ed activities we all do together, still there is the urge in every spiritually disciplined woman and man to do same-sex activities—she doing "women's" activities, he "men's" activities. When after separating into separate gender communities a couple comes together again, its love is all the more empowered by separate time with Goddess and God, as long as neither separate circle seeks to dominate the other.

• Develop rituals by which to check in with each other at daily or near-daily intervals. Make this a major priority in your relationship. Go to lunch together, without the kids, at least once a week. Do something fun together, without the kids, once a week. To be united, the Goddess and the God must spend loving time together. During creative partnership, this time is hard to find and needs rituals to protect it.

• Develop at least one significant and sacred community/ earth nurturing project to do *together*. This could involve the kids' school, an AIDS center, saving the forests. The power of the Goddess and God, working in communion, is incredible.

• Live more simply. Give away what you don't need. If you cannot cut out much of the television you watch, at least sit and watch some of what your children watch, interpreting for and with them the masks television and Nintendo characters are wearing. Through media, teach the children how maturity requires that enchantment of sterotype end and wisdom of archetype begin.

• Openly discuss, navigate, and have fun with your gender and sex differences. The average man takes considerably longer than the average woman to process emotive material. Is this affecting your relationship? Is the female partner shooting a shotgun of emotional material at the male and requiring a truthful answer immediately? She probably won't get one. Enjoy and exploit your differences. The Goddess and the God revel in their differences; those differences challenge the earth to grow.

• Own the wounds and deep fears you bring to your relationship. Know that you chose your relationship to have a safe place to heal those wounds. Also know that your relationship has enough to contend with without being the only place you bring your wounds and fears to. Goddess and God are equally wounded. Yet they come together to nurture life. Goddess and God get *some* emotional sustenance from each other, but not all. At least half or more of their emotional sustenance must come from within each of them and from external sources other than a partner.

• Try to be a little kinder. Compliment each other whenever you can. Wherever you are and whatever you are doing together, choose kindness, politeness, gentleness, when you can. Goddess and God must fight, must conflict, must clash. If they did not, earth and the energy of relationship would be in eternal stasis. Yet, Goddess and God must openly admire each other.

• Renew and revise all rituals, covenants, common projects, insights, sacred tools, and impressions of each other at least once a year. The Goddess and the God are composed of timeless energy. But they exist in time, and time changes the vessels in which divine energy flows. Renew and revise, in planned and in spontaneous ways, the relationship you have established as man and woman, on this earth, in your time.

You will know of other things you can do and have done as a couple to nurture your creative partnership. If you have not experienced this stage 7, still everything you do now in search of it and in imitation of it will hopefully lead toward it in the future. The spiritual discipline you practice in this stage will keep you strong and flexible and ready for what is coming next, a new descent that may challenge the very existence of the partnership you have worked so hard to achieve.

STAGE 8

THE SECOND CONSCIOUS DESCENT

Love bears all things . . . endures all things.
—I Cor. 13:7 (RSV)

"Your love will be tested, make no mistake," said Norma, a woman in her sixties. She had called in to a radio station talk show on which I was discussing stages of relationship. The host and I had just asked to hear from people whose creative and happy lives together had been startled, even shocked, in midstream.

She continued, "You'll get everything just right. The slip-covers will be just right on the couches, and he'll have all the tools up in the garage, and your kids will be in ballet and basketball, and the walk is swept and the sprinkler system is in and things seem so clean, so orderly. And then boom! some huge hand scoops you all up and throws you around, and you fall back down in a terrible heap. If the two of you don't work together, you're sunk. It happened to us when our middle daughter got pregnant, at fifteen. Our world fell apart. It just fell apart. Eugene became an ogre, like he didn't love his own flesh and blood anymore. I hated him for that, but I knew he had his own worries. He said it was all my fault—she was a girl, I was supposed to be looking after her.

That was his way. When he was mad at himself, he got mad at me. I just did my best to hold things together."

"What happened?" I asked. "How did things work out?"

"Well, that was twenty years ago. We're still together. We've got five grandkids. We wouldn't trade them. You just go on. You just fight to hold things together. What else can you do?"

What else, indeed? Life tests us. We do our best.

Stage 8 is about the creative life of a couple being startled, shocked, and stricken when our child gets pregnant while still a child, when one of us is severely injured, when we discover we can't have children, when one of us has an affair, when our child dies, when we enter midlife passage, when a parent we're close to dies and we explore certain feelings for the first time, when one of us gets very sick very young, when one of our children seems to get lost in meanness, depression, anorexia, drugs, a religious cult, when we birth a deformed child, when one of us loses our job or profession, when children move out of the house, when we change our previous roles, when a fire or other disaster destroys all evidence of our lives together, when war is declared and our lives must change to support it, when one of us is raped or imprisoned, when we divorce.

By the same token, the happy and creative life of the same couple might be re-formed, recatalyzed, reinvigorated, and made joyful when a common project to which we've devoted extensive life energy completes itself, when grandchildren come, when marriage matures because of the affair, when our children flourish, when disasters lead to great and renewed relationship building, when a child comes out of his/her dark rebellion, when war is finished, when new roles and sacrifices lead to new fertility of purpose, when creativity becomes redefined, when our journey deeper into joy becomes its own cause in our mature life.

No partnership grows without being challenged, over and over again, by pain and joy. Partnerships grow best when we are conscious of the challenges. The challenges are direct mirrors of the souls of the individuals involved and the soul of the creative partnership they've established.

THE SECOND CONSCIOUS DESCENT

I have found that there is a story from mythology for every possible spiritual experience people can go through. It is as if the actual world of events does not trust its own experience until it makes story of it. Or maybe human consciousness is saying, "Until we have mirrored the condition in a story, we're not sure it's real." An old Sufi storyteller told me, "The story represents the soul of the event." Without the story, the lived life is not complete.

So it is that you and I make stories of what we go through on a day-to-day basis.

"It was when your mother and I had just had you," we say to our child, "that . . ."

"When I found out I had that lump in my breast, we . . ."

"I wish it hadn't happened that way, but it was meant to be, I can see it now. . . ." And your partner says, "So can I."

Sometimes making a story of the troubles you go through as a couple is the only way to make sense of tragedy, even victory. Not to make a story of them is to repress the feelings, deny the events, destroy the relationship that has suffered and needs to be rebuilt in a new story, a story of its Second Conscious Descent.

This descent is similar to the first, yet different in a crucial way. In the First Conscious Descent, we were each pretty much on our own, seeking our own independent Self. We got support as we faced the Shadow. We had partners and allies as we built a Self. But when we were deep in the pit, the challenges we faced were predominantly challenges to ourselves. Even if we have been married for decades by the time we make the First Conscious Descent, we are still emotionally quite alone when we face the demons that come from within us, or the external demons and disasters that challenge us to grow an independent, nurturing Self. The more responsible we are, the more disciplined we are as lovers, the less we will want to drag our mate into the world of the inner demons that come from our past. We will ask our partner's support, but we will not hold hands with our partner as we descend into our own private hell, our own private refining fire. To do so would kill our relationship. Many of us, by thinking we should share *everything* with each other, including all fears, wounds, and rages, have needlessly lost lovers who were simply not ready or willing to accompany us in our very personal first descent.

In the Second Conscious Descent, however (a descent that, like the first, is usually experienced as many descents, taking place over years), we very consciously descend in communion with, holding hands with, our lover. The Second Descent challenges us as individuals, bringing up issues from the past that have never left us; but as a whole, it is a challenge that grows from, seeks joy in, and pits itself against our *partnership,* our unity. To complete it, we must work together, sacrificing equally, compromising utterly, trusting freely in our love for the other. We are going into the underworld. This time we have a partner to go with us, from the beginning of the journey till the end. We will need to practice equal parts self-discovery and personal sacrifice for our partner—a sacrifice we were not, in our regressive, underdeveloped identity, able to make in the First Descent.

Because of this basic difference between the two descents, stories of the First Conscious Descent often advise us *not* to be in a creative partnership when we make it, but instead to be in the early experimental phases of adolescence and young adulthood, the times of initiation that train us how to embody the responsibilities and joys of creation. Stories of the Second Conscious Descent, on the other hand, will often begin with energy that emanates from our creation of children or other projects we consider sacred. The Bible, from the perspective of the Lover's Journey, is a story framed by the Second Conscious Descent. So too are the Gilgamesh epic, the Hindu Vedas, and Greek and Roman myths, and so many other stories that begin with creation myths. Divine Couples create the world; all is well for a time (creative partnership); then something shadowy, startling, interruptive, shocking, evolutionary occurs. The serpent comes into the garden and tempts Eve and Adam. The shadowy force is often a blood relation or good friend of the creative couple. It is part of them. As it emerges, it sets the wheel of life, the time clock of activity in a kind of motion that even the omniscient Creator/Divine Couple had not imagined. Once this wheel of life is set in motion, the story of the Divine Couple often recedes into the background so that the story of the progeny can develop; but of course the creators often find themselves and their new relationship evolving in and through their progeny. In the stories of the Second Conscious Descent, then, as the creators of the great myths enter their Second Conscious Descent, their progeny enter their fall.

Our lives are often similar. As we move into midlife, we watch our children suffer, helping as we can, but we know that, ultimately, they're in a different season of life than we are. We try to let them make their own mistakes. Yet we too are growing through their growth. Sometimes their fall instigates our new growth—their drug addiction, their bad marriage, their accidental injury or death initiates personal redemption, should it send us into the First Descent, and/or our interpersonal challenge and joy should it send us, with our partner, into the Second Descent.

A man, Don, came into therapy with me as his son, twenty-nine, and daughter-in-law faced a huge IRS debt and charges against them. In the face of his son's fall, Don, and soon his wife, Carol, entered into a difficult process of assessing who they were and how they could best help their son. As it turned out, they saw that they had to let him go. As the son served his prison term, the couple grieved and suffered, yet also found that they became more involved in community and other family activities—activities they had not blessed before because they were so focused on their son and how they had, because they were his parents, somehow caused all his problems. They discovered new spiritual life together.

Perhaps the least-known and yet also best-known mythological story of a Divine Couple creating new spirit out of their progeny's fall comes from our own biblical history. Though historically we know mainly about Yahweh/Jehovah, archeologists and scholars like Bill Diva, Carol Meyers, and Amihai Mayar have begun to piece together the Yahweh/Asherah story, a story of God and Goddess in communion thousands of years ago.

In this story, Yahweh and Asherah created the world. Out

of the darkness they brought light, vegetation, animals, people. The goddess Asherah was associated with earth energy, the god Yahweh with sky and air. He provided the breath of life, she the waters and earth that would breathe. Together they represented creative partnership at its most fertile.

Then their children, Adam and Eve, broke from them, eating the apple, destroying the garden. What was, for Adam and Eve, Season One of relationship work would have been, for their creators, Season Three. Yahweh and Asherah, thrown into the Second Conscious Descent, were challenged to rethink their whole approach to the whole creation. Yahweh and Asherah did not emerge from their descent as a Divine Couple intact. They "divorced." Piecing together the biblical story with the new archeological evidence, we believe this divorce to have been a painful one—Yahweh became a bitter and angry god, Asherah a hermit. In our cultural consciousness, the goddess Asherah was pushed down and away and disappeared. Yahweh, in his anger, became rigid, teaching the children of Adam and Eve the Law but imbuing them also with a terrible fear of life.

When a child dies or goes down a dark path, a wife is raped or husband killed, a husband or wife loses a job, divorce is threatened, one spouse gets sick very young—when some huge piece of what holds the family, the partnership, the world intact is destroyed—all creation shudders. When the disaster is resolved—even imperfectly and after great tragedy—all creation can experience a deepening of order, as Yahweh's Law modeled, and hopefully, a quickening of joy as never before. The story of Yahweh and Asherah, in whose light and shadow we have created our civilization, is a story that emphasized the *ordering* of the Second Conscious Descent; the story of Isis and Osiris emphasizes the *emotions* of the Second Conscious Descent.

Let us return to that story now.

ISIS AND OSIRIS: PART TWO

While Isis and Osiris were conceiving their child, Horus, the story continues, Nephthys tricked Osiris into giving her his seed. She too conceived a child. Her husband, Seth, plotted his brother's demise. Seth got conspirators together, measured Osiris's body clandestinely, then built a beautiful, magical box to fit it. He held a party and invited everyone to lie in the box. "To whoever fits the box perfectly, I shall give the box with my best wishes." Osiris lay in it last. It fit him. The conspirators ran to it and nailed it shut in an instant, and Seth cast his brother out into the Nile, where the box rushed toward the sea.

The story is wise. It isn't a simple victim/villain tale. As in real life, everyone bears some responsibility. Nephthys tricks Osiris, but Osiris is not altogether a naive or innocent victim. Seth tricks Osiris and tosses the casket not into the sky or desert but into Isis's realm, the Nile. The story makes sure we understand the independent web of the story—that Osiris, Seth, Isis, and Nephthys are all parts of us, in relationship.

When the Second Conscious Descent occurs, our first instinct is often to blame our partner for the whole mess, or to blame ourselves. By "whole mess" we don't just mean the momentary event of crisis, we mean the before/during/after of our emotional interdependence.

Stories of the descent are wise about saying that everyone plays a part in this affair—this drug-addicted child, this teenage pregnancy, this depression, this midlife passage, this new crisis. There will be enough responsibility and blame to go around. Depending on the circumstances, of course, everyone must draw independent boundaries. Months or years into a crisis, the amount of personal responsibility will become clear, and perhaps one person in a couple will have to rise up and say. "Okay, I've done my part, you have to do yours to fix this." But early on in the descent, all parties gain by examining the interdependence of responsibilities and emotional reactions.

When Isis discovers what has happened to her husband, she goes into terrible mourning. She makes herself ugly. Her depression is so severe she neglects her realm. She wanders in search of him. She becomes all of us, male or female. Her emotions are ours as we see the previous creative order of our lives disappear in the face of crisis. Osiris represents that order. Seth, the shadow brother, has destroyed order. Why doesn't Isis go after *him,* confront him? Because as a part of the Divine Couple, she can see, with a wisdom that surpasses even her rage and grief, that it is someone else's destiny to confront Seth.

Isis's own river has been part of her husband's demise. She follows the water to Byblos, where she has heard Osiris is hidden. There is a tamarisk tree there that has grown up around his casket. As a divine being, he is protected. During the third season of life, and especially during the crisis/descent of stage 8, we often become acutely aware of being part of the divine web, committed and creative within it and thus protected by energies so mysterious we cannot understand them.

On the beach of Byblos, Isis hides her identity and goes through the period of humility necessary for facing a crisis that destroys order. She goes through a period of near-madness, burning the child of the queen of Byblos (though not harming it), turning into a sparrow and circling Osiris's pillar over and over. She feels her feelings, becomes them, lets them work their way through her, a role model for anyone who seeks to deeply experience feeling. Who among us is as good at this process of feeling as we would like to be? We interrupt it for self-judgment all too often, and all too early. We are afraid of the madness of our own deep pains and deep joys.

Finally, Isis comes out of her inwardness of feeling and acts; she reveals herself to the monarchs of Byblos and claims her husband's casket. Strengthened by this action, she takes further command of the situation, ordering the casket to be put on a boat and sailing the boat home. There is a claiming of power here that comes at the end of the deep emotional pain. Grief, if felt, will humble, and once it humbles, the course to follow can be seen much more clearly. In our own coupled relationships, it can be either the woman or the man who moves our crisis to action; gender does not matter here.

While sailing the casket home, Isis becomes a huge bird and, with the wind of her wings, gives Osiris the breath of life. Osiris can be seen as the order of our relationship that dies and which, after our deep work with feelings, deep humility, and painful sacrifice, regains the breath of life and restores our relationship to joy. In another interpretation, Osiris and Isis represent that relationship dynamic in a crisis wherein one partner appears caged, trapped, lacks voice and the ability to move, and the other must, at least for a time, do most of both the feeling work and the problem solving in the relationship. In both interpretations, there is profound sacrifice—we give a great deal of ourselves to keep the relationship working through the time of descent.

Staying for a moment with the second interpretation, we find ourselves face to face with the concept of duty. In many relationships, I have observed a lack of vision about the sacrifices duty requires. It used to be we taught our children that when our partner is hurting, sick, or troubled, the other stands by, sacrifices, gives more than s/he even knew was in him/her. Duty was a concept born of the philosophy of interdependence. We knew if we did our duty in one difficult circumstance, our partner would be there for us in another. Something has happened to this concept. Many of us despise our partner's helplessness—despise it because we fear it, and fear it because it reminds us too much of our own capacity for helplessness. In response to a partner's helplessness we rage, distance ourselves, forget our fidelity to our chosen bonds.

Isis does her duty, with patience. She is a model for all of us, whether male or female. She is compassion incarnate. To make the Second Conscious Descent, we must be ready to be like her, to do our duty, to be patient. We must be able to say, "At this point in my life, I am living in sacrifice to the cause of this family, this relationship, this other." We are authentic selves, forged in earlier seasons, protected by interdependent and creative partnership. We have moved far beyond our power-struggle strategy that if we gave an inch, our partner would consume us in his/her tyranny or victimization. We have the self-trust now to know how to give of ourselves utterly for the redemption of another and the redemption of our relationship, yet not lose ourselves.

There may certainly come a time in our descent when we must say to our partner, "Look, I have nothing left in me.

You're playing the victim. You have to stop." And it is certainly helpful for the helpless partner to keep a sense of humor through the crisis, to do and give even little things every day. So Isis is not a model of codependency or too much care-taking or too much enabling. Nor is Osiris the helpless victim forever. Their story of duty, compassion, and helplessness is a model of the couple who is in love for the long haul. Months go by as Isis revives Osiris, and not only their partnership but the whole world gains life. If Isis had not had the self-trust—had not been through the earlier seasons of self-development—so that she could sacrifice her energies for the time of reviving Osiris, her son Horus would not have had a father, and the world would never have regained order.

As Part Two of this story nears its conclusion, Isis gives birth to her son, Horus. The joy of Isis and Osiris at having their son is great, but it is interrupted by Seth's next rageful act. He cuts Osiris into fourteen pieces. Isis's job is not done. Sometimes we think we've gotten through the crisis, the descent, and than a new door of crisis opens and we are once again called on to do our duty. Isis continues hers, joining forces with Annubis to find the pieces of Osiris and put them back together. She finds all but his penis. She molds a penis from earthen clay. His fertility is in the earth, so this substitution is, in a sense, no substitution at all. She buries the other thirteen pieces where she finds them. She makes a sculpture of him. With Annubis's help and baby Horus looking on, Isis performs a ceremony on the sculpture that revives Osiris to anthropomorphic life.

What should we make of Annubis—Osiris's son by Nephtys (the son he never knew he had)—being welcomed by Isis as he helps her recover the fragments of his father? You might think she would be jealous or vindictive. She is not. She is grateful for the help, and she does not try to keep a son from restoring his father. Horus is not old enough yet to do his duty of restoring order. He will do it in Part Three when he confronts Seth. Right now, Annubis is the masculine agent who helps in restoring Osiris.

This masculine presence here is important. Isis wisely knows that the masculine and feminine must be balanced for order to be real, useful, complete. All of us—men who fear or abuse their masculinity, and women who fear and abuse masculinity—have much to learn from this Goddess of Life who has clearly transcended masculine/feminine power struggle. Her eye never left its concentration on balance. She knew that any realm functions well when it balances its polar forces. She knew that letting Osiris—the masculine—die would be dangerous; she knew that getting Annubis's masculine help in re-forming Osiris was beneficial.

Isis, in this moment, is like many mothers who give their sons up to their husbands in adolescence. These women know that the son must stand as much in the presence of the masculine as the feminine. Many divorced mothers find this passage in life very hard, but are doing it more and more. Films like *Boyz in the Hood* have dramatized this. In this film about inner-city life, two parents are divorced, their son ten years old. The boy's mother tells her ex-husband she is giving the boy over to him so the boy can learn discipline and how to be a man. She knows what the Isis/Osiris story says even more overtly: without equal balance of the masculine, the realm will suffer a lack of order.

That, in large part, is what's happening in our inner cities and in our culture's spiritual life. Because so many institutions are run by men, this view is often laughed down. And certainly the machine of civilization is run in large part by masculine presence. But the spiritual life of the civilization is not—75 percent of churchgoers are female, more and more families are run by single women, more and more fathers are pushed out or opt out of their children's lives. The kind of spiritual ordering that the masculine has provided families and communities, especially young males, throughout the millennia is disintegrating. In the face of this spiritual disintegration, the myth of Isis and Osiris provides a spiritual model. I believe that anyone—whether female or male—who sees the huge hole in the center of masculine spirituality in this day and age will feel called to do what Isis does: restore the masculine. Isis does it without sacrificing the feminine. All of us can too.

Before Part Two ends, Osiris, who has had little direct voice in his fate up to now, reveals to Isis something that will forever change their partnership. The underworld, he says, has no leader. Without a leader, it languishes; its unrest harms the surface world. Osiris must go to the underworld and rule it.

Imagine what Isis must have felt. After all she has gone through, she discovers that still her husband is never to be hers again in the way he had been. But she must share him now. They remain in love and continue their love. They restore their realms to fertility and happiness.

As the descent ends, our own coupleships will never be the same. Something has happened in the months and years of crisis. We look at the world and at each other anew.

Sam Keen has written, "The romantic myth, dripping as it does with drama and the promise of constant agony and ecstasy, does not teach us how love actually grows slowly as revelation deepens." During the Second Conscious Descent, we have gone through agonies and ecstasies; we have experienced dramas that were far more than what romance, even awakening, promised. We have moved far beyond promises into the deepest, most painful realities. We have seen revealed in our partner vast expanses of Shadow and of compassion we had little idea existed before.

YOUR OWN SECOND CONSCIOUS DESCENT

Remember that this descent is often many small descents over a period of years, decades. It is a descent if we make it *consciously.* It is a descent if we deal with the crisis through spiritual discipline. All of us who are married in our middle age and later life will experience crises. The key question we must ask is, "Did we fall into these crises, or did we descend?" We must ask this in the same way we ask, "Are we going to die consciously, as part of our spiritual journey, or are we just going to drop dead?"

If we *descended,* we move through the crisis with *personal courage* (personal responsibility) and *interpersonal commitment* (interdependent partnership). We have the conscious courage of an independent Self, able to stay solid, individually, through crisis; and we have the conscious commitment of a mature lover, able to be compassionate both for partner and for Self through the crisis. If we *fell,* we probably hit hard, damaged ourselves terribly, or from fear went to sleep in our falling; our identity probably dissolved and/or our interpersonal commitment dissolved. The crisis probably crushed our relationship, moving it into misery or termination.

Because so few of our relationships develop to stage 8—half end in divorce before stage 8 and many more just aren't working in whatever stage they're stuck—don't be surprised if you have not moved through this stage. Don't be hard on yourself. Don't judge yourself harshly. We damage our relationship with those kinds of judgments. The best we can do is be conscious of crises and communicate with our partner as much as possible about the great spiritual rewards consciousness can bring to crisis.

In exploring your own Second Descent, it's often helpful to make a list of the crises you and your partner(s) have faced in your partnership. Remember each, the many little ones and the one or two big ones.

At one workshop I met a couple, Ted and Marie, who had been married twenty-seven years. Late in the first decade of their marriage, their second son drowned accidentally. Marie had gone into the house for no more than forty-five seconds to turn some water on for soup. Her twenty-two-month-old child, Aaron, toddled over to a puddle, fell forward, knocked himself unconscious, and drowned. Marie remembered feeling suicidal afterward. Ted remembered feeling so much blame and rage toward Marie he wanted a divorce. With help from friends, family, and therapists, with their own strength and compassion, with discipline and with love, they descended this crisis. Almost two decades later, when I met them, they were facing a new descent—Ted had become ill and would have to give up his job. Marie said, "We went down into the dark so deep with Aaron, this new transition will not be easy, but we feel like we know it already, and we'll be conscious of its demands all the time. Losing Aaron, and working through that, has been the greatest test and greatest blessing of our relationship."

As you explore the Second Descent in your life, it's sometimes helpful to go back through your memories of your parents' lives. Your parents may not have made it to stages 6, 7, and 8. Their crises may have damaged their partnership, or made it numb, rather than empowering it in the third season. Yet one or two of their crises may have empowered them. You, as a child, would have felt the empowerment. You will now possibly remember the days and months of your family banding together, your parents working hard to keep things solid in the face of crisis, one parent seeming to sacrifice more at one moment, then the other more at another moment, as if the sacrifice was a dance between them. From that dance, you might have felt the emanation of a kind of invigorating energy. Some of the courage and commitment you have now as an individual and as a lover comes from those times when your parents modeled their Second Descent for you.

In tribal cultures, which consciously initiate young people through the earlier stages in the second decade of a person's life, stages 7 through 9 can occur much earlier than is usual in our culture. There are two primary reasons for this difference. One is our loss of spiritually conscious and complex initiation rituals. The other is the difference in longevity. We live into our seventies and eighties. Many tribal peoples and most of our own ancestors were long dead by then. Where they might have gone through stage 8 in their twenties and thirties, most of us don't go through it until later, if at all.

It is dangerous to romanticize the tribal cultures—to say they were right, we are wrong. Their lives were and are different from ours. Yet think how different our lives would be if we could initiate our young people through the first two seasons early enough that they would have thirty or more years in which to live out the creative interdependence of the third season. As we build a culture for the new millennium that takes the best of our own spiritual process and integrates the best of the lost tribal/intergenerational process, I believe we will move toward a new lifestyle in which this third season will take up two or three decades. Our lives will be joyful in a way we can only barely imagine right now.

Here are experiences of the Second Conscious Descent listed in a progression.

1. We tend to begin our descent by experiencing certain shocking acts of fate.

2. If we are conscious, we realize what is happening, verbally acknowledge it in our partnership, and commit ourselves to riding it out with spiritual discipline.

3. Each partner accepts the act of fate, the crisis, and understands that the wound grows from the partnership and/or challenges the partnership, and is therefore the personal responsibility of each partner. Power struggle rears its head but is transcended by this acceptance and agreement.

4. The labors and sacrifices of the descent are consciously divided up. This process can include unconscious rhythms of dividing, in which partners settle into a flow of sacrifice and supportiveness.

5. If for a time it appears that only one partner is in crisis, the other supports his or her work and does not see it through the lens of the fear of abandonment. The partners work through the fears they may have of each other's anger, pain, grief, sorrow, joy, or ecstasy.

6. The partners continue to care for their dependents and each other even though they are in crisis. They do not neglect responsibilities unless because of physical or mental illness. In the face of these, community steps in.

7. The descent leads the partners *and their community* toward growth, healing, and blessing. Partners in the Second Conscious Descent do not avoid or pull away from community through their descent; they find a helpful community somewhere outside their neighborhood if their neighborhood endangers them. Others in their helpful community watch them and learn from their descent; these same others learn by helping. The whole community is blessed, as if by a divine couple.

8. As the descent completes itself, the partners re-form their relationship to be different, and more profound, than it was before.

9. Sacred projects continue in stage 9 with renewed energy.

People who have been through this descent are great teachers. We need to rub up against them, hear them, watch them, support them, be blessed by them. The energy they are working with in their partnership is a kind of energy that feels mysterious to others until it is experienced.

"Nothing brought us closer than when our second son got M.S.," one father told me.

"Our family went through some horrible years," a female friend confessed. "You know, you were there. But we persevered. We survived. Now we realize how good we have it. I wouldn't have traded all those bad years—well, maybe a little! But you know what I mean. Jake and I wouldn't have what we have now, if we hadn't gone through hell."

THE EIGHTH TASK

Stage 8 of the Lover's spiritual discipline teaches us the eighth lesson of trust: *sacred commitment.*

We see that we can trust ourselves and our partner with the worst pain imaginable, the pain we feel when our creation and/or our creative partnership is attacked by fate, crisis, tragedy, and/or our own distractedness.

It is by working through this stage that we fully understand how our partner is *committed* to the wedding vows s/he admitted in the wedding—in sickness and in health, for richer or for poorer. We know this commitment in our guts now, because it has been proven to us. In earlier stages we may have assumed the commitment but had little reason except wedding vows and social rules to do so. Now we *know* it.

In this state of sacred commitment, and in the trust it brings, we can do what the Buddhist teacher, Thich Nhat Hanh, advises: "From time to time, sit close to the one you love, hold his or her hand, ask, 'Darling, do I understand you enough? Or am I making you suffer? Please tell me so that I can learn to love you properly.' If you say this in a voice that communicates your real openness to understand, the other person may cry. That is a good sign, because it means the door of understanding is opening and everything will be possible again."

Thich Nhat Hanh presents a simple ritual, one we can do at any time in a relationship. But to do it with full honesty, we must have come through a time when our whole concept of giving and receiving has changed from one of commodity to one of spiritual energy. We have, through the descent—in which we and our partners sacrificed not for "me" but for "us"—discovered how much we value each other, and discovered that sacrifice (making sacred) and commitment are about wanting to give of our Lover to our Beloved above nearly anything else. The giving we do is not dramatic. It is day to day.

It is our spiritual openness to the other.

Stage 8 provides us with the eighth element of focus for the Lover's spiritual discipline: *reformation.*

Through our work and endurance of descent, we have re-formed ourselves individually and our reformed partnership. We have discovered new realms of Sacred Tasks. We have re-formed the very order of our lives and, by emanation, of our families/communities.

Couples who practice the discipline of reformation are usually preparing to become sacred mentors to others, and can usually see the elder years on the near horizon. The discipline of reformation involves breaking down an old order and creating a new one. During this reformation, every couple goes through new covenant- and promise-making and adjustments of role. Duties are reassessed. If one partner worked especially hard, as Isis did, to take care of the other during an illness, s/he will probably ask now to do something s/he has never done, get fed in some new way, through a vacation or job change or retirement. Couples must stay in constant communication as the changes occur so that they build an exquisite balance of energies. If communication breaks apart, the couple will re-form their relationship in partial isolation from each other, and the new relationship will enter power struggle. The partner who has been taken care of may feel blindsided by his/her partner's sudden retirement from a job or sudden long vacation.

Power struggle waits during and after every couple's crisis. Because it accompanies any renegotiation of energies, it cannot be avoided. It helps every couple re-form itself as, after crisis, our sense of our own and our partner's power will probably change. If we constantly communicate—if we consciously reassert the skills of refined intimacy as passionately as we notice the reassertion of power struggle—we will re-form our relationship well. It will become that secure base we seek as we pursue our evolving love into the decades to come.

INTEGRATING THE SECOND
CONSCIOUS DESCENT

Joy in stage 9 comes in its deepest measure from the soulful feeling we have of meeting the challenges to our spiritual union with always renewing love. People who make this descent are the kind of people—rare people—we look up to; we say, "Look at that couple. There aren't many like them. When they face a difficult situation, it only seems to make them stronger."

We integrate stage 8 into our quest for joy by being open to the possibility of joyful love both in the little details and routines of everyday life with a partner, and in the vast choices and sacrifices and orderings we make and create together as partners. We are more an "us" than a "me" but don't feel robbed of "I." We are committed to making our love joyful no matter what the cost. Few people experience this amazing feeling in any ongoing way. Everyone yearns for it.

As Part Two of the story of Isis and Osiris ended, there was joy, yet still something unresolved. Some of our integration of the descent into the quest for joy awaits us as we grow older and move into the next stage of life and love.

RADIANT
LOVE

How unnatural the imposed view, imposed by a puritanical ethos, that passionate love belongs only to the young, that people are dead from the neck down by the time they are forty. . . . Where we [older people] have the advantage is in loving itself—we know so much more; we are so much better able to handle anxiety, frustration or even our own romanticism; and deep down we have such a store of tenderness.
—MAY SARTON

The more deeply and passionately two people love each other, the more concern they will feel for the state of the world in which they live.
—JOHN WELWOOD

The Japanese tell a story of gods and goddesses who look upon the world in their beneficence and see a young scholar, brilliant but easily distracted. He has committed himself to the spritual life of a monk but has not even memorized the Lotus Sutra yet! What should they do? They devise a plan. Kokuzo, a protective god, plays a major role in this plan, but the scholar doesn't know at first of either the plan or the god's protection.

The scholar simply wanders on his way, stopping at a

house for rest. In the house he spies, behind a curtain, the most beautiful maiden. He falls for her and, when she discovers him hiding there, tells her so. She asks what he does, and he explains his vocation.

"Learn the Lotus Sutra," she says to him, "then recite it to me. Let us show our love to each other only after you've done that."

A man of character, he understands her meaning. He goes away and learns the Lotus Sutra. Upon his return she is impressed but says, "I sense in you that you are not satisifed with just having learned it." This turns out to be true. Now that he has focused his discipline upon the Lotus Sutra, he has become hungry to go deeper into the world of the sutras.

She suggests, "If we were to make love now, while you are dissatisfied with yourself, it would not be the perfect union we hoped for. Why not go and study for as long as it takes for you to feed your hunger? I will write you every week, and you write me. That way we will never be apart."

He agrees to this, studying at a monastery for three years. At the end of that time, he feels he has reached a point of learning—not a point of wisdom, but a point of learning so that he needn't take dissatisfaction to his mate. He has also reached a point where she holds much less allure for him. He almost considers not going back to her.

He does make the journey, however, for he is a man who keeps promises. When he arrives at her house, she welcomes him, and they make love. When he awakens the next morning, he awakens not in a house, but on the road. The house is gone, as if it had never been here. Puzzled, he returns to the monastery and continues his studies. He becomes a great and well-known scholar.

And so it is that the divinities, radiant in their love and

applying wise trickery, help a scholar find his spiritual discipline. Kokuzo, the god who protected him, had turned into
a beautiful woman, and she had shaped the young man's
future.

Stage 9 is the time of radiant love, that time of life when
elders often seem to radiate their interdependent connection
with earth and divine energy. Often their kids are already
grown and their own partnership at the peak of its radiance.
Throughout the world there are many elder tales. More often
than not, they show gods, goddesses, Divine Couples, elder
couples or elder individuals conspiring, in common with
communal values and sacred mysteries, to teach the young.

For those people lucky enough to reach the time of radiant
love—I confess I am not one of them; I am too young yet—
those tales speak gently and powerfully. Elders in this stage
seem to have realized that their own wisdom is not arrogant;
it needs to weave itself into the tapestry of the world with
grace, often the Trickster's grace. Elders have learned in coupled relationship that often a balance of the masculine and
feminine—tricks and teachings from each gender energy in
concert—best instruct the world. While radiant love is certainly practiced by individuals who are not coupled, we'll
focus primarily on radiant couples in this chapter. What we
say about them certainly applies to many individuals. We'll
focus more specifically on elder individuals who are not coupled in the next season.

Our culture would be different if more people went
through the earlier stages and got to the time of radiant love.
But there are radiant couples around us. Think of one or
two elderly couples you know who have not only grown
old together, but have in fact become the wise ones of your

community, memory, family or culture. For some, Jimmy and Rosalyn Carter come to mind, for others the elder Waltons from the TV show, for others their own grandparents.

In mythology the power of these couples is often symbolized in Royal Marriage. It is called "Royal" because it embodies the great integration of Goddess and God. The two royal partners balance masculine and feminine in their relationship (and therefore have done so already or do so simultaneously within their individual selves) in the way modeled by the ancient Chinese Taoist symbols of yin and yang. Once yin and yang are balanced, the Chinese promise us, all the world will be balanced. Couples in royal marriage balance their own yin and yang, and from that balance radiate love into community.

In reference to family elders we might say, "She was the matriarch of the family," or "He was the patriarch of the family," or "Everything really great in my memory of family life happened when I went to Grandma and Grandpa so-and-so's house." When we say these things positively and affectionately, we are saying that those people radiated an energy that was mysterious, ineffable, and unifying. Those grandparents, those elders that even our friends liked to go visit, have come close to balancing yin and yang in their lives. The more we can be with them, the better for us and for our world. That practical teaching is at the heart of Part Three of the story of Isis and Osiris.

ISIS AND OSIRIS: PART THREE

The joy of Royal Marriage is what Isis and Osiris finally achieve. Of course, from the beginning of their marriage they radiated divine energy. They taught the mysteries, the rituals, the ceremonies that would help mortals shine with that energy. They radiated the order and compassion their world needed to spiritually flourish. Royal Marriage and radiant love are not, therefore, sudden occurrences in elder couples' lives. The groundwork for radiant love is being laid through earlier seasons, and especially in creative partnership.

But it does not often come to full radiance until after the Second Descent. You might say it cannot do so. How can we be fully radiant over all of life if we have not yet integrated, and thus become radiant toward, the Underworld? In the Second Conscious Descent, we integrate the Underworld, and become all the more wise.

When Part Two ended, we saw Isis and Osiris wiser and joyful to be reunited, but in pain too, for they were separated by the different realms over which they now had separate responsibility. Many of us in stage 8 get catalyzed to move into stage 9 because of a feeling of separateness in our partnership. We decide that it is time for one of us to retire so we can spend more time together. This is a decision made in the face of a separateness we no longer want as a couple. Or we might decide it is time to renew our vows in a very public, life-defining twenty-fifth wedding anniversary celebration. This is an act of communally recombining in the face of what may have been years of coexistent yet vague separateness. Some of this coexistent separateness may have been the result of the stresses of raising children. By the time of our twenty-fifth of thirty-fifth or fortieth wedding anniversary, all the kids may be out of the house, and we'll be ready to move to the next stage of relationship, so we vow to do it publicly and we work on it privately.

Probably because this latter scenario is so common, the myth of Isis and Osiris embodies it. No matter what age or

culture we live in, people who have children devote themselves to the children and then, once they are grown, reach a
renewed sense of devotion to their own evolving coupleship
and their larger community. Isis and Osiris did not reach their
stage 9 until after Horus was full-grown. What happened
first, after his coming to manhood, was that he defeated Seth.
He made his parents' Royal Marriage possible. Because
Horus would someday also become the Sacred King of his
parents' realm, he needed to be the one who finally defeated
the Shadow, thus proving his divine power.

Children usually don't seem to do anything so heroic to
facilitate their parents' royal marriage. But think about what
they do in fact do, even if it is subtle. Their accomplishments
give us a kind of pride we carry, as energy, in our own evolving partnership. Sometimes we judge our children too harshly, not noticing their accomplishments. When we do grow
enough to notice them, we find that their independence and
accomplishments lift great weights off our shoulders, improv-
ing our own coupled relationship and freeing up our energy
to be directed toward the larger problems of community and
world. Some people express this experience by saying,
"Once my daughter (or son) finished school and got a job, I
knew I was done. Hooray! Onto bigger and better things."
Or "Once our son (or daughter) got married, we could finally let go. It was like our lives began again. We renewed
old friendships. We took on new causes."

Our children act as Horus in another way. They often surpass and redeem us, whether we want them to or not. How
we handle their activity says much about whether we can get
to stage 9. When a child follows in our footsteps but does
better than we do at a given job or cause, or makes peace for
us in our feuding family, or challenges us to grow in some

other way, we can use that opportunity to let go and to grow. We can say, "Okay, I don't have to push at that job anymore; I don't have to fight that family fight anymore. It's time for me to turn into deeper relationship with my spouse, with volunteer work, with community and earth work." Our alternative is to say, "Damn that child! I didn't need him/her to show me up, to show the world how bad I was, to cover up my sins. I can do everything myself." Stage 9 is very much about choosing to develop radiance, to develop a new love of the larger world, a world that desperately needs our elder, radiant energies. This choice is very much like the choice to be free. Spiritually speaking, freedom cannot come to us from outside; we must consciously choose it. In the same way, we must choose to practice radiant love.

Osiris and Isis feel great pride in their son's work. The myth says that on the day Horus destroyed Seth, there was a joy in the Divine Couple, and therefore in the realm, like never before. We know we have reached stage 9 when we are capable of this new kind of joy, this almost indescribable feeling of unity. One couple said to me, "When we got married, our minister used the word *one* all the time. 'You are now One,' he said. We didn't realize what that Oneness was until after our kids were grown, and we rediscovered each other. Once that happened, we learned what joy really was, and we learned what Oneness really was." Many couples in stage 9 look back from their elder years at marital promises of Oneness and at moments during their marriages, for instance when their children were born, of quick Oneness lost soon to overwork and the wonderful stress of creative partnership and descent. Then, in later years, they feel almost as if they are, in C. S. Lewis's words, "surprised by joy." In later years, they gain the conscious experience of Oneness they'd been promised decades before.

Osiris and Isis gain it in their reunion, following Seth's demise. That reunion following a descent, which we find in so many myths and stories of Divine Couples, removes drought from the dominion, brings a people to fruition, salvation, and new rituals that ensure ongoing spiritual renewal. The myth says the Egyptian people learned from the reunited Isis and Osiris "a new religion and a new ardor for life." When we sit with, eat with, learn from, embrace, and unite our energies with those people in royal marriage in our communities, we gain this ardor for life.

I have even heard of this happening to people watching movies or television programs about older couples. A woman in a church workshop told me about watching the movie *On Golden Pond,* in which Henry Fonda and Katharine Hepburn play a couple in their late seventies. The movie ends with the elder couple reuniting its energy after much family pain. The woman who told me about watching the movie remembered weeping for joy at the movie's end. Though she was not in stage 9 herself, she could see that the couple in the movie had reached it, and seeing their evolution brought her to an insight she articulated this way: "Watching their renewed love of life I thought, 'If old people like that, with all they've faced, can do it, I can do it.' " There were many nods in the sanctuary that day, many people who had felt their own inner power grow simply by observing and understanding elders who had renewed and radiated their love. When we embrace the energy of others who are in stage 9, we gain, along with a certain admiration and humility, a very deep sense of the ongoingness of struggle, the joy that awaits, and the ardor that can be ours if we grab it. It is their tangible example of what we can become that inspires us to move through our struggles with purpose and spiritual discipline.

The other side of the coin is that the elders must also mentor and teach us so that we can learn it. Isis and Osiris *taught* their people about medicine, miracles, life after death. They consciously mentored and instructed. Just as often as younger people neglect the wisdom and radiance of elders, so too do elders neglect to teach their wisdom and radiate their energy. Often they neglect it because no one seems to listen. And often their pessimism is accurate: among all the glittering ambitions of our youth-oriented popular culture, we forget that radiant love, with its wisdom and long perspective of past and future, holds many keys to our cultural fulfillment.

Some say the single most important lesson elders in stage 9 teach us is to be grounded in the Great Cycle of Life. Without the radiant elder's perspective on that cycle, we will very easily believe we can alter the cycle through technology or, in mythological terms, some other form of "sorcery" created to surpass the divine, to deny or escape the cycle—often through addictions—or to stand outside the cycle, through a lack of personal responsibility. With the radiant elder's perspective on that cycle, we learn to see it as a cycle filled with joy.

YOUR OWN EXPERIENCE WITH RADIANT LOVE

Radiant love is a condition of relationship that does not tend to come to fruition until midlife or later, yet everyone at whatever stage of life experiences moments of radiant love. It finds expression in times when you've embodied and taught the cycle of life, felt the unity of masculine and feminine, and blessed the world through that unity. Radiant love is both a *kind* of loving and a *stage* of loving. We experience it as a *kind* of loving while we're grappling with the energies of the earlier stages. It's a kind of foreshadowing of what the *stage* of radiant love will be once we get there. And, as with all the stages of the Lover's Journey, one doesn't need to have actually attained the stage to learn valuable lessons from it.

This is especially true in efforts we make to integrate the masculine and feminine, both as individuals and as a culture. In the Lover's Journey, it is in stage 9 that we fully *experience* this integration.

Those who have not integrated masculine and feminine will tend to teach their own form of power struggle to younger people. Their mentoring can sometimes be helpful, but not in the way most people need. Especially in our age of gender transition, mentoring that is more about how to blend masculine and feminine than about how to do power struggle is crucial to marital survival. An often-divorced individual can teach and counsel others about his/her mistakes. This is valuable, but at some point people want to hear from couples who have been married fifty years. "What's your secret?" we ask them. They may not have perfect marriages, but they will have gained something that only they can bless us with.

To explore, in a very practical way, whether you've reached stage 9, see if any of the following experiences seem familiar.

• We feel centered, relatively imperturbable, very self-confident in the face of adversity. We will face trials and have bad days and even slip from self-confidence, but those moments and days do not rock us to the core.

• We are able to discern ourselves from others' projections

as never before. We understand when others' criticisms of us are really projections of their own self-judgments. We also know when they are direct teachers of some lesson we need to learn.

• We have, in our long-term partnership with another, developed one intimate mirror, our partner. We have trusted his/her assessments of us to such a great extent for so long that we have gradually come to need others' assessments less. And, in trusting that one mirror—our partner—we have developed an incredible capacity to trust our own self-discernments too. One man in his sixties put it this way: "I pretty much trust myself about how I'm doing, but when there's something I'm not sure about, I ask Alice. She fills me in when I need her." This kind of self-discernment and couples discernment can happen to people in second, third, fourth marriages; it is not the unique property of long-term monogamous couples. Yet it is a much rarer discovery in people who shift marriages, because it does require very hard work, between two people, over the long haul.

• We have discovered how to love others unconditionally. We sometimes say to our partner that we thought, in the past, we had known how this felt, but in fact have just learned. We almost feel as if we've never known how powerful mutual acceptance and unconditional love can be.

• When we are hurt or disappointed by others, we move through stages of hurt very quickly, finding forgiveness, then using its energy to discover actions that can bless the other.

• We sense that we now belong utterly—and perhaps only for a short time longer—to the tree of life. We work hard as individuals and as a couple to care for the earth, build community, and bring change and peace to the world.

• We have most probably developed a close relationship with nature, a deep need for it in our lives. Many people seek houses in the country at this stage, or at least take long walks together along the river or in the park. Many couples work toward caring for the earth and wildlife with energies they hadn't felt before.

• We teach the Lover's Journey however we have discovered it in our lives. This is a specific element we mentor people in, especially younger couples: how to love, for the long haul, with dignity, compassion, and creativity.

• We nurture family traditions/rituals with elder authority, but without obsessing. We do not operate out of the belief, "Since I know it and tell it to you you should believe me and act accordingly, and if you do not, you'll disappoint me." Sometimes this kind of authoritarianism is needed; but what we try to develop more now are strategies by which to be authoritative. These strategies use sacred tricks instead of force. In mentoring others this way, we do not take personally their responses. When they turn away from us or leave the mentorial relationship, we encourage them to stay true to themselves, which often means moving on from us. We know it is our job to give them both roots and wings.

As we are doing all this, we experience lonelinesses we haven't felt quite this way before. When our protégé leaves us, we might become depressed for a time. We may also be experiencing the beginnings of the physical decay that will haunt our next season of life. It moves us out of the sanguine quite often. And we know death is coming. Sometimes we experience a lot of frustration at not being able to do more, for ourselves, for others, for the earth. Yet when we come back to our discipline, we regain our footing and continue to bless the world.

In searching through the grid I just laid out, you may get a kind of hollow, disappointed feeling. When I was exploring stage 9 with a male client not too long ago, he cried, "I'd have to be Jesus, Mary, and Joseph to get to stage 9!" At a workshop a Buddhist woman called stage 9 and stage 10 "bodhisattva impossibilities," implying only a great saint could get to them.

If you feel that impossibility, you're not alone. Many feel it. Many feel it because they are trying to get to stage 9 by bypassing an earlier stage, and their unconscious knows it can't be done. Many feel it because they are still in a deep woundedness, despairing that they will never get out. Many feel it because they are in the stresses of creative partnership, not quite old enough yet or free enough from immediate daily commitments to be able to grandfather and grand-mother the world.

Despite this, I believe we can all practice radiant love. If we live long enough, work hard enough at the maturing challenges of intimacy, and gain enough confidence to teach our wisdom, we will radiate and bless the world with our love not only in radiant moments earlier in life, but as a stage of life that lasts many years, even decades.

THE NINTH SACRED TASK

Stage 9 of the Lover's spiritual discipline provides us with the ninth lesson of trust, the ninth piece of its sacred ground in our lives: *authority.*

We have become authorities, looked up to by our families, tribes, communities, and culture. We experience ourselves as authorities, as kings and queens. From this experience comes a kind of self-trust (which is part and parcel of a trust in the workings of the universe) that we can only imagine up to this point.

Earlier in life, of course, we may have achieved a place of authority in our field, even in more than one field, workplace, or discipline. So we have experienced ourselves as "authorities" with "reputations." In stage 9 we experience authority as an integral part of who we *are*. And our own personal sense of authority is augmented by the authority we feel as a couple.

As we might expect, the ninth element of focus in the Lover's spiritual discipline is *radiant leadership*.

We focus our energies during these years and decades of life on teaching care of soul, self, and society. Our visions of what hides and needs building in a nation's soul, an individual's self, a society's structure become essential to the disciplined guidance of our people.

By the time we get to this focus, we have most likely accomplished our professional goals. We are ready to serve without personal ambition, or at least put service first and everything else a distant second. If teachings are filled with personal ambition or a couple's unrequited dreams, they are probably not teachings that emanate and radiate from a person or couple in stage 9. People in stage 9 radiate their energy from the basis of having let go of most of their needs to be at the top of a ladder in work or have a child who becomes a doctor. People in stage 9 lead by perceiving, often unconsciously, what others and culture need, and by radiating energy that helps others and culture fill their needs. And they do not lose themselves in the process. Stage 9 leadership is a servant leadership, but it is not codependency.

INTEGRATING RADIANT LOVE

If people in stage 9 tend to have one agenda, it is the pursuit of communal peace. They have discovered that, in most situations, what the world needs in its pursuit of joy is more peace. So while people in stage 9 cut back on personal agendas, they do tend toward this one. As one old couple said to me very recently, "People need to be shown how much there is to gain from learning to be gentle."

The American Native teacher Dhyani Ywahoo speaks of the precepts of "sacred relationship." Writes Ywahoo:

> Practice of sacred relationship is practice of good relation with all in the family of life. Thus [the Creator] gave reminders to the people:
>
> 1. Speak only words of truth
>
> 2. Speak only of the good qualities of others.
>
> 3. Be confident and carry no tales.
>
> 4. Turn aside the veil of anger to release the beauty inherent in all.
>
> 5. Waste not the bounty, and want not.
>
> 6. Honor the light in all. Compare nothing; see all for its suchness.
>
> 7. Respect all life; cut away ignorance from one's heart.
>
> 8. Neither kill nor harbor thoughts of angry nature, which destroy peace like an arrow.
>
> 9. Do it now; if you see what needs doing, do it.

It takes a very developed person to embody and practice these elements. The personal practice of Ywahoo's sacred relationship, which is at base a call to *peaceful interdependence,* is something we do not—usually cannot, given the crises and battles youthful and middle-aged life throw us—integrate to a large degree into our spiritual practice until we are here in the later stages of life.

Precepts like those Ywahoo provides are examples of ways to joy that people in stage 9 seek to teach. These precepts are like the Ten Commandments of the Old Testament or the Vows of Islam. Who usually instructs the world most effectively in these codes or vows or ways? It takes a certain kind of wise, experienced, gentled individual or couple to be able to effectively teach these truths—usually older people who have integrated a great deal of the wisdom of these society-defining values into their own quests for joy. Teaching about personal responsibility and sacred life, the person and couple in stage 9 feel the joy of having fulfilled their own personal responsibilities by radiating the blessings of sacred life in the universe. Standing in this place of radiance, they have been, perhaps without realizing it, preparing for the deep solitude of a soul that seeks Season Four, the journey toward fruitful and active spiritual detachment.

Part Four

THE SEASON OF
NONATTACHMENT

Story: The Living and the Dead

As a mythologist, I've found it especially difficult to find stories about the Lover's Journey that take place in the very elder years. Most of the stories I've heard around the world, and most of the stories that we find in story collections, concern the issues and problems experienced by people in childhood, youth, and middle age. Many stories utilize older people as mentors, witches, and leaders, and quite a few do focus on elders as individuals—thus you can hear stories about a man in the elder years or a woman in the elder years—but few available stories focus on elder men and women as *loving couples*. Perhaps, centuries ago, more collected stories did; perhaps the dearth of stories of elder love and coupling is a result of our modern culling of age stories in favor of youth stories.

Whatever the cause of the dearth, it is an unfortunate one. The story I give you here, while coming primarily from Papua, is combined with elements from ancient Greek, Plains Indian, South American, Central African, and East Indian elder tales. Thus it has gone through some embellishments on its way to you. I've never done anything quite like this with a story. I feel as if, in order to find the old loving couple, I have had to interview a whole host of their relations and piece together their story that way.

If the family story of "The Living and the Dead" has suffered in its journey to you, I take full responsibility. No one, including its collector, can do anything to harm its ultimate

243

message: live fully and you shall die fully. This is the way to joy.

Once upon a time there was an elderly couple, Maria and Raoul, who lived on the outskirts of their village. They were known for their garden. Both were known to be healers. They had come to that age when people come to them to be taught by their talk and to hear, just as often, the wisdom of silences. When people came to be with them, Maria and Raoul always gave them something, usually something small. Even their own children were surprised, some say jealous, about their parents' generosity. But then, you know, Maria and Raoul gave to their children too, and their children's children. And then there came a day when they had given most of what they owned away, keeping only what they needed, and only what would not be a burden when they died.

Though Maria and Raoul were considered quite wise, not even they knew that they lived near the Way to Ioloa, the Land of the Dead. Like everyone, they assumed the actual portal to the next world was in someone else's yard! Instead, the Way, a huge hole in the earth, lay just inside their own, where two creeks merged.

When Maria grew sick, Raoul nursed her. When she died, he mourned. As he prepared to bury her, his family and friends gathered with him. He asked them to wait for a little while, for he wanted to go out with his dog and find some of the flowers he knew she liked. He wanted the wildflowers outside his own garden. It was to be a short trip, just five minutes, to that place where the creeks merged, and some of his flower seeds had flown, over the years, out past his own garden, into the wild.

When he got to the place of the merging creeks, he found his dog there ahead of him, chasing some animal. Then he saw his dog disappear into a hole. Calling his dog to no avail, he went to the hole to follow it. He went down quite a way, not knowing why he had never seen this hole before. When he got to the bottom he saw trees growing, and crops as if tended by villagers. He saw a world just like his own. He found his dog and embraced him. He saw people too, though he could tell immediately that they were shades, shadows. Fortunately, they paid him little attention, for it was evening, both above and below, that time when the dead rise to walk. They were just arousing themselves stuporously. Then he saw walking toward him his wife.

"Hello, my husband," she said, smiling. "Have you died too?" She came to him, pinched his arm, and drew blood. "You are not dead!" she exclaimed. "Why are you here?" When he told her what had happened with the flowers, the dog, and the hole, she said, "Come, hold the dog close to you lest he go after the bones of the dead, and come with me. We'll hide you so the arousing dead don't slay you to make you their own."

She took her husband and their dog to her house. From there, they watched the dance of the dead in the courtyard. It was a joyful dance, but also a fearful one. Each time they welcomed a new dead being into their midst, they tore its flesh off its bones and pulled its bones apart so that it could not be said to be of any previous living form. Then the being reshaped itself into a shadow, a shade, a ghost. Its joy came after its having been reshaped. It danced in joy. But the process of pulling apart the bones filled Raoul with terror. As in life, Maria and Raoul stayed close together, but as morning came and the dead went off to find sleep again, Maria said,

"Thank you for coming to me. Know that I am happy, and you have made me so. Know that, in our way, we will always be together. But now you must go back up to the surface, or your bones will be pulled apart. Go back without stopping."

He hugged her and, accompanied by the dog, left her. They pushed through the darkness of the tunnel, but this time he saw trees with strange flowers on them. He was afraid of the flowers, but his dog sniffed at them, then frolicked in them. Raoul, following his dog's example, enjoyed them too and picked some for later. Without man and dog realizing it, a whole cycle passed in their frolic. It was night again; the dead had arisen. They came for him. He ran with his dog to the surface, and as he climbed out of the hole, it closed up, as if never there. The dead cannot be seen mucking about on the surface.

Raoul prayed over his wife, and his community joined him. When the many days of ceremony had ended, he buried his wife with his friends and family. As the days moved forward, people saw him return to the place where the two creeks met every three days for another month. He prayed there. He let his garden wither more than he ever had, and thus his medicines gave less potency. This was known as his time of grief.

But then he arose one day to work at the creeks. As if with a last burst of energy, he built two tributaries off the two creeks into his garden. His flowers grew as never before. The medicines they gave healed the people as never before. And he was seen talking often to himself, making preparations for his journey. "I have seen the land of the dead," he was heard to say, though people thought him a little mad. "I know what flowers there are there. I know the customs there. I must now prepare myself." And so he did, until the day he died. His people spoke of him long afterward, convinced that they saw his spirit, angelic, descend into an invisible hole where the two creeks met, near evening, beside the wild-flowers.

THE ELDER'S SOLITUDE

There is a difference between becoming elderly and becoming an elder.
—REV. LINDA WHITTENBERG

. . . to see each moment for its wholeness and to appreciate it as a unique gift. That is a discipline in itself: to be still, to be loving, to know "I am in this moment creating cause for all moments."
—DHYANI YWAHOO

When I was much younger, living in Manhattan, I spent some afternoons with an elderly aunt, Lois, and, sometimes, with her long-time companion, Bob. I remember in particular one afternoon when Bob was not around and I dragged Aunt Lois to the movie *Airplane*. Throughout the satirical and sometimes tasteless movie, I laughed uproariously. As I walked her home afterward, Lois spoke politely of the movie, though I could see she hadn't liked it.

I said, "Well, it beats staying at home, doesn't it?"

"No," she said quite honestly, "not at all. It's always nice to see you, Mike, but you know, most of the time I just like being alone." My aunt, in her late sixties, had been a very active woman, forty-five years in the workforce, and full of energy, a world traveler. Very young, I didn't conceive of her as someone who could like solitude more than activity.

"But don't you get lonely?" I asked. And we got into a long conversation in which she tried to explain to me the person she had become. She said she was often alone but rarely felt lonely. "I have my memories, my close friends, family, my apartment, the city, my plants. I have Bob when we want to go out. And I have myself. I've just come to know myself. I've just come to know how to enjoy being alone. I pick and choose my activities very carefully these days. I don't need to be busy all the time. I enjoy little things like I never did. The daily quiet gives me joy."

"The movie wasn't very quiet, I guess," I apologized. "I took you to it because I thought you were lonely."

"I know," she said, smiling and patting my arm. "You're very sweet. Maybe who I am now is just not something a young person can understand."

With that, we went to her favorite little cafe to have tea.

I have never forgotten my Aunt Lois. In my life and work I have met many elders who, unlike Aunt Lois, found more misery than joy in their elder years. But I've also met many who recognized the last season of life for what it is, and they have taught me much.

There was Clarise who, when I asked, "How much time do you each spend alone now, compared to, say, ten years ago?" answered, "Five, maybe ten times," and her husband, Jim, who said, "And we don't miss the bustle at all." Jim continued, "Clarise had been trying to get me to retire for years. When I finally did, I really learned what living was about. And it wasn't about not living anymore. It was about living differently."

There was the widower, Jeremy, who told me, "I go to

church now. I guess I always did, but it was because I felt judged. Now I go because I *want* to, I like it. All the language I used to think was judgmental and shaming seems different now. It gives me strength."

There was Judy, seventy-six, a practicing Buddhist for fifteen years who was caring for her husband, a man in later stages of Alzheimer's disease. "Life is hard. It has a lot of sad times. It's everything I can do sometimes to feel good about getting old, and getting pretty sparse help, and seeing the money go, and having to take care of myself too—but don't get me wrong, son, I wouldn't trade this time. I am free of some things I never knew I could get free of. I understand what it means to practice desirelessness and nonattachment. I like being free. I like not being afraid to live." What brings you the most joy? I asked her. "That I have a lot of those moments now when everything seems to be like prayer to me."

THE SEASON OF NONATTACHMENT

Nondependence (also known as detachment or nonattachment), our fourth season, is about detaching, through spiritual practice and death, from material things and myriad relationships in search of personal connection with the divine. People in this season, like Judy, are not necessarily loners, friendless, or outside community. They are often married and doing volunteer work and supporting each other as they approach the end of life. They are still interdependent. As they get sick, they will also become increasingly physically dependent. But a new kind of spiritual energy has swept through them like a wind. It is an understanding of themselves as creatures for whom spiritual detachment and physical death are now the great teachers. The more people in this season detach from the multiplicity of the known and focus on the singularity of the unknown, the more they gain from this season. In other words, they take life seriously now by taking death seriously.

The fact that everyone dies does not mean that everyone makes the Lover's Journey to nondependence and nonattachment. Everyone who lives long enough makes some steps to detach from workplace, family, and material needs, but very few people actually experience the kind of soulful and joyful nondependence that we see a few mainly old people realize. I say *"mainly* old people" because there are some who seem to achieve nondependence very young in life, such as those who have sought it in a monastic lifestyle. But for most of us, nondependence does not come into its own until we search for the deep solitudes of elder life.

What keeps the vast majority of us from experiencing Season Four, even in our seventies and eighties? I think the greatest obstacle is that if we don't learn to quest for joy with our mates, children, tribes, friends, and earth, how can we learn to face death from a strong foundation? How can we face death with the deep sense that we have truly and fully lived and in so living embraced that essential core of life energy within us, our own soul, that death cannot take away? How many of us get to old age with the sense that we've lived a full life of the soul? Few. Embroiled as individuals and a culture that denies death, we miss, or at best stumble through, most of the spiritual growth of the last season of living.

It does not need to be this way.

THE LIVING AND THE DEAD: PART ONE

Maria and Raoul are known in the village for their garden. They tend it, they share its beauty and its medicines. They have come to that age when they practice wise silences. They have come to that age when rather than their going out toward others, others come more toward them. They are generous, giving away everything but what they need. They provide for their own blood relations, but without overdoing it. They are part of their whole community, but they mark their lives most clearly by relinquishments and their search for solitude.

In the story's brief description of them is a rich vision of stage 10. They are elders, as they probably were in stage 9, but now their eldership is more a wisdom that has its source in solitude than one that has its source in the activities of radiant love. Often old people report feeling as though there are two distinct kinds of eldership, one busy, the other reflective. Both go on in elders simultaneously, of course; to distinguish stage 9 eldership from stage 10 eldership is, therefore, artificial. And yet, it is authentic. As one elder woman, seventy-three, put it, "I remember being very busy after my kids were grown. I was with the grandchildren a lot. I was volunteering; we were moving to Florida and making new friends. Now I'm not as busy. Now I'm quieter. Now I sleep a lot more. There's a difference." When I posited to an elder man, seventy-six, that there was a difference between active and solitary eldership, he agreed in this rather enigmatic way: "When I was in my most active phase, I always felt I was leaving something behind that I had to retrieve. I felt like I had to go back for it. Now I don't feel like I've left that thing behind as much anymore." I took this to mean that letting go of some of the interdependent needs for creative activity opened up a way for him to become nondependent.

Maria and Raoul are generous in their search for solitude. This generosity is a mark of stage 10. Elders in this stage understand that nonattachment has a literal interpretation. We must be ready to give things away. Many elderly people are not able to do this. Having lived lives in various kinds of deprivation, they now hoard. It is hard for them to reframe prosperity to mean solitude, elder self-reflection, generosity of wisdom and material goods. I have no controlled study to prove this, but it is my observation that elderly people who hoard goods are also parsimonious about sharing wisdom. It is only through gaining a sense of nonattachment that wisdom keepers are prosperous enough spiritually to be able to freely bless those who ask for blessing.

Just by hearing Part One of the story and seeing the elders, Maria and Raoul, described there, we can experience blessing ourselves even if we are young. They teach us that all of us could use more of a sense of prosperity in our lives. All of us would feel and create more joy if we knew solitude better, sought the mystical more, paid more attention to our own medicines (created in our own garden—our internal life) than we depended on the medicines of the external world. All of us would enjoy life more if we had more elder models. And all of us can spend more time with them, if we try. Especially when they are in stage 10, they need us to come toward them, with respect, with discernible needs, with a love of wisdom, and with patience.

As the story continues, we learn that Maria and Raoul live right next to the portal that opens their lives to the world of the dead. Like most of us, they assume that portal is somewhere else far away—at St. Peter's gate, or in a fearful dark forest, or in a disease that "can't happen to me"—but death, in the Lover's Journey, is always right on the border of our own spiritual "property." Death holds our hand all through our lives. Maria and Raoul don't know yet that death is so near. But soon they will. Soon they will make the Third Conscious Descent—not after journeying across a continent, but starting from right where they stand.

MONALITY

So elders who move well in stage 10 are moving into the knowledge that death is with them always. They are preparing to deal with their fear of death and the mystical rewards of breaking down the duality between life and death. What internal shift makes it possible for them to accomplish this? It is a shift that reunifies the inner world of the elder. Earlier stages of life have required subservience to the intellectual process of duality discernment. Child raising, creative partnership, the workplace—all these require us to penetrate the depths of dualities and discern ethical, moral principles and politics through them. These same stages of life can give us intuitions of the essential oneness that underlies it all, but we cannot be completely engaged in the activities of life and simultaneously maintain constant intuition of that "monality." So in the wonderful wisdom of the Lover's Journey, there is a stage of life when we have, for all intents and purposes, finished the activities that require the rigors of duality discernment; we come to a time when we can fall, through solitude, into the intuition of oneness, monality, pure grace.

Stage 10, at its best, provides this grace. East versus West, masculine versus feminine, good versus evil, perceptive versus judgmental, reason versus passion, perpetrator versus victim, science versus spirit, matter versus energy, soul versus body, these dualities can dissolve. The kind of cosmic compassion we develop for ourselves as we spend our time in solitude teaches us to feel compassion for both perpetrator and victim, both good and evil, both science and spirit. We have not become naive, we have emancipated our innocence. We have not become stupid, we have let go of the need to know. We have not become more other—for example, more masculine or more feminine—we have become more in tune with our own intuitions of oneness and thus less concerned with labels. We have not become *more* passionate or *more* reasonable; we have integrated both. And we have not become more open to evil or less open to good, more willing to allow "wrong" and less willing to allow "right." We have simply come to that moment of mystical consciousness that shows us how *everything* is sacred, *everything* is divine. We experience monality and mysticism as saints and bodhisattvas have modeled them for us.

Few of us truly get to stage 10. The Buddha and Jesus seem to have done so. Muhammad and Baha'ullah, Hildegard of Bingen, and Mother Teresa seem to have done so. They are models for all of us. They have seemed to come to a point in their lives where they have broken down even the biggest duality—the duality between mystery and meaning. Their sense of mystery is their sense of meaning. In that oneness, they can, at least in theory, approach the duality of life and death as no duality at all.

YOUR OWN ELDER'S SOLITUDE

Rev. William H. Houff writes in *Infinity in Your Hand:*

> "One of the most common and painful emotional afflictions arises through our attachment to unmet expecta-

tions. How often I sit in my study [as a pastoral counselor] and listen to people mourn the disappointment, unkept promises, and betrayals of life! Inevitably, as such sorrows are poured forth, blame and indignation mount until the burden is nearly unbearable. "He made me angry." "She made me guilty." "They left me with poor self-esteem." So goes the litany of complaints and recriminations—all relics, all irretrievable. Yet they dominate and distort the only time we have: now! So it is that we squander the present. So it is that we fashion our own prisons. How seldom we pause in our pain to recognize that our present feelings are our own, and we can do something about them.

Nobody "makes" us feel anything.

Rev. Houff, an elder in his sixties speaking from a stage 10 perspective—a perspective that encourages personal responsibility and "living in the now"—is not unsympathetic to people's pain. Yet if we have not reached stage 10 or have not had moments of touching its mystical energies earlier in life, we will accuse Houff of a lack of empathy. Our challenge, as we explore our own stage 10, is to explore the extent to which we take *personal responsibility* for our actions, and practice in our spiritual discipline the *essentiality of the present*. People in stage 10 tend no longer to blame others for their own sufferings. Part and parcel of this self-evolution is their ability to "be here now," not back there, not somewhere else, but *here*.

Are elements of the following list part of your spiritual practice, or have you felt them in the elders you've known?

• A contentment to be solitary.

• A sense of finally knowing what beauty is.

• A new revision of intimacy systems to ensure time and place for solitude.

• An urge to tell one's life story to kin and world.

• Detachment from previous life work (retirement).

• A great deal of time spent in personal rituals of connection to earth and Mystery. A mystical time. A relaxing time. Creative-active structures like gardening, golf, knitting, journaling are popular. Creative-contemplative structures like long walks and long prayer are also popular during this elder time.

• Some elders in this time report conversations with the unseen (animal spirits, gods, ancestors).

• Some elders gain in their solitude specific visions to offer the young. As in stage 9, these elders teach and mentor and grandparent.

• This can also be a time of the passing on of birthright/ earthright to the community.

Much of the loneliness elders feel in our culture is due to a cultural void of spiritual practice for elder solitude. Elders are often left alone without they themselves or people around them understanding the essentiality of their role not only as elders, but as elder students of solitude and sacred mystery. Elders who are integrated into community bless the young and themselves through mystical understanding, an understanding that allows them to let go of anxieties and material and time prisons. With one eye focused on what is to come in the world of the dead and the other eye still focused on the world of the living, the elder in solitude has much to teach us.

THE TENTH SACRED TASK

Stage 10 of the Lover's spiritual discipline teaches us the tenth lesson of trust: *relinquishment.*

To trust myself and the universe completely, I must relinquish what I have gained and what has kept me in its grasp.

The most extreme form of elder in this task is the Hindu sannyasi who, with begging bowl and staff, leaves his family and home and all material things to live out his life in wandering. While most of us won't go to this extreme, still the sannyasi's path teaches us that we must be willing to give up just about anything to evolve to this next deep place of trust.

Stage 10 provides us with the tenth element of focus for the Lover's spiritual discipline: *reflective solitude.*

In our solitude we reflect on our own lives, the lives of community, our mystical connection with all Being, and our smallness in the face of Mystery. As earlier attachments fall away, so do earlier answers, politics, and enmities. In our solitude we slow down enough to see that nearly everything we experienced in earlier life as "other" can now be seen reflected in our own mirror.

So it is that in this time we are not just alone, we are at the center of the universe, reflecting all that is. This is the role we most associate with saints and elder teachers, shamans and prophets, who we use as our doorway to a leap of faith in ourselves. They have stood in the slow solitude of their own reflection so well we utterly trust them. The fact that some of the gurus we trust turn out to be untrustworthy will not, I hope, daunt our elders in their reflectivity, and the rest of community in their search for the right reflector.

INTEGRATING THE ELDER'S SOLITUDE

How utterly joyful it is to break down the duality between living and dying! What incredible empowerment a few people among us do experience as a result of this breaking down. I pray that when I am an old man, I will experience it. I know that while I have quick moments of sensing it, I must not disrespect my elders by pretending that I, in the busyness of my middle-age life, can exist in stage 10 as they can. Yet I'm proud of myself and anyone who can integrate stage 10 modeling, and its joys of relinquishment and solitude, into any individual's everyday life.

May Sarton says this about an individual soul in its quiet: "I sometimes feel I am melting into the lovely landscape outside my window. Am floated. For an hour I do nothing else but rest in it. Afterwards I feel nourished. I am one with those old gentle hills."

Elders in this time of life integrate stage 10 into their quest for joy by giving a great deal of their life functioning over to it. Their gardens call to them with voices from both the living and the dead, if they would but listen. And they can spend time in those gardens without losing the wonderful functionings of grandparenting, of mentoring, of bridge-playing, of swimming, of dinners at a senior center. Relinquishment, reflectivity, and solitude don't require the end to active life. Elders who balance their activities with solitude and elders who spend sometimes too much time in solitude all know that they are already in such physical decay the *choice* of solitude may quickly diminish. They need to live in the solitude happily for what it is now, right now, for death does await.

The rest of us integrate the elder's solitude into our quest for joy by listening to, being with, putting faith in, and learning from our elders. Often young people don't know which elders to trust. When we meet elders who have experienced the deep solitude of stage 10, we have encountered people of such rich gifts that it is our responsibility and privilege to be present to those people and their gifts, not only for our good or theirs, but because joy is a difficult thing to make in the world. Whoever holds a piece of it is due our respect.

THE THIRD
CONSCIOUS
DESCENT

*The confrontation with death—and the reprieve from
it—makes everything look so precious, so sacred, so
beautiful that I feel more strongly than ever the im-
pulse to love it, to embrace it, and to let myself be
overwhelmed by it. . . . I wonder if we could love
passionately, if ecstasy would be possible at all, if we
knew we'd never die.*
—ABRAHAM MASLOW

*I have watched many cling desperately to a rapidly
degenerating body, hoping for some incredible miracle,
anguished by a deep longing for fulfillment never
found in life. I have also met those whose death was
an inspiration to all about them. Who died with so
much love and compassion that all were left filled with
an unnamed joy for weeks afterward.*
—STEPHEN LEVINE

The Italians tell a story of Francis, who, as an old man, was
approached by Death. Instead of being afraid of her, Francis,
who knew it was his time, said, "Bless you. I have seen the
world; I've had my fill of everything." He asked to say last
good-byes, then to be taken. Death refused this last request,

261

but Francis, who had been given a magic sack and stick by a fairy long ago, ordered Death to jump into the sack. Because of the sack's magic, Death had to do so. As she disappeared into the sack, the queen of the fairies appeared. She granted Francis his wish for a last day to make his good-byes. She then told him it was time to destroy the magic sack and stick. After he said his good-byes and burned the sack and stick, Death rose around him like smoke and took him away.

As we move through the last season of life, we confront death. We confront the deaths of our friends as we confronted the deaths of our parents and relatives in moments throughout our earlier lives. If we have partners, we confront their deaths. Then we confront our own. How shall we face the loss of our partner and seeming loss of ourselves? Every culture since the beginning of consciousness has wrestled with this question, and every individual too.

Francis models a joyful and blessed death. It is that power of blessing we seek as we weaken, decay, break hips, get confined to wheelchairs. It is that blessing we seek as we watch partners wither and die, trying to quiet their anxieties and treat their pain, all the while feeling we cannot take the sorrow of losing them, but indeed must handle more and more of it. It is that power of blessing we seek as we bury our partners and prepare ourselves to return to the dust. How joyful it must be to be able to say, "Death, bless you, I'm ready," and "Death, bless you, my partner's ready." How shall we discover that joy in our lives, in our relationships, and in a culture for which sickness and decay are the worst maladies, aging is by social definition a kind of leprosy, and the moment of death is something to experience as terrible?

Francis meets the source of his power at his end, and that goddess tells him to give up all power (the sack and stick) before he dies. She is guiding him to integrate death and himself into death; she is saying, "Since dying and death will take your power anyway, be conscious of your surrender of power, make that surrender empowering." He gives up the sack and stick. He says his last good-byes. Without regret, and touched by joy, he dies.

Each of us would perhaps like to be this goddess for our mate and partner. We would like to be able to help lead our partner toward inner resources that help him/her die joyfully. But to fill this role, we have to be able to make peace with death and dying ourselves. How can we, when we are so terrified of it? Without being able to help our partners bless their deaths, we are much less able to bless our own when our time comes.

Stage 11 is very much about helping make our partner's death into a Third Conscious Descent. Among the ancient Greeks, heaven (Elysium) was not up in the sky but under the ground. This is a wonderful metaphor of joyful death for stage 11. This stage is not just about getting old, getting sick, helping a loved one die, and dying ourselves. It is about the journey to the heaven–underground, the Elysium. It is about the quest for joy in our time of physical decay and service to a dying one. Think how different our lives would be if all old people became elders, and all elders made the Third Conscious Descent.

THE LIVING AND THE DEAD: PART TWO

When Maria grows sick, the story says, Raoul nurses her. There is no indication in the story that he initially helps her toward conscious dying or that she helps him help her. They who had been so conscious during stage 10 are, at first, un–

conscious in the face of her sickness and death. Then she dies, and it is after the fact of her death that both make the journey toward conscious dying.

If we just see the story one way, we will say, "So she died, then he went into the underworld looking for her, poor guy, he missed her so. The story is about his not letting go." And of course it is, in that interpretation. The story teaches that we must let go of the loved one. As Dag Hammerskjold put it, "Our love becomes impoverished if we lack the courage to sacrifice its object." The death partner, Raoul, can never find joy if he stays stuck. He must learn to let go of Maria.

So that's one interpretation, but let me suggest another. What if, for a while, we saw Maria's death and life underground as her entrance into the world of sickness, dying, and death? What if all the time spent in death's underground is time the two partners are spending trying to make her sickness and dying a conscious part of their lives? This is not an unusual interpretation. In fact, all over the world—Native America, Africa, India—we find stories that show old age, sickness, and dying to be unconscious phenomena until partners actually journey to the underworld *together* and *understand* what they are going through.

I have found the death journey to be divided into two primary categories, those in which the death place is clearly different from the surface world (Elysium, for instance, in Greek tradition, is a clearly different place than the land of the living), and those in which the death place is a re-creation of the land of the living. In the former, the idea is that people's souls are actually going to that death place, that heaven underground or heaven in the clouds. In the latter, the idea is that people's souls are "going" to a re-creation of their former lives because they are really still in their former lives, still learning lessons there.

The story of Maria and Raoul fits this second category. It is a village that looks exactly like the village on the surface world that Maria and Raoul inhabit. So let us spend some time viewing the journey this old couple makes as a journey into the dark process of dying itself.

In this interpretation, we learn how to move hand in hand into *conscious* dying. Maria and Raoul are in the underworld, which is the dark world of dying and learning the process of making dying joyful. As it teaches its lessons, it wraps the journey in fear, especially the fear of the helper (the death partner). Throughout his time underground, Raoul is afraid for himself and Maria is afraid for him. The story does not romanticize the death process. It doesn't say, "Dying, the Third Conscious Descent, will be a happy, wonderful time in your life." It is honest to say that there is great pain here, great fear. Navigating that fear, putting it to rest, and discovering the flowers—the symbol of joy—despite it are crucial to making the process conscious.

The conscious dying process is also befriended by the dog. Dogs often represent that part of ourselves that is grounded, close to the earth, able to sniff out what we are seeking sometimes long before we actually arrive to notice we have been seeking it. The dog finds the way into the conscious dying process; the dog finds the way into the descent; the dog finds the safety of the flowers that reward the descent. The dog is that part of each of us that leads unconscious dying to become conscious. The dog is that part of us that has the courage to leap down into the hole. How do we develop this part of ourselves in a culture that seems to negate it? How do we embrace the dark caverns of dying and death? First we must know we have it within us, the power to make the death journey into a spiritual event, a soulful descent.

Edith, whose husband had Alzheimer's, said this to me: "I can either approach this whole thing as a tragedy or a comedy. He doesn't remember me or anybody consistently. At first, it just hurt me. Now, as he gets even sicker and closer to dying, I let myself drift along with him. I try to become the innocence that's in him. I see how hard it all is for him, how frustrating for him. He gets enraged at his own incompetence. I clean up after him; I try to befriend him. I don't hang on to the idea that there's only one way to see him—as my competent husband. Once I let go of that, I see all sorts of other things. We have a new relationship. Unless you've experienced this, young man, I don't think you can understand."

When I spoke to Edith six months later, her husband had died. She herself had just turned eighty. She said, "Living without him and facing my own death are much easier because I let myself die with him." It took me a long time to understand this. Finally I understood my own confusion about the word *die*. When she said, "I let myself die with him," I heard negativity. But what she really meant was, "I went through the dying process with him and came out cleansed, empowered, and ready for my own journey." Edith was an unusual woman. Most people, even most elders, do not realize that they, like Raoul, must go down into the underground with their dying partner; and that they must not only go down into an underground of sorrow, frustration, and hopelessness, but an underground where they observe the dance of death, and find, as they help their partner make peace, their own peace.

Raoul stays underground with his wife and watches the

dance. In real time he and she are together in the conscious dying process for perhaps months. In the story, it's just one day/night cycle. When it is done, she thanks him for being with her, they speak their last words, and he sets off to return to his world. He leaves her in her peace and he finds the joy he seeks in the flowers. Edith found the flowers too. That is what she was saying to me. Raoul's story focuses us on the joy the death partner experiences. Stage 12 and its stories will help us explore the joy the one who dies, Maria, experiences. For now we follow Raoul into the flowerbed, then find him chased by the dead ones. The story is telling him it is time to fully reawaken to his own life, fully let Maria go, and return with his dog to bury his dead.

You'll notice that this whole Conscious Descent occurs before Maria is buried. Raoul dies with her while she is dying; once he and she have made peace, he can bury her and go on with his life. The dead remain dead and the living continue living. This becomes possible because living and dead have gone through the conscious dying process together. This is a very different process than the one we often see where people physically bury their partners without burying them emotionally. They become like the living dead. Their mourning remains repressed and eats them up. The model of dying as a Conscious Descent invites us to focus our energies on reinventing our relationships—to remain partners or lovers or wife and husband, but now to take on new roles, as dying one and death partner.

These roles do not mean that Maria and Raoul must be smiling all the time—that would be more repression than joy. In reference to her work, Elisabeth Kübler-Ross writes, "There are millions of people who have the illusion that a patient is 'better off' if surrounded with an air of 'all is well';

that is, if we visit terminally ill patients only with a smile on our face and cheerful, superficial conversation or silence." She continues, "[As a culture] we have no problems getting them the very best in physical care and attention, but most often neglect their more painful emotional and spiritual turmoil." Finding joy in the descent is about navigating that turmoil together.

MAKING THE DESCENT WITH YOUR PARTNER

Because chapter 12 will focus heavily on the experience of the one dying, let us focus here on the spiritual discipline that, if practiced by the death partner, fulfills his/her personal responsibility to make death a conscious process of finding meaning and joy.

• Protect at all costs your partner's right to death with dignity.

• Forgive yourself for the mistakes you've made during your life with your partner, and forgive your partner.

• Meditate, pray, and converse with your dying partner on letting go of regrets. Help your partner to let go and let go yourself.

• Help your partner visualize his/her death journey. Encourage him/her to bring into daily practice the wealth of vision that imagination can bring to the experience of death, whether through art, writing, reading, or making up stories.

• Nurse and provide for your partner without becoming enmeshed in your partner's life. Take care of your own needs as well as your partner's.

• Get help in understanding your own fear of abandonment, for any death of an intimate partner will trigger that fear. Confront and move through your sense of blaming yourself for your partner's suffering. It is natural to feel some self-blame and some survivor guilt. Get help in working through those responses to a partner's dying. Turn to your own spiritual practice as you seek the discipline to move through your pathological responses to your partner's death.

• Make the dying one comfortable by attending to his/her surroundings. Even if the hospital is the place of death, make it a comfortable space.

• Keep the dying one in contact with spiritual growth by making his/her surroundings a ritual space. This is not just about comfort; this is about filling the dying one's space with sacred objects—whether photographs of elder relatives and intimate family or knitting needles or medals or favorite canteens or newspaper clippings or religious objects or whatever you know is sacred to the dying one.

• Give the dying one permission to die. This is essential, even if the partner is in a coma. Speak to the partner and give permission. Many loved ones will suffer a great deal because we are grasping at them and they therefore do not feel they can die.

The *strength* and the *compassion* we need to fill our role as death partner rarely comes if we don't have a spiritual practice to support them. Often, because we do not, in earlier life, approach our love as a spiritual discipline, and do not have spiritual practices in place, we do more spiritual and emotional harm to the dying one we love than we wish to do. We make what can be a descent through pain and joy into a fall of agonizing self-destruction.

The dying one, for his/her part and if s/he is physically conscious and able, needs to engage in spiritual practice as deeply as does the partner. The dying one, if capable, needs to ask for what s/he needs, without assuming the partner will know. The dying one, if capable, needs to be personally responsible for his/her dying process. It is something s/he is the primary actor in. The death partner is, like a birth partner, actively involved; but the partner is not the primary actor. Even though the death partner tries to help death's door open smoothly for the dying one, still the partner cannot see the door as clearly.

We are going to die. When we practice love and life as spiritual disciplines, that fact scares us less. We begin to prepare for death early, in the same way we prepare for the coming of a child into our house and family. We study death. We embrace it; we talk about it; we let it feed life with new meaning.

In the Lover's Journey model, we are laying out an ideal course, with death arriving in old age. Yet we all know that many people die young or "before their time." How does the Third Conscious Descent apply to them? we might ask. It still applies, very much so. There is a certain maturity toward death we cannot accomplish until we've been through the earlier stages of life and love—yet the basic principles of caring for the dying, of being compassionate and strong, and of maintaining spiritual practice apply no matter how old the dying one is. And the basic principles of dying apply too. Once I had the honor of meeting Scott, a seven-year-old with terminal leukemia. He put his family at ease with his dying and did not crush his own needs in the process. It was as if, in a mythic way, he were born to die—born to model conscious and joyful dying for the rest of us.

If you are someone who works with the dying, you have learned many of their lessons. The culture needs you to teach these. You have probably learned to have few expectations, to be patient and kind, to hold boundaries, to speak no ill, to encourage dying ones to make peace with family and friends. You have probably learned ways to process your sadness and grief so that you can move on. You have probably heard ranting and raving. You've seen people slip into depressions and comas. You've lifted bodies from bed to bed that once were more than skeletons and now are bone on bone. If you work with the dying or spend time with the dying, you've gone through the initial stages we all go through in the presence of death—stages based in our fear of loss. You've come to that point where you value the life that is being lived in the face of death. Hospice workers tell me one of the most valuable things they have learned and try to teach is this: *The dying one is very much alive and is ready to find a kind of joy s/he never imagined before the dying process began.*

If we keep our energies focused on that principle, death will remain a terribly stressful experience, but also the next stage of growth.

THE ELEVENTH SACRED TASK

Stage 11 of the Lover's spiritual discipline teaches us the eleventh lesson of trust: *salvation.*

I learn to trust the universe so fully I know I am a valued part of it no matter what I have done in my life. It is in this stage that we are truly able to understand what in ourselves we take into the next world for cleansing. By trusting that we can be whole no matter how we've suffered or created suffering, we trust ourselves to die in peace.

Salvation is a lesson of trust everyone, no matter the biological age or stage of life, needs to know about. Yet there is a special intensity to that lesson in stage 11. When I know I am saved as I stare into the face of death, I truly understand the joy of that trust.

Those religions that consider salvation the primary lesson of trust in a person's life from cradle to grave—literal-minded Christians are a group that does this now—view the human life process as completely untrustworthy, utterly terrifying. These groups do not understand that there are stages of trust development; that for a ten-year-old child to obsess about how he will be saved for his sins is like saying to him, "You are about to die every minute of the day, so you are always on the edge of destruction. And since you're always on this edge, you'd better focus your deepest energies on how to transcend that destruction." This view forces on us the belief that we are the living dead. The best part of ourselves is in heaven, the worst on earth.

No matter our age, it is useful to bring into our spiritual practice the notion that we do make mistakes for which we consider ourselves accountable. But that is a very superficial view of salvation, as many dying people understand. Those who are dying face the need to be "saved"—to feel they are attached to an undying whole, no matter what they've done—in a way that the ten-year-old, innocent child, even the forty-five-year-old at the peak of creativity, cannot understand. When someone dying cries out, "I'm saved," s/he is crying out, "Oh, Lord, how wonderful, I belong!" To trust life so completely that we can feel we belong in it even as we face its end is to know great joy.

Stage 11 provides us with the eleventh element of focus for the Lover's spiritual discipline: *release.*

I am challenged to trust myself, my world, the universe, and Being by practicing spiritual release from all that has previously been trustworthy—myself, my world, my universe and being.

I am being asked to consciously move through a process of separating myself from everything that once told me "I am," and in releasing any control I have over knowing that "I am," I come to embrace a new way of knowing that "I am," a way that only dying can bring me. The dying one must release his/her family, social role, house, natural surroundings, body. The death partner must release the dying one. If they do it consciously, death will be joyful.

INTEGRATING THE THIRD CONSCIOUS DESCENT

Many people die suddenly, and so they and their partners have little time to make this descent, to integrate it into their life journey and their quest for joy. Their circumstances will, hopefully, inspire the rest of us to attend to the needs of the descent during our elder's solitude or earlier in life so that, should we die suddenly, at least we and our partner have made strides toward understanding what we believe salvation is, how we would like to release and be released.

In order to integrate stage 11, we must change our way of viewing death. This short chapter is far too small a place to accomplish that vision. Stephen and Ondrea Levine, Elisabeth Kübler-Ross, Raymond Moody, Krishnamurti, Anya Foos-Graber, and many others are already moving in that direction, toward that vision. My sense is that our culture will not see that it needs to consciously integrate dying and stage 11 until it realizes that life is a quest for joy in the first place.

Until that moment, the culture will be ruled by those voices and policies that fear death throughout every instant of life, that shame us for sin and prosletyze us for salvation, without ever having understood that there are stages to living and to dying—and that those stages, even as our bodies dissolve, guide us to life, deep core life, even ecstasy.

INITIATION
INTO COSMIC
CONSCIOUSNESS

Love is God, and to die means that I, a particle of
love, shall return to the general and eternal source.
—LEO TOLSTOY

I have never met anyone quite like Lillian. Here is what she
said to me: "I'm afraid, yes, I guess I am, but only the way a
body is afraid. With tremblings and shiverings and my organs
failing. That's what everyone sees of me right now but I'm
seeing something else. My soul is ready for a new adventure.
My soul is ready to come alive. I've lived a good life. Now
it's time to die. See that? I wish you could see that."
Throughout her elder years, Lillian and her husband had suffered many small ailments but nothing severe, until John died
of a sudden heart attack. That was twenty-two years before
Lillian died. Lillian lived those twenty-two years in a great
deal of solitude, but still, until her eyes went, drove her light
blue Ford Granada to her bridge parties and to the store. She
walked a great deal. Some of her family was nearby, kids,
grandkids, great-grandkids. She spent time with them when
she could. There were always family gatherings to go to,
gatherings in Spokane or in Seattle, five hours away. She
went to the ones in Spokane and in Seattle until sometime in

her early eighties, when she just didn't want to travel anymore.

Lillian had had many jobs in her life—receptionist, secretary, teacher, volunteer coordinator—and had served on numerous committees and boards in her first few decades in Seattle, then in the next few decades in Spokane. What she said she remembered at ninety-two, dying of cancer, was not the jobs but the people. "You do a lot of things with your life," she said to me, "and they amount to something at the time. But what you remember is the people you did them with." She showed me her collection of photographs. "Look at these pictures. You don't see many pictures of jobs, do you? It's people you remember." Even as the cancer ate her bone marrow, Lillian remembered her life fondly and blessed the people who came to see her in a million ways.

At Lillian's funeral, in the sad aloneness that accompanies most funerals in our culture, I said good-bye to her with the hope that she had found a new place for herself, a place of mystery that ends the Lover's Journey for one lifetime and begins some next stage of it barely known to our world. Burying her just three days after she died, and after her body had been the complete focus of her dying—embalmed by a mortician who never knew her and did not pray over her—her family spent little time with the passage of her soul, the initiation of her consciousness into the next world. Watching this process, I thought of boys and girls in our culture who are barely initiated into adulthood, thrown into that next mystery without much care for their souls. We spend little time training those children for spiritual life. We spend even less time caring for the souls of our elders as they seek spiritual death.

THE LIVING AND THE DEAD: PART THREE

In the story, this care of the dead one's soul is crucial to the dying process. The surviving lover helps the dead lover become initiated into cosmic consciousness (the divine). He grieves, then lets her go, then begins his own process of initiation into that consciousness. This is not only the last stage of a physical human life, it is also the last stage of the Lover's Journey. Each of us begins our own initiation into the Great Mystery by first helping another through.

For Raoul, there is a last burst of energy. In story time it seems to last only a little while. In our own lives, it may last a few years. Having seen the world of the dead, Raoul knows how to prepare himself. In the same way, if we strive to consciously learn about the death process, we will begin to feel we've seen the land of the dead; we'll be prepared. If we care for dying people, we'll see it another way.

One elder man said to me, "As I spent those last months with my wife, I felt like I was looking through her into the world I am going to go to soon. Caring for her, learning from her, I feel better prepared. I'm less scared. I've always had my faith, but this is something different. Now I *know* something else is out there, and I'm excited." I had seen this same excitement when I was a boy, probably six years old. I saw an elder Hindu man in a hospital who, when asked if he was afraid of dying, said, "Why should I be? I'm finally going to rejoin the universal!"

When we seek to see the world of the dead, through whatever our exploration or spiritual practice, we realize that we are about to be initiated into something wonderful, the very essence of our own being made large in the spirit world. Despite our fear, we feel joy. Some religions seek to help us find this time of joy, this burst of energy.

Raoul makes practice of his death preparation. He inspires all of us to make our own death a spiritual practice, which of course implies finding mentors, priests, friends, family to help us in our practice. In this way death becomes communal practice.

Then he dies. His community is convinced it sees his soul make a journey through a spirit hole where the two creeks meet. His journey continues. His community and family presumably care for his passage in ceremonial ways, so that he can be initiated into the cosmic consciousness that is everywhere, without and within.

Until a few centuries ago, our own ancestors believed there was a death journey. Over the last few hundred years, this belief became the object of charges of superstition. In the last few decades, through the work of Raymond Moody, Elisabeth Kübler-Ross, and others who have tracked "after-death" experiences all over the world, we are seeing the return of interest in the last stage of the Lover's Journey. That interest is a return of interest in joy itself. It promises to lead us toward an attitude toward dying that says, "Death is mournful but it is also joy." What a different world that would be to live in. Once we can unlearn our terror and denial of death, we can see its joyfulness; once we do that, say the shamans, we can send the spooks to the other world, and find a greater joy in life again too.

YOUR OWN INITIATION INTO COSMIC CONSCIOUSNESS

What is it like to die? In the *Tibetan Book of the Dead,* the death initiation into cosmic consciousness, the bardo journey, takes forty-nine days. During this time, the dead one moves from early stages of dissolution of his/her earthly being to the last stage, rebirth—reincarnation. During this whole process, the soul is mentored, faces adversity, discovers luminosity of inner being, becomes the universal radiance (merges with the divine in four phases of mergence), is reborn. Sogyal Rinpoche, in *The Tibetan Book of Living and Dying,* gives a very accessible analysis of the process. Some people find *The Tibetan Book of the Dead* itself difficult to read. Sogyal Rinpoche's book is not.

The Tibetan way of dying is only one of many ancient and many tribal sources of death wisdom available to us. It compares uncannily with our own modern death wisdom, made recently popular by Dannion Brinkley's book, *Saved by the Light.* A man who died twice, the first time as a result of being hit by lightening, Brinkley made it through many of the stages of death initiation before coming back to life. After a very long physical and emotional rehabilitation, Brinkley has become an associate of Raymond Moody, a pioneer of after-death study.

Wherever we look, whether in the ancient mind or the mythic story or modern scientific process, we find evidence of stage 12, initiation into cosmic consciousness, even in Christian heritage. We find experiences of the soul leaving the body. (This experience may begin, as some scientists argue, in the brain's experience of letting go—its projection of images of angels, white lights, and so forth, as oxygen leaves it). We find the soul understanding where it has been and where it is going. We find it merging with the universal. Even in Brinkley's experience, we find it reborn—in his case, back into his present body.

World sources seem to agree on at least a four-phase process:

1. Physical death
2. Absolute Self-knowledge
3. Mergence with the Divine
4. Rebirth

Not to prepare for this initiation process, world wisdom tells us, and not to build a death culture to aid in this process, is to condemn ourselves to ignorance, the great danger.

What can each of us do to aid our own initiation and the initiation of others? Here are some suggestions, culled from world wisdom.

• Gain in life a sense of ourselves as divine. This brings true humility, power, and joy at the end of life.

• Accept and/or develop a vision of the death journey. Do it verbally and through other available media.

• Make last comments to the living (sometimes this manifests in our own lives or in the lives of old people we know as incessant memory storytelling, "rambling").

• Make practical preparation for dying (wills, living wills, and so forth) so that, without distraction, we can teach our community how to focus on the death initiation we want.

• Make clear what community we want and need around us as we die. We have the deciding choice as to whom we want with us. We need to be as generous as we can in exercising this power. Often we need to make it in the spirit of forgiveness.

• Realize that if never before, now is the time to focus on what brings us joy.

• Feel free to detach from others, especially while dying (instinctual clinging to others can occur during this time, but still we must detach and gain acceptance for detaching). In a culture that practices love not as spiritual discipline but rather as emotional enmeshment, we often don't feel free to detach when we need to. We feel we must help the living, the survivors, to feel okay about our dying. This compassion is essential, but it must also be accompanied by healthy detachment. Our dying days are not a time when we gain the lion's share of our joy by feeling compelled to do what others want us to do.

• Prepare for spiritual detachment from the body. This will often mean telling others when you want to die and what kinds of medical interventions you will not allow. The medical prowess to put off death is not a prowess the Lover necessarily needs to enjoy. The Lover knows its time of death, and welcomes it, for the Lover knows that there comes a time to love death as much as it loved life.

• Move through the threshold into the land of the dead and enjoy the initiation into cosmic consciousness.

All this is easier said than done, yet it remains worth doing. Many people who work with the dying help prepare them by offering artistic tools—painting, poetry writing. Many people as they die experience last bursts of creative energy about dying itself. Many poets write late poems about the death journey. D. H. Lawrence's "Ship of Death" is a wonderful model of creative efforts we can each make to "know" our own death—visualize it—before we die. In spending some of our last creative human energies on visualizing our happy deaths, we build a ship of death for ourselves. As you die, seek to find others who have the courage to talk about and visualize death. Spend time with them envisioning death. Help others to see your comfort with dying, so that they may

learn from your dying, rather than fear it and turn away from
it and from you.

THE TWELFTH SACRED TASK

Stage 12 of the Lover's spiritual discipline teaches us the
twelfth lesson of trust: *unity*.

*Dying is done joyfully when we have faith that, through its diffi-
cult initiation process, we become one with what we have always
been: cosmic consciousness.*

Disciplines and practices that help us trust the process of
our own unifying-with are disciplines and practices that re-
move our clinging to the human life that is passing away and
teach us how to embrace the "new" (it has always been) life
energy we are set to embrace.

Stage 12 also provides us with the twelfth element of focus
for the Lover's spiritual discipline: *rebirth*.

*When we move through the initiation into cosmic consciousness as
if we moved through the birth canal into a new birth, we experience
a rebirth that gives us new focus.*

That rebirth may be reincarnation, it may be Brinkley's
new life purpose, it may be a million other things we do not
yet know about. But we can know with certainty—we have
only to notice how the life-death-rebirth cycle works in nature for proof of its existence—that we, like everything else
alive, will be reborn somehow. Focus on that rebirth gives us
direction as powerfully as trusting the process of dying itself
gives us a sense of grand unity.

INTEGRATING STAGE 12

Our mission must be to bring death into the forefront of the
vast public dialogue about how to live. Until we do, the Lov-

er's Journey will not be complete, and great shares of human love will not find life. Each of us finds more joy in our lives by getting to know and by aiding more dying people. If we remain in early stages of the Lover's Journey, we are so ruled by the doctrines of enmeshment that we will be too afraid to stay with dead people and love them and help them make their passage; the dying and the dead will just trigger our impatience and our fears. But as we mature in the Lover's Journey and better understand spiritual discipline and detachment, we will yearn to know the dying and gain their wisdom.

For those who are themselves dying, integration of stage 12 involves a great deal of life review, a great deal of consciousness seeking, a great deal of wisdom giving. The closer the dying get to the actual death and initiation into cosmic consciousness, the more mysterious knowledge they gain and can convey. It is not an explainable phenomenon. It just is. Lillian, as she moved closer to her initiation, grew wiser and, with the help of a body that had not lost its faculties, gave others, including me, more joy than she ever could have imagined. "I'm determined to die happy!" Lillian once told me.

I believe she did.

EPILOGUE

He who binds himself to a joy
Does winged life destroy
But he who kisses the joy as it flies
Lives in eternity's sun rise.
—WILLIAM BLAKE

You seek joy in your own way. You give yourself permission to live joyfully in your own way. You live out your Lover's Journey in your own way. It may not exactly resemble the journey I have laid out here, yet I think it will resemble it in many ways.

I hope you'll let this book give you more permission than you had to live joyfully. I hope you'll let it inspire you to make joy in your relationships. I hope you'll refer to the Lover's Journey map when you need to. Some things written in it may glide over you now, but ten years from now, when you enter that new stage, those things might make you say "Aha!" When Mr. and Mrs. Harrison began me on my search for joy, I could not have known it would lead me to this map. But I'm glad it did. I hope, if nothing else, they have inspired both you and me to seek joy in every moment of life—not the fake smiles we put on, but the kind of joy that grows from practicing life and love as a spiritual discipline.

As you grow older, I hope you see yourself integrating the

earlier stages of the Lover's Journey into your elder years. I hope all of us can teach young people to grow from dependency to independence to interdependence to nondependence, feeling solid in having a map for our journey without making the map into a religious obsession. If we can teach love as a spiritual discipline to our youth without crushing them in dogma, we will start them out on a life we can be most proud of. They, in their innocence, know what we often forget: love is a spiritual discipline we practice because we need to, not because we are told to.

We live in a time when past teachings and energies can come together as they never could before. We have never known so much about love as we do now. We have never tasted individual freedom as we taste it now. We have never known as much about the biology of intimacy as we know now. We have never had the confidence to leave oppressive religions and roles behind as we do now. We have never ended a millenium as we end this one—confused, yes, but energetic, and better able to communicate our energy than ever before.

We are at the right time and place for great optimism about love. We are at the right time to see ourselves as lovers who, in our very DNA and every cell, carry millennia of wisdom about joyful loving, wisdom that wants to guide us out of the gender wars and violence, the blaming and shaming, the coping mechanisms and addictions, the disappointments and fears of intimacy to a full-fledged embrace of ourselves as individual spiritual beings who can find fulfillment in the structure, discipline, nurturance, and spiritual freedom of a quest for joy.

SELECTED READINGS

Abrahams, Roger D. *African Folktales*. New York: Pantheon Books, 1983.

Afanasev, Aleksandr. *Russian Fairy Tales*. New York: Pantheon Books, 1945.

Apuleius, Lucius. *The Tale of Cupid and Psyche*. Translated by Robert Graves. Boston: Shambhala Publications, 1992.

Batten, Mary. *Sexual Strategies*. Los Angeles: Tarcher/Putnam, 1992.

Becker, Ernest. *The Denial of Death*. New York: The Free Press, 1973.

Bly, Robert. *Iron John*. Reading, Mass: Addison-Wesley, 1990.

Bradshaw, John. *Homecoming*. New York: Bantam Books, 1990.

Branden, Nathaniel. *The Psychology of Romantic Love*. Los Angeles: Jeremy P. Tarcher, 1980.

Brazelton, T. Berry, and Bertrand G. Cramer. *The Earliest Relationship*. Reading Mass.: Addison-Wesley, 1990.

Brinkley, Dannion, with Paul Perry. *Saved by the Light*. New York: Villard Books, 1994.

Budge, E. A. Wallis. *Legends of the Egyptian Gods*. New York: Dover, 1994.

Cameron, Julia. *The Artist's Way*. Los Angeles: Tarcher/Perigee, 1992.

Campbell, Joseph. *The Hero with a Thousand Faces,* second edition. Princeton, N.J.: Princeton University Press, 1968.

———. *Historical Atlas of World Mythology*. New York: Harper & Row, 1983.

———. *Myths We Live By*. New York: Bantam Books, 1988.

———., commentator. *The Complete Grimm's Fairy Tales*. New York: Pantheon Books, 1972.

Campbell, Susan. *The Couples Journey*. San Luis Obispo, Calif.: Impact Publishers, 1980.

Cashford, Jules. *The Myth of Isis and Osiris*. Boston: Barefoot Books, 1993.

de Chardin, Pierre Teilhard. *The Creative Imperative*. Millbrae, Calif.: Celestial Arts, 1986.

Dominguez, Joe, and Vicki Robin. *Your Money or Your Life*. New York: Viking, 1992.

Eisler, Riane, *The Chalice and the Blade*. New York: Harper & Row, 1987.

Eliade, Mircea. *Rites and Symbols of Initiation*. New York: Harper & Row, 1975.

Erdoes, Richard, and Alfonso Ortiz. *American Indian Myths and Legends*. New York: Pantheon Books, 1984.

Estés, Clarissa Pinkola. *Women Who Run with the Wolves*. New York: Ballantine, 1992.

Farrell, Warren. *The Myth of Male Power*. New York: Simon and Schuster, 1993.

Feinstein, David, and Stanley Krippner. *Personal Mythology*. Los Angeles: Jeremy P. Tarcher, 1988.

Fisher, Helen. *Anatomy of Love*. New York: Fawcett, 1992.

Foos-Graber, Anya. *Deathing*. York Beach, Me.: Nicolas Hays, 1989.

Grey, John. *Men Are from Mars, Women Are from Venus*. San Francisco: HarperSanFrancisco, 1993.

Gurian, Jay P., and Julia M. Gurian. *The Dependency Tendency*. Lanham, Md.: University Press of America, 1983.

Gurian, Michael. *Mothers, Sons, and Lovers*. Boston: Shambhala Publications, 1993.

———. *The Prince and the King: Healing the Father-Son Wound*. Los Angeles: Tarcher/Putnam, 1992.

Goldberg, Herb. *The New Male*. New York: Signet Books, 1979.

Greenberg, Jay R., and Stephen A. Mitchell. *Object Relations in Psychoanalytic Theory*. Cambridge, Mass.: Harvard University Press, 1983.

Hamilton, Edith. *Mythology*. New York: New Directions, 1942.

Hammarskjold, Dag. *Markings*. New York: Alfred A. Knopf, 1964.

Haule, John R. *Pilgrimage of the Heart*. Boston: Shambhala Publications, 1992.

Hendricks, Gay, and Kathlyn Hendricks. *Conscious Loving.* New York: Bantam, 1990.

Hendrix, Harville. *Getting the Love You Want.* New York: Harper Collins, 1990.

Herdt, Gilbert H., ed. *Rituals of Manhood: Male Initiation in Papua New Guinea.* Berkeley, Calif.: University of California Press, 1982.

Hildegard of Bingen. *The Book of Divine Works with Letters and Songs.* Translated by Matthew Fox. Santa Fe, N.M.: Bear & Co., 1987.

Hillman, James. *Revisioning Psychology.* New York: Harper & Row, 1975.

Horn, Holly. *Asherah: Shaking Loose the Goddess.* Self-published, 1991.

Houff, William H. *Infinity in Your Hand.* Spokane, Wash.: Melior, 1989.

Houston, Jean. *The Search for the Beloved: Journeys in Sacred Psychology.* Los Angeles: Jeremy P. Tarcher, 1987.

Johnson, Robert A. *We.* New York: HarperCollins, 1983.

Jung, C. G., ed. *Man and His Symbols.* New York: Doubleday, 1986.

———. *Psychology and Religion.* Princeton, N.J.: Princeton University Press, 1958.

Kaplan, Louise J. *Oneness and Separateness: From Infant to Individual.* New York: Touchstone, 1978.

Keen, Sam. *The Passionate Life.* New York: Harper & Row, 1983.

———, and Anne Valley-Fox. *Your Mythic Journey.* Los Angeles: Jeremy P. Tarcher, 1978.

Kipnis, Aaron R., and Elizabeth Herron. *Gender War/Gender Peace.* New York: William Morrow, 1994.

Kübler-Ross, Elisabeth. *Living with Death and Dying.* New York: MacMillan, 1981.

———. *Death: The Final Stage of Growth.* New Jersey: Prentice Hall, 1975.

Lawler, Robert. *Voices of the First Day.* Rochester, Vt.: Inner Traditions International, 1990.

Lee, John. *Facing the Fire.* New York: Bantam, 1992.

Leonard, Linda Schierse. *The Wounded Woman*. Boston: Shambhala Publications, 1983.

Levine, Stephen. *Who Dies?* New York: Anchor/Doubleday, 1982.

Margulis, Lyn, and Dorion Sagan. *Mystery Dance*. New York: Summit Books, 1991.

May, Rollo. *The Cry for Myth*. New York: W. W. Norton, 1989.

————. *Love and Will*. New York: W. W. Norton, 1969.

Miller, Alice. *For Your Own Good*. New York: Farrar, Straus and Giroux, 1983.

Moir, Anne, and David Jessel. *Brain Sex*. New York: Laurel, 1989.

Moore, Robert, and Douglas Gillette. *King, Warrior, Magician, Lover*. San Francisco: HarperSanFrancisco, 1990.

Moore, Thomas. *Care of the Soul*. New York: HarperCollins, 1992.

Murdoch, Iris. *The Black Prince*. New York: Viking, 1973.

Nicholson, Shirley, ed. *Shamanism: An Expanded View of Reality*. Wheaton, Ill.: Quest Books, 1987.

O'Flaherty, Wendy, trans. *Hindu Myths*. New York: Penguin, 1975.

Pearson, Carol. *The Hero Within*. New York: Harper & Row, 1989.

————, and Bill Page. *A Male/Female Continuum: Paths to Colleagueship*. Laconia, N.H.: New Dynamics, 1986.

Rico, Gabriele. *Pain and Possibility*. Los Angeles: Jeremy P. Tarcher, 1991.

Rilke, Rainer Maria. *Letters to a Young Poet*. Translated by Stephen Mitchell. New York: Random House, 1984.

Rubin, Lillian B. *Intimate Strangers*. New York: Harper & Row, 1983.

Sagan, Carl, and Ann Druyan. *Shadows of Forgotten Ancestors*. New York: Random House, 1992.

Sams, Jaime, and David Carson. *Medicine Cards*. Santa Fe, N.M.: Bear & Co., 1988.

Sarton, May. *As We Are Now*. New York: W. W. Norton, 1973.

————. *The House by the Sea*. New York: W. W. Norton, 1981.

Scarf, Maggy. *Intimate Partners*. New York: Random House, 1987.

Sell, Emily Hilburn, ed. *The Spirit of Loving*. Boston: Shambhala Publications, 1995.

Sewell, Marilyn, ed. *Cries of the Spirit*. Boston: Beacon Press, 1991.

Sogyal Rinpoche. *The Tibetan Book of Living and Dying*. New York: HarperCollins, 1993.

Solomon, Marion F. *Narcissism and Intimacy*. New York: W. W. Norton, 1989.

Stern, Daniel N. *The Interpersonal World of the Infant*. New York: Basic Books, 1985.

Stone, Merlin. *When God Was a Woman*. New York: Harvest, 1976.

Storm, Hyemeyohsts. *Seven Arrows*. New York: Ballantine, 1972.

Tannen, Deborah. *You Just Don't Understand*. New York: Ballantine, 1990.

Thich Nhat Hanh. *Peace Is Every Step*. New York: Bantam, 1991.

Trueman, Terry. *Sheehan*. Spokane, Wash.: Siobhan, 1992.

Trungpa, Chögyam. *Cutting Through Spiritual Materialism*. Boston: Shambhala Publications, 1987.

Turner, Victor. *Ritual Process*. Ithaca, N.Y.: Cornell University Press, 1977.

———. *The Forest of Symbols: Aspects of Ndembu Ritual*. Ithaca, N.Y.: Cornell University Press, 1967.

Tyler, Royall. *Japanese Tales*. New York: Pantheon, 1987.

Uysal, A. E., ed. *Selections from Living Turkish Folktales*. Ankara, Turkey: Ataturk Kultur, Dil Ve Tarih Yuksek Kurumu, 1989.

von Franz, Marie-Louise. *The Interpretation of Fairy Tales*. Dallas: Spring Publications, 1970.

———. *Puer Aeternus*. Boston: Sigo Press, 1981.

Welwood, John. *Journey of the Heart*. New York: HarperCollins, 1990.

Wexler, David B. *The Adolescent Self*. New York: W. W. Norton, 1991.

Winnicott, D. W. *Human Nature*. New York: Schocken Books, 1988.

Woodman, Marion. *The Ravaged Bridegroom*. Toronto: Inner City Books, 1990.

Yolen, Jane, ed. *Favorite Folktales from around the World*. New York: Pantheon Books, 1986.

Ywahoo, Dhyani. *Voices of Our Ancestors*. Boston: Shambhala Publications, 1987.